Reformed
and Always
Reforming

Acadia Studies in Bible and Theology

Craig A. Evans and Lee Martin McDonald, General Editors

The last two decades have witnessed dramatic developments in biblical and theological study. Full-time academics can scarcely keep up with fresh discoveries, recently published primary texts, ongoing archaeological work, new exegetical proposals, experiments in methods and hermeneutics, and innovative theological syntheses. For students and nonspecialists, these developments are confusing and daunting. What has been needed is a series of succinct studies that assess these issues and present their findings in a way that students, pastors, laity, and nonspecialists will find accessible and rewarding. Acadia Studies in Bible and Theology, sponsored by Acadia Divinity College in Wolfville, Nova Scotia, and in conjunction with the college's Hayward Lectureship, constitutes such a series.

The Hayward Lectureship has brought to Acadia many distinguished scholars of Bible and theology, such as Sir Robin Barbour, John Bright, Leander Keck, Helmut Koester, Richard Longenecker, Martin Marty, Jaroslav Pelikan, Ian Rennie, James Sanders, and Eduard Schweizer. The Acadia Studies in Bible and Theology series reflects this rich heritage.

These studies are designed to guide readers through the ever more complicated maze of critical, interpretative, and theological discussion taking place today. But these studies are not introductory in nature; nor are they mere surveys. Authored by leading authorities in the field, the Acadia Studies in Bible and Theology series offers critical assessments of the major issues that the church faces in the twenty-first century. Readers will gain the requisite orientation and fresh understanding of the important issues that will enable them to take part meaningfully in discussion and debate.

Reformed
and Always
Reforming

The Postconservative Approach
to Evangelical Theology

ROGER E. OLSON

Baker Academic
Grand Rapids, Michigan

Published by Baker Academic
a division of Baker Publishing Group
P.O. Box 6287, Grand Rapids, MI 49516-6287
www.bakeracademic.com

Printed in the United States of America

Library of Congress Cataloging-in-Publication Data
Olson, Roger E.
    Reformed and always reforming : the postconservative approach to evangelical theology / Roger E. Olson.
        p.   cm. — (Acadia studies in Bible and theology)
    Includes bibliographical references and index.
    ISBN 10: 0-8010-3169-9 (pbk.)
    ISBN 978-0-8010-3169-4 (pbk.)
    1. Evangelicalism. I. Title.
BR1640.O455 2007
230′.04624—dc22   2007017173

Contents

Introduction

The thesis of this book is simple but controversial: *it is possible to be more evangelical by being less conservative*. It's simple in that it can be expressed so concisely and straightforwardly. It's controversial because many people, both evangelicals and non-evangelicals, will find it counterintuitive and some will contest it. For a long time the terms "evangelical" and "conservative" have been inextricably linked both in the popular mind and among scholars. To be evangelical, so many think, is to be socially, politically, ethically, and theologically conservative.

However, much depends on how one defines "evangelical" and "conservative." As we will see, these terms are essentially contested concepts. They beg description. No one can simply assume their meanings. Much of the burden of this introduction will be to define and describe these terms theologically and, of course, these definitions and descriptions will be my own, although I rely on noted authorities. The rest of the book will demonstrate how it is possible to be more evangelical by being less conservative or at least how one can be evangelical without being conservative (as these terms are defined here).

What This Book Is About

This is a book about theology and not sociology, politics, or even ethics. These may come into play from time to time, but for the most part evangelical theology is our concern here. Therefore, unless noted otherwise, "evangelical" here means evangelical theology. And theology means *reflection on divine revelation in order to believe rightly and understand what is rightly believed.* Theology is process; doctrine is raw material and product. Theology examines doctrines (beliefs about God) and produces doctrines, often by reaffirming, restating, or revising older ones.

Books have already been written attempting to demonstrate that it is possible to be more evangelical by being less conservative politically and economically. A clear case is Jim Wallis's book *The Politics of God: Why the Right Gets It Wrong and the Left Doesn't Get It.*[1] Largely due to the popular media, many Americans equate evangelicalism with the so-called Religious Right or a conservative political agenda focused on abortion and homosexuality. Wallis argues that it is possible to be authentically evangelical in one's faith and religious commitment while being liberal politically. He is not alone in that contention; evangelical speakers and writers Ron Sider and Tony Campolo have been making the same case for years.

This book attempts to do for evangelical theology what Wallis, Sider, and Campolo have done for evangelical social ethics and politics. By no means do I wish to compare myself with those esteemed gentlemen, but my project is similar even if more feeble in its outworking. Many evangelicals now accept that one can be fully, authentically evangelical and lean "leftward" politically—especially on issues such as poverty relief, war, and capital punishment. At the same time, however, many or perhaps most evangelicals who think about theology assume that in theology "evangelical" and "conservative" are inseparably conjoined.

People ask me what kind of evangelical I am. Simply to identify oneself as evangelical is no longer sufficient; there are too many types and styles of being evangelical in America and in the world. Asbury Theological Seminary professor Kenneth Collins is surely right that "there are many ways of being evangelical in America today, and evangelicals delight in that diversity and celebrate

---

1. Jim Wallis, *The Politics of God: Why the Right Gets It Wrong and the Left Doesn't Get It* (San Francisco: HarperSanFrancisco, 2005).

such richness."[2] Well, the second half of his statement may not be true for all evangelicals. Especially some conservative evangelicals seem to want to enforce a greater degree of conformity if not uniformity on all evangelicals. However, Collins is right that by and large evangelicals enjoy their diversity, especially in terms of differing worship styles, forms of church government, and views on secondary doctrinal matters such as the order of events in the "last times" (surrounding the return of Christ), baptism, and the Lord's Supper.

Evangelicalism is undeniably diverse. It is no longer—if ever it was—sufficient simply to say "I'm an evangelical." Some have adopted the modifier "conservative" to further pin down what kind of evangelical they are, especially in terms of theological orientation. One contemporary example is theologian Wayne Grudem of Phoenix Theological Seminary. His massive one-volume *Systematic Theology* has become a standard text in theology courses in many evangelical colleges, universities, and seminaries.[3] Grudem explicitly identifies his style of theology as "conservative evangelical" and applies that label to the tradition within which he works. This tradition, he claims, goes back to Luther and Calvin and includes at least thirty-four major nineteenth- and twentieth-century systematic theologies.[4]

Few evangelical theologians have been willing to step forward and declare that they are not "conservative evangelicals." So powerful is the connection between the two terms that to separate

2. Kenneth J. Collins, *The Evangelical Moment: The Promise of an American Religion* (Grand Rapids: Baker Academic, 2005), 14.

3. Wayne Grudem, *Systematic Theology: An Introduction to Biblical Doctrine* (Grand Rapids: Zondervan, 1994).

4. Grudem, *Systematic Theology*, 17. See appendix 4, pp. 1224–30 for the complete list of Grudem's approved conservative evangelical systematic theologies. All of these, he says (p. 17), belong to the conservative evangelical position and hold to the inerrancy of the Bible. However, among the thirty-four are Dutch theologian G. C. Berkouwer, American United Church of Christ theologian Donald G. Bloesch, and American Wesleyan theologians Charles W. Carter (who edited a two-volume Wesleyan systematic theology under the title *A Contemporary Wesleyan Theology* [Grand Rapids: Francis Asbury, 1983], including an essay on Scripture by Wesleyan theologian Ralph Earle) and H. Orton Wiley. All of these expressed serious doubts or reservations about the concept of biblical inerrancy. Their inclusion in Grudem's volume as "conservative evangelicals" who held or hold to biblical inerrancy is questionable.

them seems tantamount to a declaration that one is not evangelical. However, a few evangelical theologians have openly dared to call themselves "postconservative evangelicals." A major thrust of this volume is to examine what that means; how can a theologian or theology be evangelical and not be conservative?

The History of the Term "Postconservative Evangelical"

The label "postconservative" first appeared (or should have appeared but didn't) in 1973/1974 with the writing of a little book by Jack Rogers, then a Fuller Theological Seminary professor. Rogers intended its title to be *Confessions of a Postconservative Evangelical*, but when the book was published in 1974 the prefix was dropped and the title became *Confessions of a Conservative Evangelical*.[5] Near its beginning he says,

> "Conservative" is a good word. It marks continuity with the past, preservation of enduring values, holding on to what has been proven with time. In this sense I am still a conservative. I want to "hold fast what is good" (I Thess. 5:21). There is another sense in which the word "conservative" is used. The dictionary defines "conservative" as "tending to favor the preservation of the existing order and to regard proposals for change with distrust." Being conservative in that sense leads to conservat*ism*. That is the sense of being conservative which has marked much of my past. That is the sense of being conservative which I want to put behind me. That is the sense of being conservative which confuses Christianity with our culture. Salvation is not found in the *status quo*. From apostolic times Christians have challenged the existing order.[6]

This quote demonstrates why the intended title with the prefix "Post-" was more appropriate. The entire volume is Rogers's theological autobiography, focusing on his journey out of conserva-

---

5. Jack Rogers, *Confessions of a Conservative Evangelical* (Philadelphia: Westminster, 1974). When I read Rogers's book during my seminary education I had the uneasy feeling that the title did not fit the book. I confirmed the title change in conversation with the author, who is now professor of theology at San Francisco Theological Seminary and a leader of the Presbyterian Church (USA).

6. Ibid., 11.

tive evangelicalism into something else that can only be labeled "postconservative evangelicalism." The label "postconservative" did not catch on; perhaps it would have if it had been included in Rogers's book title.

The next appearance of the label, so far as I have been able to determine, was in Baptist evangelical theologian Clark Pinnock's 1990 volume *Tracking the Maze: Finding Our Way through Modern Theology from an Evangelical Perspective.* There Pinnock delineated a taxonomy of three main approaches to theology in the modern age: liberal, conservative, and moderate. This is fairly standard fare for mapping modern theology, although it runs the risk of lumping together into broad categories rather different theologians and styles of theology. When he turns to describing the "Moderates," Pinnock divides them into subcategories: "Postliberals" and "Postconservatives." The latter category includes Vatican II Roman Catholic theologians and the new evangelicals who emerged out of fundamentalism.[7] In other words, there Pinnock was using "postconservative" as synonymous with "postfundamentalist." In my opinion this is not a very helpful use of postconservative; the traditional way to describe the new evangelicalism that emerged out of and away from fundamentalism beginning in the 1940s with the founding of the National Association of Evangelicals is postfundamentalist or neoevangelicalism.

Although I read Pinnock's book, I somehow forgot his use of the term "postconservative." When I wrote an article titled "Postconservative Evangelicals Greet the Postmodern Age" for *The Christian Century* I thought I was inventing a new term.[8] Only later did I discover Rogers's earlier intended use of it and Pinnock's earlier use of it in *Tracking the Maze.* However, I claim some right of ownership of the term to describe a certain style of doing evangelical theology (which includes both Rogers and Pinnock) because Rogers never actually used the term in print,

---

7. Clark Pinnock, *Tracking the Maze: Finding Our Way through Modern Theology from an Evangelical Perspective* (San Francisco: Harper & Row, 1990), 66–74.

8. Roger Olson, "Postconservative Evangelicals Greet the Postmodern Age," *The Christian Century*, May 3, 1995, 480–83.

to the best of my knowledge, and Pinnock's use of it was somewhat problematic. Postconservative surely must mean something more specific than postfundamentalist when many, if not most, postfundamentalist evangelical theologians call themselves conservative!

After my article appeared, the term took on something of a life of its own. It was vilified by some, ignored by others, and adopted by a few. The present volume is in part a response to those who vilified the term without correctly understanding it. I hope some who I consider postconservatives will be more willing to use it as I clear up some of the confusion surrounding it.

Not long after my article mapping out postconservative theology appeared in *The Christian Century*, conservative evangelical theologian Millard Erickson published *The Evangelical Left: Encountering Postconservative Evangelical Theology*. I found the title ironic since postconservative evangelical theology seeks to escape the "left/right" categorization into which all theologies have been forced during the modern age by the Enlightenment. Erickson treated postconservatives as accommodators to the Enlightenment[9] when, in fact, they are by and large trying to disentangle theology from the influence of the Enlightenment and modernity. It is postmodernity rather than modernity with which most postconservatives engage in critical and constructive dialogue. Postconservatives emphatically do not consider themselves part of an "evangelical left." To them, "left" and "right" in theology are both defined by the Enlightenment and modernity, which are increasingly being challenged and marginalized by postmodernity. I did not recognize in Erickson's book a fair elucidation or critique of what I understand to be postconservative evangelical thought.

In 1998 nonevangelical theologian Gary Dorrien used the label postconservative in his *The Remaking of Evangelical Theology*.[10] Chapter 5 is titled "Postconservative Evangelicalism: Dialogues in Search of a Generous Orthodoxy." There the author captured the

9. Millard Erickson, *The Evangelical Left: Encountering Postconservative Evangelical Theology* (Grand Rapids: Baker Academic, 1997), 33.
10. Gary Dorrien, *The Remaking of Evangelical Theology* (Louisville: Westminster John Knox, 1998).

spirit of my meaning of "postconservative evangelical theology" almost perfectly, equating it with a style of or approach to being evangelical in theological work. He compared it rightly with postliberalism in terms of a movement beyond original roots, using narrative theology as a device for escaping some of the conundrums and dead ends of traditional theology.

Dorrien rightly contrasted postconservative evangelical theology as a style with its main competitor for doing evangelical theology away from modernism: paleo-orthodoxy or "catholic orthodoxy" (as exemplified in the works of Thomas Oden and Donald Bloesch). He also rightly made clear that these are not absolute alternatives; they overlap in many areas. Both value community and tradition, although in different ways.

Dorrien captured the spirit of postconservative evangelical theology well when he expressed the complaint of many postconservatives about conservative evangelical theology:

> Evangelicals are prone to fret that everything will be lost if they have no ground of absolute certainty or no proof that Christianity is superior to Islam or Buddhism. This fear drives them to impose impossible tests on Christian belief. Inerrancy or the abyss! It also drives them to invest religious authority in a posited epistemological capacity that exists outside the circle of Christian faith. The truth of Christianity is then judged by rational tests that are not only external to Christian revelation but given authority over revelation.[11]

In 2003 British theologian Dave Tomlinson published a book that introduced the label "postevangelicalism": *The Post-Evangelical*.[12] There the author argued for a departure from evangelicalism by so-called emerging Christians associated with the new emergent church network. However, many of Tomlinson's concerns, and at least some of what he proposed, echo the style I labeled postconservative evangelical.

---

11. Ibid., 201. It should be noted here that Donald G. Bloesch agrees with this critique of much of conservative evangelical theology without adopting the postconservative approach or style.

12. Dave Tomlinson, *The Post-Evangelical* (El Cajon, CA: EmergentYS Books, and Grand Rapids: Zondervan, 2003).

I, for one, have no interest in tossing aside the good label "evangelical" or even attaching the prefix "post" to it; I consider myself an evangelical Christian and take a backseat to no one in waving the evangelical flag. I understand Tomlinson's and others' disenchantment with the term evangelical; it has been associated closely with fundamentalism, televangelists, and Religious Right political activism by the media and in the public mind. However, I do not think the situation calls for discarding or moving away from the term "evangelical," which may be misunderstood but has no good substitute. Our task as evangelical theologians is to correct those who misunderstand and misrepresent our label; it is not to give up on it.

Two volumes of theology appearing in 2005 explicitly adopted the label "postconservative evangelical" and applied it to their styles of doing theology. John R. Franke's *The Character of Theology: A Postconservative Evangelical Approach* represented a daring proposal for "doing theology today" (the title of the first chapter) that engages constructively with the best of postmodern thought understood as nonfoundationalism, a term to be defined and described later here. Capturing the spirit of postconservative evangelical theology quite well, Franke described it as "[a] theology with an inherent commitment to the reforming principle [that] maintains without reservation that no single human perspective, be it that of an individual or a particular community or a theological tradition, is adequate to do full justice to the truth of God's revelation in Christ."[13] Franke's proposal so closely parallels my original intention in introducing the concept of postconservative evangelical theology that my task in this volume will be to move behind and beyond it. I will attempt to take a broader view (by delineating a postconservative style) and push beyond what Franke has already written by underscoring postconservative theology's skepticism toward the authority of tradition. Franke expresses a more traditionalist mood in his section, "Tradition: Theology's Hermeneutical Trajectory."[14]

13. John R. Franke, *The Character of Theology: A Postconservative Evangelical Approach* (Grand Rapids: Baker Academic, 2005), 79.
14. Ibid., 154–63.

Also appearing in 2005 was a major proposal for rethinking evangelical theological methodology by Kevin J. Vanhoozer, titled *The Drama of Doctrine: A Canonical-Linguistic Approach to Christian Theology*. There the Trinity Evangelical Divinity School theologian expresses dissatisfaction with the traditional "two-party system of conservative and liberal" theologies because it "no longer seems adequate to describe what is taking place."[15] He describes his own project as postconservative: "The present book sets forth a postconservative, canonical-linguistic theology and a directive theory of doctrine that roots theology more firmly in Scripture."[16] Vanhoozer's proposal and project is, indeed, both postconservative and evangelical in several ways. For example, his theory of revelation is postpropositional without falling into the trap of denying that propositions of revelation exist. Yet his approach is more specific than the style of theology I labeled postconservative in 1995. It represents one postconservative approach, not postconservative evangelicalism as a whole, which is broader and more inclusive.

I will not even attempt to list all the articles, columns, editorials, and web pages that have used the term "postconservative" in a variety of ways since 1995. Some conservative evangelicals have rejected the term out of hand as impossible; for them "conservative" and "evangelical" cannot be separated. They cannot conceive of such an animal as postconservative evangelicalism; it would be the same as postevangelicalism. One conservative evangelical writer speculated, without citing any references, that postconservatives are on a trajectory toward accepting sexual perversion and outright heresy if not apostasy into evangelical churches. Other more cautious evangelical writers have simply expressed discomfort with the term itself. When I wrote an article for a major evangelical magazine about the phenomenon, I had to call it "reformist evangelical theology," as the term "postconservative" was distasteful to the editors. My friend Stanley J. Grenz, who was, to my mind, the epitome of a postconservative evangelical theologian, was reluctant to have the label applied to him or his theological work.

15. Kevin J. Vanhoozer, *The Drama of Doctrine: A Canonical-Linguistic Approach to Christian Theology* (Louisville: Westminster John Knox, 2005), xiii.
16. Ibid.

A Brief Account of Postconservatism

I am confident that some of the discomfort with the term "postconservative evangelical" will be eased by elucidating its meaning more clearly and carefully than has happened so far. That is the burden of the present volume. I hope to persuade readers that there is a style of doing evangelical theology that cannot fairly be described as conservative; postconservative is one way, and perhaps the best way, to describe it. Although there are significant differences between them, postliberalism and postconservatism share something in common. Postliberalism is an attempt to move beyond the confines of liberal theology without rejecting everything about it. Postconservatism is an attempt to move beyond the limitations of conservative theology without rejecting everything about it. Both make critical but also constructive use of some aspects of postmodernity in freeing their host theologies (liberal and conservative) from the shackles of the Enlightenment and modernity.

Who are some of the leading proponents of postconservative evangelical theology? Here I hesitate. The term has been so widely and profoundly distorted by its critics that some postconservatives do not want it attached to them. In some cases, being perceived as postconservative has hindered careers in theology. Rather than create a box category with heavy boundaries, I prefer to regard postconservative theology as a "fuzzy" category defined by a gravitational center without definite boundaries. (I will discuss how it is possible to have a center without a circumference—something to which some conservatives have objected—in a later chapter on the nature of evangelicalism.) In other words, I do not regard postconservative evangelical theology as an organization or a club with members. There is no headquarters or membership list. It may even be the case that no single individual is completely or perfectly postconservative; it might be best to speak in terms of postconservative moves in theology rather than postconservative theologians.

Contrary to Millard Erickson, I consider postconservative evangelicalism not so much a movement as a mood. It is a style of doing theology; some theologians follow or embody that style more than others. I've already mentioned two evangelical theologians who explicitly adopt the term for their theological proposals and projects: John Franke and Kevin Vanhoozer. In addition to Franke and Vanhoozer, I consider a number of other evangelical theologians and writers postconservatives in the sense that their styles of doing theology seem to move beyond strict adherence to the "received evangelical tradition." For them the fact that something is the "established evangelical position," to use Erickson's language, does not settle the issue. I will name some of them later in this introduction. They are willing to subject any doctrine or practice of the churches and of Christians to new scrutiny in light of God's Word. They do not pay lip service to the Reformation concept of *sola scriptura* or *prima scriptura* (Scripture as the supreme source and norm for faith and practice); they are determined to follow it by being open to new ways of thinking about anything insofar as fresh and faithful interpretation of Scripture demands it. That is why it is possible to be more evangelical by being less conservative: insofar as "conservative" denotes firm adherence to tradition and unwillingness to consider new theological ideas even in the light of fresh and faithful interpretation of Scripture, being conservative is contrary to the spirit of evangelical faith, which elevates the Bible above tradition.

The Meaning of "Conservative Evangelical" Here

It is impossible to understand the postconservative mood in evangelical theology apart from conservatism. The essence of conservatism in theology is a determined—if often implicit and unacknowledged—adherence to tradition. It is the establishment of a magisterium, whether formal or informal, that exercises prior restraint over the critical and constructive tasks of theology. Very few evangelical theologians admit that they recognize or follow such a magisterium and most deny it. But their conservatism shows in their tendency to slam down any and every new proposal for revisioning Christian doctrine by appeal to what has always been believed by Christians generally or by what evangelicals have traditionally believed.

Evangelical conservatism is exemplified by the various essays and most of the responses in the volume *Evangelical Affirmations*, edited by Kenneth S. Kantzer and Carl F. H. Henry.[17] The essays represent speeches given at a conference sponsored by the National Association of Evangelicals and Trinity Evangelical Divinity School in 1989, attempting to identify and codify an evangelical doctrinal consensus. Some of the leading speakers at the conference and authors of the essays, such as Henry, the dean of conservative evangelical theologians, explicitly equated authentic evangelicalism with conservative, orthodox theology.[18] Most of the speakers and writers decried the fragmentation of evangelicalism, especially a supposed widespread deviation from evangelical orthodoxy, and attempted to clarify essential evangelical beliefs. For them, "evangelical integrity" is at stake in identifying who is "in" and who is "out" of the evangelical club.[19] The goal of the conference was the establishment of firm evangelical boundaries. In identifying these boundaries, appeal was often made to what evangelicals have always believed.

Of course, as so often happens in such conferences (others of which I have attended), the organizers drew in only those speakers and writers who would probably endorse a certain vision of authentic evangelical faith. Notably missing from this conference, as from others like it organized by conservative evangelicals, were well-known and highly regarded progressive evangelicals who might prove to be flies in the ointment or troublers of the house of Israel. For example, the 1989 Evangelical Affirmations Conference and the 1990 volume of the same title included no evangelical theologian who would critique the controversial concept of biblical inerrancy. Predictably, plenary (as opposed to partial) inerrancy crept in as one of the affirmations that define authentic evangelical faith.[20] This happened more in the speakers'

17. Kenneth S. Kantzer and Carl F. H. Henry, eds., *Evangelical Affirmations* (Grand Rapids: Zondervan, 1990).
18. Ibid., 17–19.
19. Ibid., 513.
20. In his contribution to *Evangelical Affirmations*, titled "Who Are the Evangelicals?" Carl Henry argued against broadening the definition of "evangelical" to include those who depart from the full truthfulness of Scripture. Who he had in mind is unclear; he may have meant adherents of "partial inerrancy," or evan-

and writers' expositions of the affirmations than in the actual wording of the affirmations, but the volume makes clear that the participants in this conference desire inerrancy to be included as part of the evangelical identity.

Throughout the volume, appeal is made repeatedly to what evangelicals have generally believed, to an alleged evangelical consensus. The door is closed to further reflection or reconsideration. Although the signatories to the affirmations deny that it is intended as a creed or binding confessional statement for ordination or church membership, they surely knew it would be used by administrators of evangelical institutions in making decisions about hiring and continuing employment. Although most evangelicals probably do adhere to the nine affirmations to some degree, the attempt to invest them with authority based on traditional interpretation and historical evangelical consensus is what makes postconservatives uneasy. This is functionally to place a set of human statements on the same plane with Scripture; they become a written magisterium placed on a pedestal above question or reconsideration even on the basis of fresh and faithful biblical scholarship.

Conservative evangelical theology, then, is the style of doing theology that relies heavily on authoritative tradition and rejects or consciously neglects the critical and constructive tasks of theology except insofar as "critical" means rejecting new formulations and revisionings of beliefs. In the late twentieth and early twenty-first centuries, conservative evangelical theology

---

gelicals who deny inerrancy in favor of the infallibility of Scripture. He admitted that infallibility is the term used in the National Association of Evangelicals' statement of faith, but argued that it was not meant as a disavowal of inerrancy. However, questions arise about Henry's polemic and his rhetoric of exclusion. For example, Scottish theologian James Orr was embraced as an evangelical by B. B. Warfield of Princeton, who championed inerrancy and to whom most inerrantists appeal, but Orr did not believe in biblical inerrancy. And what about Wesleyans like Nazarene theologian H. Orton Wiley, who criticized inerrancy as too problematic a concept? Was he not an evangelical? And what about the many evangelicals who do prefer to use the term "infallibility" to describe the Bible's truthfulness? Does their reluctance to adopt inerrancy as a shibboleth make them less evangelical? In personal correspondence Henry denied that he applies inerrancy as a *sine qua non* of authentic evangelicalism but also suggested that any avowal of errors in the Bible is tantamount to calling the Holy Spirit a liar. This is the spirit of conservative evangelicalism; it breathes the same air as fundamentalism even if it is not quite as toxic.

takes either of two main forms. First there are the biblicist evangelicals, for want of a better label, who believe that revelation is primarily propositional (facts and statements of fact) or at least that propositions form the core of that part of revelation that is relevant for theology. These evangelicals attempt to move directly from the Bible to doctrine, supposing that doctrines are revealed among the facts of the Bible and need only to be collected, systematized, and presented in understandable form.

These conservative evangelical theologians tend to follow the methodology of nineteenth-century Princeton theologian Charles Hodge. Very often, if not usually, they appeal to something like a "received evangelical tradition" of hermeneutics and doctrine to fend off new interpretations and formulations and to consolidate agreement about a fairly detailed list of core doctrines. For them, correct doctrine is the essence of Christianity and of evangelical faith.

To some extent or other the following theologians seem to me to embody this style of theology—which is not to say they are all alike in every way. They are traditionalist and biblicist even if at times they depart from that approach and make postconservative moves in theology, such as reconceiving a particular attribute of God or introducing a nonmainstream idea. To a very great extent they are influenced by "the stout and persistent theology of Charles Hodge," to borrow the title of an article by conservative evangelical theologian David Wells.[21] Other conservative evangelical theologians include Carl F. H. Henry, Kenneth Kantzer, J. I. Packer, Wayne Grudem, Norman Geisler, and D. A. Carson.

By no means is this meant to be a rogues' gallery. Nor do I mean to suggest by listing them in this manner that there are no differences among them. For example, some take a presuppositionalist approach to apologetics and theology while others prefer an evidentialist approach, a significant difference. My only reason for putting their names together here is to identify for readers some of the evangelicals whom I and other postconservative evangelicals consider conservatives. My impression is that none of these gentlemen would object to being labeled conser-

21. David Wells, "The Stout and Persistent Theology of Charles Hodge," *Christianity Today*, August 30, 1974, 10–15.

vative evangelicals, but I am open to correction. Whether they would appreciate my characterization of their style of theology as biblicist and traditionalist is perhaps more debatable. I hope they are receptive to it. All seem concerned to protect the propositional nature of revelation as primary, and they seem to believe it is relatively easy with training and skill to move from biblical exegesis to establishment of sound doctrine without the aid of other sources and norms such as tradition, philosophy, or culture. Grudem's approach in *Systematic Theology* is typical:

> Systematic theology involves collecting and understanding all the relevant passages in the Bible on various topics and then summarizing their teachings clearly so that we know what to believe about each topic. . . . It attempts to summarize the teachings of Scripture in a brief, understandable, and very carefully formulated statement.[22]

I do not labor under the misconception that all conservative theologians or even those in my brief list agree entirely with Grudem about this (or anything else). However, the idea that doctrines are to be mined out of the Bible and that evangelical doctrines are simply biblical teachings and not the secondary language of the church on the basis of revelation is typical of the conservative approach to evangelical theology. So is frequent appeal to an evangelical faith once and for all delivered as a negative norm for ruling out new ideas.

A second type of conservative evangelical theology is represented by traditionalists who identify an ancient, ecumenical doctrinal consensus—or such a consensus plus the teachings of the magisterial Reformers (Luther, Calvin, et al.)—as a source and norm alongside of Scripture, even if subordinate to Scripture for establishing and defending evangelical doctrine. This approach to conservative theology has been called "paleo-orthodoxy" by one of its main adherents, Methodist theologian Thomas Oden. The main difference between this style of conservative theology and the alternative outlined above is its explicit identification of tradition as a governing authority for evangelical theology. The tradition being invoked is not the "received evangelical tradition"

22. Grudem, *Systematic Theology*, 21, 23.

or "established evangelical doctrine" but the consensus of the early
church fathers including the ancient ecumenical creeds. Some
of these theologians add the magisterial Reformers' consensual
teachings and the main Reformation confessional statements, insofar as they agree with one another (e.g., the Lutheran Augsburg
Confession and the Reformed Heidelberg Catechism).

Along with Oden, Baptist theologian D. H. Williams and evangelical Episcopal theologian Robert Webber represent this approach. In spite of significant differences, all three believe some
ecumenical consensus of early (and perhaps Reformational) theologians and councils represents the interpretive lens through
which all Christians should read Scripture. In other words, as
Protestants, they do not explicitly place tradition on the same level
as Scripture in terms of authority, but they do believe modern
Christians should respect the church fathers and early Christian
councils (and perhaps sixteenth-century Reformers) and should
even regard these sources as authoritative for biblical interpretation. In practice this means the critical and constructive tasks of
theology ought to be conducted in light of what the church has
already decided about crucial doctrinal matters. Representative
of this approach to conservative evangelical theology is Oden's
The Rebirth of Orthodoxy: Signs of New Life in Christianity, where
the author warns all doctrinal revisionists that their innovative
interpretations "will not gain easy consent in the company of
those who have been formed by the earliest attesters to the truth
of God's coming in history."[23] Throughout the book Oden makes
clear that, in his opinion, all truly important theological questions
were answered and controversies settled by the church fathers and
their councils. Fresh, innovative theological thinking is treated as
dangerous and suspect—if not toxic—to authentic Christianity.

Common Features of Conservative Evangelical Theology

What do all these conservative evangelical theologians have in
common? It would be dangerous to lump them all together; they

23. Thomas Oden, *The Rebirth of Orthodoxy: Signs of New Life in Christianity*
(San Francisco: HarperSanFrancisco, 2003), 31.

are very different in many ways. However, certain features appear commonly among them. First, there is a tendency to treat correct doctrine—orthodoxy—as the essence of authentic Christianity and of evangelical faith. Along with that in varying degrees is a tendency to treat orthodoxy as a rather rigid phenomenon and to respond in a fairly brittle manner to even the most innocent innovators on the ground that they may be at the top of a slippery slope to apostasy down which their followers will almost inevitably slide.[24]

Second, conservative evangelical theologians tend to treat revelation as primarily propositional. Thus they tend to gloss over the personal and eventful nature of revelation as well as the revelational power of stories, images, and speech acts.

Third, these theologians tend to elevate some tradition, whether implicitly or explicitly, to the status of a magisterium for evangelical theological identity. For some it is a perceived "received evangelical tradition," while for others it is a more ancient "ecumenical consensus." The effect is to close off fresh theological reflection leading to revisioning of doctrines.

Fourth, because of this tendency toward traditionalism, conservative evangelicals tend to be suspicious of the constructive task of theology; to a very large degree they reject or neglect attempts to construct new doctrinal formulations or reconstruct old ones. They tend to be defensive of what they perceive to be traditional evangelical orthodoxy, and they spend a great deal of time and energy patrolling evangelical boundaries.

Fifth, they tend to view evangelicalism as a bounded set category; people are either in or out, and it should be relatively easy to tell who is which. Many conservative evangelical theologians write and speak as if the evangelical theological guild were a club with membership and rules. They seem to feel that, at least occasionally, self-identified evangelical theologians should be publicly identified as pretenders and stripped of their right to be considered authentically evangelical.

Sixth, conservative evangelicals tend to regard the "evangelical tent" (especially of theologians) as relatively smaller than the

24. This is expressed, for example, in Millard Erickson's critique of "the evangelical left," in which he warns of "a further shift leftward" by postconservatives' followers (*The Evangelical Left*, 133–42).

number of those who call themselves evangelicals. They worry a great deal that evangelicalism is becoming too broad and thin and they often go about attempting to restrict the scope of authentic evangelicalism to those who adhere to a certain concept (such as Scriptural inerrancy) that they regard as crucial for the health and well-being of evangelical Christianity, even if it is not an item of traditional Christian orthodoxy or explicitly taught in the Bible.

Seventh, these theologians tend to be highly suspicious of both modernity and postmodernity even if they are themselves influenced by modernity, which many postconservatives suspect is the case. In most cases they agree among themselves that ancient or traditional is best and that the postmodern spirit is relativistic and therefore destructive of authentic Christian faith, which consists of absolutes known with a high degree of certainty. Doctrinal pluralism is anathema and these theologians tend to see it at work in many places, including among evangelicals. A good example of this feature of conservative evangelicalism is Donald Carson's *The Gagging of God: Christianity Confronts Pluralism*, which is a stimulating if flawed critique of the contemporary theological scene.[25] In my opinion Carson sees defection from authentic evangelical absolutism where it may not exist.

Eighth, conservative evangelicals tend to think that it is possible to do theology relatively uninfluenced by history and culture. They are antihistoricists in a fairly extreme way. Historicism in this sense is belief that all ideas are historically, socially, and culturally situated so that they are amenable to reconsideration and revision within a different context. While conservative evangelicals often admit that the gospel must be contextualized (Carson and Erickson especially play on this note), they draw back from any idea that every doctrinal and theological formulation or method is culturally embedded. They prefer to believe in and look for a transcultural expression of the gospel; theology ought to be global rather than local (except in terms of language and application).

25. D. A. Carson, *The Gagging of God: Christianity Confronts Pluralism* (Grand Rapids: Zondervan, 1996).

Ninth, conservative evangelical theology tends to remain close to its fundamentalist roots even as it repudiates the cultish and sectarian aspects of fundamentalism. Most of the theologians I identify as conservative evangelicals will reject this feature of conservative evangelicalism. They do not like to believe that they remain close to their fundamentalist roots. In some cases it is not so much a matter of not having moved far enough away from fundamentalism as of having moved toward fundamentalism from a background in liberal theology. I admit this is a matter of opinion and perspective, but postconservative evangelicals worry that postfundamentalist evangelicals (i.e., establishment evangelical theologians) have one foot stuck in fundamentalism and sometimes "conservative evangelical" is just a euphemism for "fundamentalist," a label that almost no theologian wants to wear.

To be sure, insofar as fundamentalism signals anti-intellectualism, an aversion to critical thinking, and separation from secular society and from Christians affected by secularism and liberalism, most conservative evangelical theologians are not fundamentalists. However, many conservatives share with fundamentalists a tendency toward harsh, polemical rhetoric and angry denunciations or ad hominem arguments when writing about fellow evangelicals with whom they disagree. The words "heresy" and "heterodoxy" and charges of departures from the true faith are all too frequent in some of their writings. An example appears in Carson's *The Gagging of God* with regard to fellow evangelical Stanley Grenz, who to his dying day in March 2005 affirmed the supernatural inspiration and even inerrancy of Scripture. Carson wrote, "With the best will in the world, I cannot see how Grenz's approach to Scripture can be called 'evangelical' in any useful sense."[26] He provides no detailed reasons or arguments to support this criticism, which is of a kind that can be very damaging within the sometimes volatile political arena of the evangelical academy. Such statements are far too frequent among conservative evangelicals, and they smack of the tactics of fundamentalism.

Tenth, and finally, conservative evangelical theology tends to be done in the grip of fear of liberal theology. That is not to say

26. Ibid., 481.

liberal theology is good, but only that it is possible to allow it too much power. It is not uncommon to hear or read a conservative evangelical theologian warning of Friedrich Schleiermacher, the father of liberal theology, when discussing more progressive or postconservative evangelicals and their theological work. Conservatives tend to insist on placing every theologian and theological proposal on the spectrum of left to right as defined by attitudes toward modernity, with liberal theology representing maximal accommodation to modernity within a Christian theological framework. By and large, conservatives have trouble conceiving of any theology that is not tied to modernity in this way and thus neither "left" nor "right." Postliberalism (the Yale School of Theology) is a case in point; conservatives hardly know what to do with it and it is often ignored because it cannot be placed on their spectrum.

A caveat about this delineation of conservative evangelical theology is in order here. I do not mean to paint all conservatives with the same brush; one or more of these common features will not fit individual conservative theologians. They are not all present to the same degree in individual conservatives. However, my own broad and fairly deep experience with evangelical theology has led me to view these as relatively common features that to some degree mark most conservative evangelicals who work in theology.

What Conservatives and Postconservatives Have in Common

Postconservative theology attempts to move beyond these features insofar as they represent limitations and hindrances to healthy theology. Most postconservatives view these features as limiting factors and hindrances. That is not to say they reject them wholesale; it is a matter of degree.

What do postconservatives have in common with conservatives so that they are all evangelicals? Evangelical historian David Bebbington has identified four hallmarks or "core convictions" of evangelical Christianity: biblicism, conversionism, crucicentrism (cross-centered piety), and activism in evangelism and social transformation.[27] Mark Noll, one of the best-known and most influential historians of the evangelical movement, agrees with Bebbington about these four common features of evangelicalism:

> These core evangelical commitments have never by themselves yielded cohesive, institutionally compact or clearly demarcated groups of Christians. But they do serve to identify a large kin network of churches, voluntary societies, books and periodicals, personal networks, and emphases of belief and practice.[28]

In other words, the four hallmarks are not sufficient to sustain enduring evangelical organizations, but they are agreed-upon common features or family resemblances that identify evangelicals within different organizations.

Conservative and postconservative evangelicals agree about these core convictions; that is what makes them evangelicals. Of course, some conservative evangelicals—to say nothing of fundamentalists—may think this too minimal an account of what makes someone evangelical. Many of them want to add a strong confessional element so that being evangelical requires a fairly detailed doctrinal component. That was apparently the concern that drove the conveners and participants of the aforementioned Evangelical Affirmations Conference in 1989. Nevertheless, there is fairly broad agreement among observers of the evangelical scene that these four convictions define evangelical faith. Postconservatives as well as conservatives adhere to these convictions enthusiastically.

Postconservative Evangelical Theology and Theologians

The common features of postconservative evangelical theology will be fleshed out throughout this volume. In many ways they are

27. D. W. Bebbington, *Evangelicalism in Modern Britain: A History from the 1730s to the 1980s* (London: Unwin Hyman, 1989), 1–17.
28. Mark Noll, *The Rise of Evangelicalism: The Age of Edwards, Whitefield and the Wesleys* (Downers Grove, IL: InterVarsity, 2003), 19.

simply the reverse of the hallmarks of conservative evangelical theology outlined above. For example, postconservatives tend to regard the essence of authentic Christianity and evangelical faith as transforming experience and a distinctive spirituality (e.g., a personal relationship with Jesus Christ that results in amendment of life toward holiness) rather than correct doctrine. In other words, orthopathy (right experience) is prior to orthodoxy in defining true Christianity. The influence of pietism is evident in postconservative evangelicalism. Also, postconservatives tend to regard revelation as something more than propositions; the main purpose of revelation is transformation rather than information. The essence of revelation may be thought of as God's acts in establishing covenant with people and redeeming them through Jesus Christ. No postconservative denies a propositional element to revelation, but many are uncomfortable with the conservative emphasis on propositions as the most important feature of revelation.

Who are the postconservative theologians? Again, one should not think of postconservative evangelicalism as a box or bounded set category. But there are some evangelical theologians whose works reveal a trend away from fundamentalism and traditionalism and toward a desire to make the Word of God fresh in a creative and constructive encounter with culture. They tend to think the constructive task of theology is always unfinished, and that the call of the theologian is to rethink traditional concepts and categories in every generation and culture. They are not relativists, but they eschew an absolutism that enshrines human formulations of belief in incorrigible terms as if theology were a museum. They tend to be open to postmodernity and work with a nonfoundational approach to theology; they are less concerned with rational certainty than with the blessed assurance wrought by the inner testimony of the Spirit of God.

Some evangelical theologians who could be considered postconservative in this sense, even if they do not apply that label to themselves, include Stanley Grenz, Clark Pinnock, Kevin Vanhoozer, John Sanders, John Franke, Amos Yong, Nancey Murphy, James McClendon, Miroslav Volf, Henry (Hal) Knight, and Brian McLaren.

Like the conservative theologians previously cited, these do not constitute a monolithic block; they are a diverse group of theologians who share a common spirit of adventure but not unfettered theological experimentation. All are committed to the Bible as theology's primary and controlling source and norm. All work within a supernatural life- and worldview centered on God's revelation of himself in Jesus Christ "in [whom] all things hold together" (Col. 1:17 NRSV). All proclaim salvation through Christ and conversion as a supernatural work of the Holy Spirit by grace through faith alone. None is liberal or "on a liberal trajectory," contrary to some conservative critics. Yet they all feel perfectly free and even compelled to move beyond traditional boundaries when the Spirit calls through Scripture, for all of them believe there is a difference between every human interpretation of Scripture and revelation itself. No doctrine is in itself sacrosanct; all doctrines are open to reexamination, and the constructive task of theology is never finished because God always has new light to break forth from his Word.

The present volume will attempt to explicate this approach to theology to which I have applied the phrase "postconservative evangelical." The practitioners of this theology, many of whom are influenced to some degree by last-generation evangelical theologian Bernard Ramm (d. 1993) and who often quote British theologian Lesslie Newbigin, constitute the loose group or collection of theologians who inspire this work. My intention here is to examine some of their contributions and create a portrait (not photograph) of the postconservative evangelical approach to theology.

Mediating Evangelical Theologians

Do all evangelical theologians fall into one of these two broad categories? Is every evangelical theologian either conservative or postconservative? Certainly not. Two who fall between and share characteristics of both styles of theology are Donald G. Bloesch and Alister McGrath. Bloesch has been quietly working along his own lines without joining any coalition or network of evangelical theologians for twenty-five to thirty years. He taught at the University of Dubuque School of Theology (Presbyterian) for many years until his retirement. His voluminous outpouring of publications about evangelical theology and of evangelical faith has influenced many conservative and postconservative evangelicals. Most recently he has completed his magnum opus, a seven-volume system of theology collectively titled *Christian Foundations*.[29] Bloesch is conservative by the standards of his own denomination (United Church of Christ) but progressive by traditional evangelical standards because he denies biblical inerrancy (except as truthfulness in all matters pertaining to faith and practice) and leans noticeably toward Karl Barth in some respects. His theology is a form of "evangelical neoorthodoxy." Interestingly, however, conservatives are fond of him because of his strongly confessional stance; he regards evangelical faith as having a strong confessional component and he is defensive of traditional doctrinal formulations and even traditional language of God in worship and prayer. It would be difficult to peg him as either conservative or postconservative. He wears both aspects or works with both styles.

Oxford University theologian Alister McGrath has produced several works of evangelical theology and is widely regarded as fairly conservative; he is a fan of conservative theologian J. I. Packer and defends conservative theological positions from within his own Anglican identity. However, in books like *A Passion for Truth: The Intellectual Coherence of Evangelicalism*, McGrath raises strong objections to some features of conservative evangelical theology and, together with postconservatives generally, complains about its tendency toward captivity to Enlightenment modes of thinking:

> Despite all its criticisms of the theological and exegetical programmes of the Enlightenment, evangelicalism seems to have chosen to follow it in this respect. The narrative character of Scripture has been subtly marginalized, in order to facilitate its analysis purely as a repository of propositional statements, capable

29. Donald G. Bloesch, *Christian Foundations*, 7 vols. (Downers Grove, IL: InterVarsity, 1992–2004).

of withstanding the epistemological criteria of the Enlightenment. . . . Throughout its history, evangelicalism has shown itself
to be prone to lapse into a form of rationalism.[30]

Like Bloesch, McGrath is critical of the influence of modern
rationalism in the form of epistemological foundationalism,
which manifests in a craving for rational certainty either through
empirical-historical evidences or logical deduction from a priori
truths (rational presuppositions). And like Bloesch, McGrath is
defensive of traditional orthodoxy and reluctant to support fresh
theological construction or innovation.

Surely there are other evangelical theologians who cannot
be comfortably labeled either conservative or postconservative.
Nevertheless, these are two styles of theology competing for
the hearts and minds of evangelicals and especially of young
evangelicals. Among the young stand arrayed two groups of
evangelicals. On the one hand are those increasingly committed
to a fairly aggressive form of Reformed theology with a strongly
Puritan flavor, influenced by J. I. Packer, R. C. Sproul, John Piper,
D. A. Carson, and other "confessing evangelicals." On the other
hand are those fascinated with the experimentations of worship
found in the "emerging church network" led by Brian McLaren
and influenced by Stanley Grenz. The latter are often—though
not always, to be sure—receptive to open theism (that God does
not know the future exhaustively and infallibly) and inclusivism (that some may find salvation by God's grace through Jesus
Christ without ever hearing the gospel explicitly proclaimed or
taught).

My Credentials for Writing about Evangelical Theology

What gives me, Roger Olson, the right to write about these
approaches to and styles of theology? What do I know about
evangelicalism and evangelical theology? You, the reader, have a
right to know. Why should you accept that I know what I'm talk-

30. Alister McGrath, *A Passion for Truth: The Intellectual Coherence of Evangelicalism* (Downers Grove, IL: InterVarsity, 1996), 105–6.

ing about? Although I do not wish to "blow my own horn" here, I feel the need to lay out my evangelical credentials and reveal my own history with evangelicalism and evangelical theology so that you know "where I'm coming from" and thus can decide what credibility to attach to my work.

I was born into the home of a Pentecostal pastor in Iowa. There were no boundaries between my home life and my church life. Our church was deeply involved in the local evangelical association (a local affiliate of the National Association of Evangelicals) as well as with the multidenominational evangelical organization Youth for Christ. We supported Billy Graham crusades as well as other evangelistic efforts of non-Pentecostal evangelicals. My earliest memories include attendance at citywide and statewide evangelical gatherings. During my teen years I was heavily involved with Youth for Christ, where I rubbed shoulders with people of all ages from many denominations. My uncle was president of our denomination for twenty-five years and during that time he served on the national governing board of the National Association of Evangelicals; he and I talked for hours about the meanings of "evangelical," "fundamentalist," and "liberal," and what made us Pentecostals evangelicals.

I attended and graduated from an evangelical Bible college where I began to read evangelical literature, including the now defunct but then very influential *Eternity* magazine, founded by Donald G. Barnhouse. There I came into contact with the articles and editorials of numerous well-known evangelical scholars. After college I attended and graduated from an evangelical Baptist seminary, North American Baptist Seminary, where a parade of evangelical scholars came before me in classes, chapels, conferences, and through their writings. One of my professors (on a visiting basis) was the well-known and influential evangelical pastor and theologian James Montgomery Boice of Tenth Presbyterian Church in Philadelphia. As assistant pastor of an independent evangelical and charismatic congregation, I was deeply involved in the city's evangelical ministerial association and served on the steering committees of several evangelistic outreaches of leading evangelists who visited our city.

Throughout my doctoral studies, including a year studying theology with Wolfhart Pannenberg in Germany, I stayed in touch with evangelical groups and read voraciously among the evangelical theologians of the 1970s and 1980s. Early on I was influenced more by Donald Bloesch and Bernard Ramm than by Carl Henry. I was privileged to audit a doctor of ministry seminar led by Ramm not long before he died, and Bloesch and I became friendly acquaintances. Eventually, during my fifteen-year stint teaching theology at Bethel College and Seminary in St. Paul, Minnesota, I began to write articles for *Christianity Today* and eventually became editor of the evangelical *Christian Scholar's Review*. I coauthored two books with evangelical theologian Stanley Grenz and cochaired the Evangelical Theology Group of the American Academy of Religion. Because of my passion for all things evangelical, an editor of Westminster/John Knox Press invited me in 2002 to write *The Westminster Handbook to Evangelical Theology*. That reference work was published in 2004. I have written numerous articles and book reviews related to evangelical theology and delivered numerous papers to professional society meetings about evangelical theology. My *The Pocket History of Evangelical Theology* was published by InterVarsity in 2007.

I remember well my shock and dismay when Harold Lindsell's *Battle for the Bible* was published in 1976.[31] I read it together with Dewey Beegle's *Scripture, Tradition and Infallibility* during the summer of 1977.[32] The two volumes take radically different stances with regard to biblical inerrancy. I was shocked by the aggressiveness of Lindsell's volume, which attacked all who dared to call themselves evangelical while denying strict biblical inerrancy. That included most of my seminary professors and many of my spiritual mentors! The word inerrancy was not part of our vocabulary in at least my branch of Pentecostalism, but there was no doubt in my mind we were evangelicals. I saw a creeping return to dominance of Reformed fundamentalism as Lindsell's book brought about a heresy hunt among evangelicals.

31. Harold Lindsell, *Battle for the Bible* (Grand Rapids: Zondervan, 1976).
32. Dewey Beegle, *Scripture, Tradition and Infallibility* (Grand Rapids: Eerdmans, 1973).

Throughout that furor over inerrancy and evangelical identity, I determined to remain evangelical and to allow no one to push me out of that camp while remaining true to my pietistic, Arminian heritage that did not place value on the kind of rational certainty sought by the aggressive neofundamentalists trying to take over the entire evangelical movement. It has been a struggle. Now, at age fifty-four and secure in a tenured position at a major Baptist university, I am ready to declare quite publicly which side I am on. I have not significantly changed my theological beliefs since my seminary days and I remain a committed evangelical. But the adjective "conservative" no longer adequately describes the kind of evangelical I am. Of course, like all evangelicals, I am conservative in the overall scheme of Protestant theology. I find little common ground with real theological liberals. I believe in the supernatural inspiration of Scripture and its full authority over all matters of faith and practice. I believe in the Trinity and the deity of Jesus Christ. I believe salvation is by God's grace alone through faith alone by means of Christ's cross alone. I believe Jesus Christ suffered a penal substitution for sinners, providing atonement for humanity's sin. I believe in the virgin birth and in Christ's bodily resurrection, including the empty tomb. I believe in the supernatural gifts of the Holy Spirit and in miracles of healing, provision, and rescue in answer to prayers. I believe God is the providential ruler and governor of all of nature and history. I believe nothing can happen without God's permission. I believe Christ will return in power and glory to judge the world, and I personally adhere to the premillennial interpretation of the kingdom of God in relation to Christ's return.

Does all that make me conservative? Certainly—compared to liberals and secularists. But within the evangelical movement I am probably not a card-carrying conservative, in spite of my traditional beliefs, because I adhere to a "big tent" view of evangelicalism that includes many people who don't agree with me about some secondary matters of doctrine and because I am not enamored with the foundationalist project of theology that captivates the followers of Charles Hodge and the "Old Princeton School" of theology. Most important, I suppose, I believe in the full equality of women in home, church, and society (I grew up with women ministers all around me!), and I do not believe "inerrancy" is a useful term for describing the Bible's truthfulness.

I hope you will dare to continue reading and that you will, in the seven chapters that make up this book, consider what postconservative evangelical theology means and how it is possible to be more evangelical by being less conservative when "conservative" is understood in a certain way as characterizing a certain style of doing theology.

1

The Postconservative Style of Evangelical Theology

Much was already said about conservative and postconservative evangelical theology in the introduction. Here I will go further in articulating the style that marks postconservative evangelical theology. What characteristics mark it as different from conservative or conventional evangelical theology? Who are some of the leading postconservative evangelical thinkers and how have they manifested these characteristics? Is this a movement or a mood in evangelical theology? These and other issues will be addressed directly or indirectly in this chapter as I attempt to paint a portrait of postconservatism. I must first deal with some preliminary considerations, however, including the important question, Who is an evangelical theologian?

The Identity of an Evangelical Theologian

No doubt some astute readers are beginning to wonder whether the theologians whose style of theologizing I'm labeling postcon-

servative really deserve the label "evangelical." And does postconservative theology deserve to be called evangelical? Before plunging into a full-scale description of this style of theology, then, it
will be helpful and even necessary to discuss how to identify an
evangelical theologian and an evangelical theology. What justifies
calling a theologian or a project in theology evangelical? This
question naturally arises because of the conventional tendency
to connect "evangelical" with "conservative." If a theologian or
theology is not conservative can he, she, or it be evangelical?
How closely should these concepts be linked?

Here I will propose two controversial theses: *evangelical
theology is theology done by an evangelical theologian*, and *an
evangelical theologian is someone who claims to be evangelical, is
generally regarded as working within the evangelical network, and
adheres to David Bebbington's four cardinal features of evangelical faith plus one* (to be explained later). First of all, evangelical
theology is theology done by an evangelical theologian. What
else? How else should evangelical theology be defined?

Some conservatives wish to identify and guard boundaries
around evangelical theology by investing it with strong confessional content. For them, an evangelical theologian is someone
who is theologically trained, who contributes critically and constructively in the field of Christian theology, and who adheres to a
set of beliefs or doctrinal affirmations that constitute orthodoxy.
This is clearly the thrust of the Evangelical Affirmations document as interpreted by the speakers and most respondents at
the conference of the same name sponsored by the National Association of Evangelicals and Trinity Evangelical Divinity School
in 1989. The movers and shakers of this conference, if not all of
its participants and signers of the document it produced, clearly
intended to invest the concept "evangelical" with strong and
stable doctrinal content. For them, evangelical theology is first
and foremost orthodox Christianity. The conveners and leaders of
this conference—as several others like it before and since—were
concerned that "not only on the outside, but even within our own
ranks, some confusion exists as to exactly who are evangelicals."[1]

1. Kenneth S. Kantzer and Carl F. H. Henry, eds., *Evangelical Affirmations*
(Grand Rapids: Zondervan, 1990), 29.

They frequently expressed dismay at the rampant diversity of interpretation among evangelicals. The Affirmations document produced by the conference was intended to "represent evangelical truths that specially need to be asserted and clarified in our day."[2] An anonymously written essay in the book produced out of the conference, titled "The Evangelical Affirmations," made clear that anyone who disagrees with any of these nine affirmations may not be authentically evangelical. The affirmations are primarily doctrinal in nature. Carl Henry, one of the leaders of the conference, asserted that "evangelical" describes those who adhere to a basic structure of cognitive content with regard to doctrine.[3]

This way of identifying who is an evangelical theologian and what justifies calling a theology evangelical is problematic in that it closes the door to reform of the doctrinal structure and adds extrabiblical content to the canon of divine revelation, even if that is not explicitly admitted or stated. A major principle of the Reformation was *reformata et semper reformanda*—reformed and always reforming. How is continuing reform of evangelical faith and life possible if being evangelical requires firm adherence to a humanly devised cognitive structure of doctrinal content? That is, if being evangelical necessarily includes being orthodox, how can orthodoxy itself be reformed by evangelicals?

Conservative evangelical theologian D. A. Carson recognizes the diversity within evangelicalism and regards it as a problem. He is not alone; I think it is safe to say that all conservative evangelicals are uncomfortable with diversity, especially the scope of diversity one finds within the evangelical movement. In *The Gagging of God* Carson writes, "Contemporary evangelicalism, consistent or confessional or otherwise, embraces a wide range of people (including some who would not readily apply the label to themselves), but not all of their theological opinions."[4] In other words, like many other conservative evangelicals, Carson draws a distinction between "sociological evangelicalism" and "authen-

2. Ibid., 30.
3. Ibid., 515–16.
4. D. A. Carson, *The Gagging of God: Christianity Confronts Pluralism* (Grand Rapids: Zondervan, 1996), 449.

tic doctrinal evangelicalism" (my terms). Great diversity exists within the evangelical movement even in regard to beliefs, but authentic evangelical theology is more limited and controlled and must not be allowed to be as pluralistic as those who associate with the evangelical movement. For Carson, as for most conservative evangelicals, the doctrinal pluralism within the evangelical community raises a crucial question: "Properly speaking, the question then becomes, How much of the historic evangel can be abandoned before it is no longer evangelicalism?"[5]

By "historic evangel" Carson seems to mean a specific content of doctrinal belief such as the nine Evangelical Affirmations produced by the 1989 conference and spelled out in the 1990 book of the same name. (He does not specifically mention that conference or its Affirmations in this context, but he was at the conference as a presenter and his presentation is contained in the book produced by the conference.) In *The Gagging of God* Carson probably speaks for most, if not all, conservative evangelicals when he complains that in the pluralism of the evangelical movement the traditional theological content of evangelicalism is being reduced to the vanishing point.[6] He argues that "until recently evangelicalism has tried to define itself primarily in theological categories, and that . . . emphasis seems to be changing among many who still attach themselves to that label."[7] As Carson sees it, "there are as many problems among evangelical intellectuals [theologians and biblical scholars] as in evangelical populism [folk religion], if of a slightly different sort. In both cases, the product is less and less 'evangelical' in any useful historic or theological sense."[8]

Another conservative evangelical theologian who shares Carson's concern and who was also prominent at the Evangelical Affirmations conference in 1989 is David Wells of Gordon-Conwell Theological Seminary. His 1993 volume *No Place for Truth; or, Whatever Happened to Evangelical Theology?* expresses similar displeasure with doctrinal pluralism among evangelicals and

5. Ibid., 447.
6. Ibid., 453.
7. Ibid., 456.
8. Ibid., 453.

especially evangelical theologians. He accuses evangelicals in general of an "unabashed desertion of the cognitive substance of faith" (i.e., orthodoxy) and evangelical theologians of fascination with novelty. Wells waxes eloquent in his jeremiad about this pluralistic situation within the evangelical theological guild:

> Evangelicals who seek to work the theological craft in a way that is recognizably historical and who keep the intellectual company of Athanasius, Augustine, Luther, Calvin, Wesley, Edwards, Hodge, and the like [meaning conservatives like himself] are often quite baffled by all the other company they seem obliged to keep in contemporary evangelicalism. The new interests and appetites can be brought into relation with historical evangelical or Protestant faith only by a mighty exercise of the imagination and, not infrequently, a tactful aversion of the gaze. Must we swallow these new interests, as we had to swallow vegetables we hated when we were young, in order to preserve our place at the table? There is a yawning chasm between what evangelical faith was in the past and what it frequently is today, between the former spirituality and the contemporary emptiness and accommodation.[9]

It is difficult not to sympathize with such a stirring complaint, but not all evangelicals see things Carson's and Wells's way. What is that "way"? To summarize, these and other conservative evangelical theologians believe that "evangelical" ought to be a concept heavily invested with cognitive content; Christian orthodoxy ought to be part of its very definition and that orthodoxy should be fairly detailed. Doctrinal change is a bad thing; it detracts from the power of evangelical faith and leads toward greater declension from faithfulness if not apostasy from Christianity. The only way to rescue evangelicalism from sheer emptiness is to draw back from theological creativity and doctrinal innovation and draw firm and narrow doctrinal and theological boundaries around the movement that forbid significant change and diversity.

Wesleyan theologian Kenneth J. Collins sees things differently. Without in any way jettisoning doctrine or reducing it to

9. David Wells, *No Place for Truth; or, Whatever Happened to Evangelical Theology?* (Grand Rapids: Eerdmans, 1993), 134–35.

irrelevance, he defends the diversity within evangelicalism and defines the concept broadly so as to encompass a wide range of theological viewpoints: "Simply put, there are many ways of being evangelical in America today, and evangelicals delight in that diversity and celebrate such richness."[10] Obviously he is not thinking of conservatives like Carson and Wells! Collins adds, "American evangelicalism is a movement that embraces distinctiveness and difference and yet has an overarching unity that is displayed in the common bonds of witness, fellowship, and purpose."[11] In concert with many postconservatives, Collins declares that "there is no evangelical metanarrative."[12] The unity of evangelicalism does not lie in a detailed orthodoxy; it is not a closed circle of people who think or believe exactly alike. Rather, evangelical unity may be found in certain shared themes. Collins explicates them in terms of "four enduring emphases" common to evangelicals throughout history. These constitute an "evangelical ethos" that pervades the movement and unifies it in spite of significant dynamism and diversity:

> (1) the normative value of Scripture in the Christian life, (2) the necessity of conversion (whether or not dramatic or even remembered), (3) the cruciality of the atoning work of Christ as the sole mediator between God and humanity, and (4) the imperative of evangelism, of proclaiming the glad tidings of salvation to a lost and hurting world. Indeed, each of these four themes has repeatedly emerged in the literature, with more or less emphasis, as evangelicals have grappled with their own identity. They are, therefore, integral to any assessment of the evangelical ethos. They are broad enough to account for evangelical pluralism and yet particular enough to define evangelical self-understanding.[13]

Like all postconservative evangelicals, Collins expresses strong interest in and deference for traditional Christian orthodoxy in its broad outlines. The way I would put it is that every evangelical

10. Kenneth J. Collins, *The Evangelical Moment: The Promise of an American Religion* (Grand Rapids: Baker Academic, 2005), 14.

11. Ibid.

12. Ibid., 22.

13. Ibid., 21.

theologian worth his or her salt is deferential toward orthodox doctrine as spelled out in the Great Tradition of Christian belief, the ancient ecumenical doctrinal consensus plus the consensus of the sixteenth-century Reformers.[14] But it is not a closed book or a set of commandments written in stone; orthodoxy is not revelation itself. Orthodox doctrine is the product of human reflection on God's revelation and therefore is open to reconsideration in light of faithful and fresh readings of God's Word. In fact, I would go so far as to add this characteristic to the four ethos-constituting evangelical themes that Collins cites and that are nearly identical to those spelled out by David Bebbington, as noted in the introduction. A fifth common theme of the evangelical ethos is: (5) deference to traditional, basic Christian orthodoxy within a higher commitment to the authority of God's Word in Scripture as the norming norm of all Christian faith and practice. It seems to me that most postconservatives agree with my fifth theme even if they have not officially added it to the minimal account of four unifying themes or hallmarks. This is where I think the conservatives are right and wrong. Conservatives such as Carson and Wells are right that correct doctrine matters and that authentic evangelical faith includes a strong commitment to orthodox doctrine. But they are wrong insofar as they elevate traditional doctrinal orthodoxy to incorrigible status where it is functionally infallible and therefore equal with divine revelation itself.

Of course, few, if any, conservative evangelical theologians admit to doing this. But the attitude toward orthodoxy is manifest in their writings. Typically they occasionally pay lip service to Scripture's place above doctrinal tradition, including orthodox tradition. Listen to Carson, sounding very postconservative:

> Our attempt to "contend for the faith that was once for all entrusted to the saints" must never be cast as *merely* a conservative call to an earlier period of the evangelical movement . . . but to the

14. See Jaroslav Pelikan, *The Emergence of the Catholic Tradition 100–600: The Christian Tradition 1* (Chicago and London: University of Chicago Press, 1971), 332–57; Roger E. Olson, *The Mosaic of Christian Belief: Twenty Centuries of Unity and Diversity* (Downers Grove, IL: InterVarsity, 2002).

Bible itself. In principle it [Carson's program] recognizes that parts of the movement may at any time be in error, and that all things must constantly be brought back to Scripture: that is the importance, of course, of the 'formal principle' of evangelicalism.[15]

Carson sounds downright progressive when he says that the Bible and not some historical position from the past must be the touchstone for determining what is authentically evangelical. But he goes on to treat the traditional intellectual, theological content of evangelicalism (viz., orthodox doctrine) as the defining characteristic of true evangelical faith.

Clearly, then, there are at least two ways of viewing who is truly evangelical that bear on how to recognize a theologian or theology as authentically evangelical. One way, which I here somewhat loosely call "conservative" even though it may not be the traditional way, is to view authentic evangelical theology as a continuation and faithful expression of evangelical orthodoxy. As Millard Erickson argues, part of being faithful is to express traditional beliefs in contemporary idiom.[16] But being evangelical in theology requires adherence and not only deference to orthodox doctrines. What this amounts to, in my opinion and in the opinion of many postconservative evangelicals, is a traditionalism that enshrines Protestant orthodoxy as it was developed in the post-Reformation period by Protestant scholastics and especially by the Old Princeton School theologians in the nineteenth century as an incorrigible intellectual content of authentic evangelical faith. In this approach, then, not all who call themselves evangelical or who are generally recognized as associated with the evangelical movement are genuinely evangelical.

The second approach is shared by many postconservative evangelical thinkers and observers of the evangelical scene, myself included. An evangelical theologian is someone who works within and from the evangelical movement and who therefore shares in its ethos as defined by the five common themes or core commitments. I agree with conservatives that "evangelical"

15. Carson, *The Gagging of God*, 449.
16. Millard Erickson, *Christian Theology*, 2nd ed. (Grand Rapids: Baker Academic, 1998), 76–80.

cannot be compatible with anything and everything. I have met some theologians who say they are evangelical but whom I do not recognize as such because I know that they do not work from within or out of the evangelical movement and that they deny or ignore one or more of the common themes of the evangelical ethos. Their feet are not planted in the evangelical movement's history or ethos. But, in general, my tendency is to acknowledge as an evangelical theologian anyone who calls himself or herself evangelical and really does live and worship and work within or out of the evangelical movement and who enthusiastically breathes the same spiritual air as the evangelical movement as a whole (i.e., its ethos).

The alternative to this second approach is functionally to close the door to reform and enshrine a fairly detailed set of orthodox doctrinal affirmations as equal in authority with revelation itself. In other words, I see a tension within the conservative approach that breaks it down as ultimately unworkable. That tension is easily recognized in Carson's analysis and critique of evangelicalism. On the one hand, conservative evangelicals admit *sola scriptura*—that Scripture alone stands as the final source and norm of theology so that every doctrinal formulation, however ancient and accepted, is subject to correction by Scripture. On the other hand, they label as less than fully or authentically evangelical any theologians or theological proposals that diverge from manmade orthodoxy. How then can an evangelical theologian subject ancient and accepted doctrines to critical scrutiny and propose revisions in the light of faithful and fresh biblical understanding without automatically being condemned as nonevangelical?

The only way to leave a door open to doctrinal reconsideration and revision in the light of Scripture is to define the evangelical attitude toward orthodox doctrine as one of respect and deference but not slavish adherence. This is exactly the approach taken by most postconservative evangelical theologians. Quite contrary to the criticism that they engage in unfettered theological experimentation cut off from Christian tradition, postconservatives generally regard the Great Tradition of Christian belief as a secondary source and norm for Christian theology. Typical is Clark Pinnock's high recommendation of that Tradition—as distinct from traditions—in *Tracking the Maze: Finding Our Way through Modern Theology from an Evangelical Perspective*: "Evangelical theology derives strength from its steadfast loyalty to the doctrines of classical Christianity."[17] He adds, "Historic Christianity is committed to objective theism. By this I mean that we are committed not just to a way of life, but to specific beliefs that are true to reality. Our creed is not just a poetic expression of an ideal we subjectively hold, but a claim about what is really there."[18] Pinnock makes clear, however, that this "loyalty" and commitment to a content of belief takes second place to a higher loyalty and commitment to revelation in Scripture, which may at any time require a revisioning of doctrine. This is expressed in his description of the so-called Wesleyan Quadrilateral (Scripture, tradition, reason, and experience) as his preferred theological method, with Scripture standing over and above tradition: "Scripture offers the unique access to the story of redemption and then, in turn, funds tradition, reason and experience, as God's Word is remembered, experienced, and thought about."[19]

One can find similar expressions of the primacy and priority of Scripture over any and every tradition combined with a high regard for the Great Tradition of Christian teaching and belief in the writings of Stanley Grenz and other postconservative evangelical thinkers. The relationship between Scripture and tradition in postconservative evangelical theology will be examined in detail in a later chapter.

What makes a theologian evangelical, then, is not strict faithfulness without mental reservation or reconsideration to doctrinal orthodoxy. That would, in effect, add doctrinal orthodoxy to the canon of Scripture! Rather, what makes a theologian evangelical is that he or she works enthusiastically from within the evangelical movement and enthusiastically embodies the ethos of evangelicalism as defined by its five common characteristics or themes.

17. Clark Pinnock, *Tracking the Maze: Finding Our Way through Modern Theology from an Evangelical Perspective* (San Francisco: Harper & Row, 1990), 119.
18. Ibid., 143.
19. Ibid., 71.

Two Historical Styles or Approaches to Evangelical Faith

When attempting to define or describe evangelicalism there is no escaping history; to define or describe the movement or its theology apart from its history would be to engage in an abstract exercise. That is why the work of Mark Noll and other evangelical historians—and some historians who are not self-identified evangelicals—is crucial. We cannot understand what it means to be evangelical today while ignoring the movement's historical roots and development. But this is not a book of history, so I will focus only briefly and, I confess, inadequately on one major historical fact that continues to have an impact on evangelicalism and the theologies it produces. The evangelical movement of today can be traced back to European Pietism, a movement rooted in the Reformation but that attempted to add to Protestantism an experiential dimension of conversion and personal relationship with Jesus Christ. Noll, perhaps the most widely recognized and astute historian of the movement, roots it in the Great Awakenings of Britain and the American colonies in the 1730s and 1740s. However, he acknowledges three main antecedents of those revivals that birthed and shaped evangelical Christianity: Puritanism, Pietism, and Anglican Evangelicalism.[20] With regard to his own use of the terms "evangelical" and "evangelicalism," he says, "It is a usage designating a set of convictions, practices, habits and oppositions that resemble what Europeans describe as 'pietism.'"[21] In other words, Noll, like many other historians of evangelicalism, seems to recognize one antecedent—Pietism—as primary in shaping the evangelical ethos.

However, Noll, like virtually every other historian of evangelicalism, gives much credit to British Puritanism for shaping the movement and its ethos. Pietism tended to be inwardly focused in its experientialism. Its outlook on salvation was heavily influenced by synergism, what is sometimes called Arminianism even though this basic outlook on salvation predates Arminius to Melanchthon and the Anabaptists. Puritanism tended to be

---

20. Mark Noll, *The Rise of Evangelicalism: The Age of Edwards, Whitefield and the Wesleys* (Downers Grove, IL: InterVarsity, 2003), 51–75.
21. Ibid., 17.

more publicly focused and its outlook on salvation was definitely
Reformed or Calvinistic. These two strands of Protestantism
flowed together in the Great Awakening, which was the crucible
of evangelicalism as it has come down to us today. What arose
was a movement informed by both Pietism and Puritanism, and
therefore full of tension, but marked by the common conviction
that "God could actually, actively and almost tangibly transform
repentant sinners who put their trust in him."[22]

Both Pietism and Puritanism included experiential compo-
nents. Both reveled in the experience of the transforming grace of
God, even if in very different ways. Jonathan Edwards and John
Wesley, the two "godfathers," as it were, of the evangelical movement, were both influenced by Pietism and Puritanism. Along
with the experiential component streaming into evangelicalism
from Pietism and Puritanism came a strong interest in correct
doctrine and orthodoxy from Protestant scholasticism. The post-
Reformation orthodox Protestant thinkers embedded within
Puritanism lent to evangelicalism a commitment to doctrinal
correctness with a strongly Reformed flavor. Examples include
William Perkins and John Owen. John Wesley injected into the
evangelical movement his own non-Reformed, Arminian commitment to doctrine in the form of his own revision of Anglican
confessionalism. Wesley was no scholastic, but he did have a
strong interest in doctrine and some later Methodist theologians
practiced a kind of scholastic method of theology.

According to postconservative evangelical theologian Henry H.
Knight, these roots of the evangelical movement have contrib-
uted to it a "pervasive tension" between Protestant scholasticism and Pietism that accounts for much of the tension and
turmoil within the movement today: "Because evangelicalism is
informed by both the scholastic and pietist traditions, it is beset
by an internal tension."[23] I like to say that evangelicalism is an
unstable compound because of this dual inheritance; these two
powerful impulses combined uneasily within it. On the one hand
are people of influence who are primarily committed to the Prot-

22. Ibid., 65.
23. Henry H. Knight III, *A Future for Truth: Evangelical Theology in a Postmodern World* (Nashville: Abingdon, 1997), 24.

estant scholastic tradition in its Puritan form. They may be and often are also influenced to some degree by Pietism. The interactions between Pietism and Puritanism are complex and obscure, but few doubt that they did influence each other. These evangelicals tend to be Reformed and strongly confessional in their doctrinal orientation. Sometimes they find it difficult to abide their fellow evangelicals who are unlike them in these regards. Typical of this strand of evangelicalism is the Alliance of Confessing Evangelicals that publishes *Modern Reformation* magazine. These evangelicals wince at popular revivalism, synergistic folk religion, and progressive evangelical thinkers who experiment with new ways of thinking about God, the Bible, and salvation (e.g., open theism, partial inerrancy, and inclusivism).

On the other hand are heirs of Pietism and revivalism who revel in transforming experiences of God's Spirit, Jesus-piety, and a sometimes seemingly cavalier attitude toward tradition. Typical of this strand of evangelicalism is the Jesus People movement of the early 1970s and the Pentecostal-Charismatic movements; one might also throw in the quite different emerging churches network, the large and diverse house church movement, and the seeker-sensitive churches. Evangelicals of this style often have trouble understanding and sympathizing with their more intellectually serious and doctrinally concerned evangelical brothers and sisters who call themselves "confessing evangelicals."

The vast bulk of evangelicalism lies somewhere between these expressions, combining aspects of each. It is not uncommon to find both styles within a single evangelical organization or congregation. A growing suburban evangelical church, or one seeking to grow, may have two Sunday morning worship services: one somewhat liturgical in the Reformed style, reciting creeds and confessions of faith with hymns and doctrinal sermons, and the other informal, sensitive to spiritual seekers, aiming at provocation of spiritual affections with chorus singing, group praying, testimonies, and drama. However, these two impulses—one toward evoking experience of God and the other toward inculcating correct beliefs—tend to fall into conflict with each other over time. That certainly has been the case within the wider evangelical movement as a whole.

What, then, is evangelicalism? I am not asking about its invisible and intangible essence, which is disputed by individuals and groups within the movement; I'm asking about the movement. Mark Noll describes evangelicalism in its earliest years and now as "a large kin network of churches, voluntary societies, books and periodicals, personal networks, and emphases of belief and practice."[24] Who can dispute it? All anyone can do is add to it: publishers, parachurch organizations, mission societies and agencies, ecumenical groups, Bible study and church renewal organizations, evangelistic enterprises, and so on. Evangelicalism is a vast and diverse collection of individuals, churches, and groups. So vast and diverse is it that some have questioned whether there is such a thing as "the" evangelical movement or whether evangelicalism is a movement of movements. Evangelical historian Nathan Hatch declares, "There is no such thing as evangelicalism."[25] In his considered scholarly opinion,

> The evangelical world is extremely dynamic, but there are few church structures to which many of its adherents or leaders are subject. The evangelical world is decentralized, competitive, and driven by those who can build large and successful organizations. It is this instability that I think is problematic for theological integrity.[26]

And yet, in spite of Hatch's denial, something akin to a real movement does exist for better or worse, and in spite of all its blooming, buzzing confusion (like nature), it needs a name. We call it evangelicalism. It is marked by the five common themes delineated above and its theological side, broadly conceived, is composed historically of two ingredients that conflict with each other: Protestant (mostly Reformed) orthodoxy and Pietism, which is for the most part synergistic as well as experiential. Much of the tension and turmoil that goes on in the evangelical world can be traced to its nature as an unstable compound of inextricably linked but competing styles and emphases.

24. Noll, *Rise of Evangelicalism*, 19.
25. Nathan Hatch, "Response to Carl F. H. Henry," in Kantzer and Henry, eds., *Evangelical Affirmations*, 97.
26. Ibid., 98.

The Postconservative Style of Evangelical Theology

I have just argued that the evangelical movement has always been characterized by a tension-filled combination and juxtaposition of two ingredients without which it would not be evangelicalism. How does postconservative evangelical theology fit into this? My thesis is that what I call postconservative evangelical theology is by and large a derivation of the Pietist side of the evangelical movement. It is theology that grows out of that ingredient just as conservative theology grows out of the Puritan-Protestant orthodoxy ingredient. That is not to say that conservative evangelical theology is not at all influenced by Pietism; many conservative evangelical theologians are pietistic in their personal lives of devotion. Nor is it to say that postconservative evangelical theologians lack any interest in Protestant orthodoxy; many of them express strong appreciation for the contributions of orthodox theologians of the past. However, illumination of these two styles of theology within evangelicalism might arise from a brief journey to the not-too-distant past.

Many conservative evangelical theologians write and speak as if there was a time when "evangelical theology" was virtually synonymous with the Old Princeton School of theology as represented by the theological dynasty that ran from A. A. Alexander to Charles Hodge to Benjamin Warfield to J. Gresham Machen, who finally broke with Princeton to found Westminster Theological Seminary. And some of them write and speak as if "evangelical theology" should forever remain little more than new expression of that same theology. I'm reminded of a sign on Interstate 35 between Austin and San Antonio, Texas, touting the delights of a tourist town called Gruene (pronounced "Green"). The town's motto is, "Gently resisting change since 1872." Coincidentally, that was the year the first volume of Charles Hodge's *Systematic Theology* was published.[27] Postconservative evangelical theologians suspect that conservatives—since 1872!—want nothing in evangelical theology to change. However, during that same era there were other evangelical theologians at work who were not

27. Charles Hodge, *Systematic Theology* (1872; repr., Grand Rapids: Eerdmans, 1973).

of the same ilk; their contributions are not as warmly highlighted by many establishment evangelical theologians even though their influence was considerable, especially on pastors and laypeople within the evangelical movement. They were the theologians of the experiential, revivalist side of the movement, and their ranks included A. B. Simpson, founder of the Christian and Missionary Alliance; Oswald Chambers of *My Utmost for His Highest* fame; influential Methodist theologian and university president Lorenzo McCabe; E. Y. Mullins, who authored many books of theology and who was the unrivaled dean of Southern Baptist theology for almost a half century; and H. Orton Wiley, who was the standard theologian of the Holiness movement in the first half of the twentieth century. These and other theologians worked more within the experiential and Pietist side of the evangelical movement and did not employ a scholastic method. Many of them had little use for concepts such as biblical inerrancy, which to them seemed like an overly rationalized approach to Scripture. Postconservative theology has not simply popped up out of nowhere; it is rooted in this side of the evangelical story. In particular, progressive Wesleyan theologians such as Henry Knight and Kenneth Collins, as well as Arminian Baptists such as Clark Pinnock and Stanley Grenz, stand on the shoulders of these theologians.

To a very great extent, then, conservative evangelical theology is an extension of the concerns, methods, and style of the Old Princeton School of Reformed theology, even if some of its adherents are Baptists or Free Church members. That style continues that tradition of seeking after a certain kind of rational certainty to support faith and govern theological work. It does so by defending tradition and propositional revelation in a relatively aggressive manner. It extends that tradition by constructing highly coherent and closed systems of theology that protect and defend a perceived "received evangelical tradition." It imitates that tradition by underscoring and highlighting the cognitive content of revelation and evangelicalism as primary over the experiential and personally transformative aspects of revelation and evangelical faith. It continues that tradition by drawing firm and rather narrow boundaries around what it perceives to be authentic evangelicalism, as defined by correct doctrine, and questioning the credentials of evangelicals who dare to work outside those boundaries and challenge traditional doctrinal formulations. Its central feature and style could be described as "contending for the faith," where "faith" is understood in terms of a traditional content of belief linked to Protestant orthodoxy. Like the Old Princeton School of theology—and fundamentalism, to which it remains rather closely related—conservative evangelical theology works unconsciously under the spell of the Enlightenment and modernity, although it denies doing so.

Postconservative theology grows out of different soil but works just as much within the larger evangelical ethos and movement. In the rest of this chapter I want to explicate this style of theologizing by discussing several of its common features. Individual theologians are postconservative to a greater or lesser degree. I do not think of them as paragons of postconservatism—although Pinnock and Grenz come close. Some of the common, unifying features of postconservative theology will be fodder for later chapters. Here I will deal with them only in a cursory manner to give readers a sense of the postconservative style of doing theology.

First, postconservatives, like conservatives, presuppose revelation, but they consider its main purpose to be *transformation* more than *information*. This emphasis colors everything else. Of course, conservatives also believe that revelation is intended to transform, but they emphasize the importance of revealed information: facts. Carl Henry, the dean of evangelical theologians in the second half of the twentieth century, embodies the conservative style with regard to how revelation is understood. In his programmatic little book *Towards a Recovery of Christian Belief*, he writes, "Divine revelation is a mental activity" in that it involves "intelligible disclosure."[28] Another conservative evangelical theologian, Paul Helm, argues that revelation aims at knowledge: "Revelation is a cognitive concept. It has to do with knowledge, with an actual or possible mode of knowledge."[29] Most conservative

---

28. Carl F. H. Henry, *Towards a Recovery of Christian Belief* (Wheaton: Crossway, 1999), 55.
29. Paul Helm, *Divine Revelation* (Westchester, IL: Crossway, 1982), 27.

evangelical theologians would agree with Henry and Helm; divine special revelation, in contrast to general revelation in nature, is theology's primary source and norm and is the communication of information for the purpose of creating knowledge. Of course, they would also argue that this knowledge given by revelation is transforming, but postconservatives wonder if knowledge is the only or best means of transforming persons.

Postconservatives do not reject a propositional, factual, and informational aspect to divine revelation, but they wish to stress that revelation is given primarily for the purpose of redemption through personal encounter and relationship, and that nonpropositional aspects of revelation can be useful for theological endeavor. They do not want to reduce revelation to communication of information, a view they regard as truncated. Pinnock speaks for most postconservatives when he says, "The primary point of revelation was not to communicate truths or to prove there is a God but to announce something that had happened."[30] Pinnock similarly asserts, "Revelation . . . encompasses historical actions, verbal disclosures, and personal encounters."[31] The Bible, then, is not a "book full of timeless truths"[32] but a revelatory vehicle that contains many types of revelation, all of which surround and support that which is primary in Scripture: narrative. Many postconservative evangelicals are enamored with narrative theology, which emphasizes the power of story (not necessarily fiction!) to transform people in a way propositions do not. Others such as Kevin Vanhoozer add to that revelation as event in the form of divine speech acts, which not only communicate information but at the same time, and more importantly, do something; they are creative and transformative beyond the cognitive realm. According to Vanhoozer, in concert with all postconservatives, "The words of the Bible are not simply carriers of information but *means of transformation*."[33]

The point is that postconservatives worry that conservative theology is too caught up in the idea of cognitive Christianity

---

30. Pinnock, *Tracking the Maze*, 159.
31. Ibid., 171.
32. Ibid., 175.
33. Kevin J. Vanhoozer, *The Drama of Doctrine: A Canonical-Linguistic Approach to Christian Theology* (Louisville: Westminster John Knox, 2005), 70.

to the neglect of Christianity as a personally transforming and personally involving relationship, rooted in revelation as God's self-giving by means of a complex of dramatic actions, including but not limited to communication of truths.

A second common characteristic of the postconservative style of evangelical theology is a certain vision of what theology is all about. For postconservatives theology is a pilgrimage and a journey rather than a discovery and conquest. Also, for them the constructive task of theology is always open; there are no closed, once and for all systems of theology. Again, Pinnock best represents the postconservative style of theology as a pilgrimage. For him, theology is always at best both "conservative and contemporary." By "conservative" he means faithful to Scripture and respectful of tradition. Later, in *Tracking the Maze*, he invested the label with more baggage along the lines I have developed here. By "contemporary" he means constantly ready to reconsider old formulations and create new ones in light of new discoveries and different contexts. He wrote in *Christianity Today*, "Scripture is normative, but it always needs to be read afresh and applied in new ways."[34] Pinnock explicitly admits that his theological work has been and continues to be a journey. He has been ready to start over at any time, at least since a profound theological conversion during the 1970s, stimulated by his encounter with the charismatic movement and his turn away from Augustinian-Calvinism to Arminian theology. Some have labeled him a "moving target," but postconservatives, who do not all necessarily agree with all his proposals, respect his willingness to change.

Pinnock speaks for all postconservatives when he asks, "Why do conservatives assume that the received doctrinal paradigms created by human beings like ourselves are incapable of improvement?"[35] And postconservatives can only agree when he critiques the conservative theological mind-set: "How awfully easy it is for people who think themselves in possession of God's infallible Word to transfer some of that infallibility to themselves. . . . And how easy for them, to respond to anyone who questions

34. Clark Pinnock, "An Evangelical Theology: Conservative and Contemporary," *Christianity Today*, January 5, 1979, 23.
35. Pinnock, *Tracking the Maze*, 51.

any aspect of their fortresslike position with righteous anger and adamant rejection."[36]

Contrary to some critics, postconservative evangelicals do not exercise unfettered theological experimentation, nor do they reject the search for objective truth. They do, however, believe that taking risks in theological endeavor with thought experiments is not a sin. Vanhoozer has especially promoted a greater appreciation for the role of imagination in theological work. According to Vanhoozer, imagination, far from being the devil's playground, is a gift of God used by the biblical authors (e.g., in poetry and parable) and useful for the theologian whose task is to pick up where Scripture leaves off and "look along" and not only "at" Scripture.[37] Evangelical theology especially needs to rediscover and "rehabilitate" imagination's role for "faithful improvisation" on the theo-dramatic themes of biblical revelation.[38] In other words, for Vanhoozer as for other postconservative evangelicals, although for him in a distinctive way, theology is not so much "thinking God's thoughts after him" or constructing timeless and closed systems of thought but creative performance based on the "dramatic script" of canonical revelation plus the Great Tradition of Christianity: "Theology asks: What are we, as followers of Jesus, to *believe, say, and do* so as to continue the theo-drama into new cultural and intellectual scenes?"[39]

Vanhoozer's proposal for understanding the task of theology is thoroughly postconservative, and he labels it so. Somewhat startling, given his location, is his description of the task of theology in relation to Scripture and tradition; it well expresses the postconservative spirit or style of evangelical theology but in his own inimitable idiom:

> Faithful performance and creative improvisation need not be at odds with one another; the biblical script itself is a record of previous improvisations—of God, of the prophets, and of the apostles—that display creative fidelity. The best improvisation,

36. Ibid.
37. Kevin J. Vanhoozer, *First Theology: God, Scripture and Hermeneutics* (Downers Grove, IL: InterVarsity, 2002), 37.
38. Vanhoozer, *Drama of Doctrine*, 338.
39. Ibid., 311.

like the best translation, is precisely the one that displays narrative continuity (*ipse*-identity) with what went on before. Theology is no different.[40]

Lest anyone misread this as conservative, the author goes on to say, "The canon is the norm of theology, but it need not follow that theological understanding be confined to the past," and, "a good performance [whether theological or dramatic] *discovers* potential meaning that is really there, in the text [Bible], though previously hidden."[41] I see very little significant difference between Pinnock's vision of theology as an ongoing pilgrimage involving risk and Vanhoozer's vision of theology as creative performance involving imaginative improvisation based on the revelatory text. Both admit that no humanly conceived doctrinal system is final and that new performance is always required.

Postconservative evangelical theology, then, unlike conservative theology, regards the constructive task of theology as ever unfinished. We cannot finally close the door to the possibility that our previous discoveries and conquests or our previous performances are flawed; reconsideration and reconstruction of doctrines in the light of God's revelation in Jesus Christ and in Scripture is required by our own finitude and fallenness and not by culture or any defect in given revelation.

A third characteristic of postconservative theological work is a discomfort and dissatisfaction with the reliance of conservative evangelical theology on Enlightenment and modern modes of thought. This is a great irony, of course, as most conservative theologians decry the Enlightenment and modernity. David Wells, for example, lays most of the blame for evangelicalism's decline into pluralism and lack of prophetic voice at the feet of its accommodation to modernity.[42] Many other conservative evangelicals similarly diagnose evangelicalism's ills. Modernity is the common whipping boy of fundamentalism and conservative evangelicalism. The great irony, however, is that, according to many astute observers of conventional evangelicalism, the

40. Ibid., 344.
41. Ibid., 351, 352.
42. Wells, *No Place for Truth*, 115–36.

movement is itself strongly influenced by modernity. Mark Noll takes note of this debt to the Enlightenment: "In . . . significant ways, evangelicalism was itself an authentic expression of Enlightenment principles."[43] Alister McGrath has insightfully explored this "evangelical Enlightenment" phenomenon of covert modern influence on the evangelical movement even—or perhaps especially—in its conservative apologetics and theology: "Certain central Enlightenment ideas appear to have been uncritically taken on board by some evangelicals, with the result that part of the movement runs the risk of becoming secret prisoner of a secular outlook which is now dying before our eyes."[44]

McGrath identifies these "central Enlightenment ideas" that unduly and covertly influence conservative evangelical theology and pins them especially on the theologies of the Old Princeton School of Reformed theology (Hodge et al.) and Carl Henry. According to McGrath, these and other conservative evangelicals have worked with an Enlightenment-inspired philosophical method known as foundationalism that prizes rational certainty and elevates propositions and coherent systems almost to idols. Foundationalism stems from the philosophical contributions of Enlightenment thinkers René Descartes and John Locke; it rejects as dubious all but knowledge based on self-evident truths of reason or evidences of the senses. It is obsessed with rational certainty and tends to rule out of bounds truth claims based on faith and revelation stemming from the inner testimony of the Holy Spirit through spiritual experience. McGrath and others find this general philosophical method covertly at work in much conservative evangelical thinking.

Postconservative evangelical theologians have raised red flags over this issue and declared that evangelical theology needs to be liberated from the Enlightenment and that some forms of postmodern thought can help in that liberation process. Henry Knight, Stanley Grenz, John Franke, Brian Walsh, Richard Middleton, and a host of other postconservatives have called for this and worked hard to achieve it. Their common concern is that

43. Noll, *Rise of Evangelicalism*, 150.
44. Alister McGrath, *A Passion for Truth: The Intellectual Coherence of Evangelicalism* (Downers Grove, IL: InterVarsity, 1996), 173.

conservative foundationalism and propositionalism elevate something alien to revelation above revelation as the criterion of truth, and that Christianity gets reduced to a philosophy, to the extent that these Enlightenment-inspired methods and commitments drive evangelical thinking. This aspect of postconservative evangelical theology will be explored more fully in a later chapter.

A fourth common characteristic of the style of evangelical theology called postconservative is its vision of evangelicalism itself. As already seen, conservative evangelical thinkers tend to limit the boundaries of authentic evangelicalism. This was the whole purpose of the project and proposal of the 1989 Evangelical Affirmations conference and document. Later, in the early twenty-first century, the Evangelical Theological Society took up the question of evangelical boundaries and tested them by considering whether to strip two members of their membership status, although in the end they were allowed to keep their memberships. Who is "in" and who is "out" is an obsession with some conservative evangelicals. For many of them the "tent" of authentic evangelicalism is small, even if the "tent" of the evangelical subculture is too large.

Postconservatives view evangelicalism as a centered set category rather than as a set having boundaries.[45] That is, the ques-

---

45. I am borrowing from Paul G. Hiebert in making this distinction between "bounded set" and "centered set" categories. However, I am adapting his contribution and using it critically. He says that centered sets must have boundaries but that the boundaries are defined by the center (*Anthropological Reflections on Missiological Issues* [Grand Rapids: Baker Academic, 1994], 124). He also writes about "fuzzy sets" that have no boundaries. My centered set category is a combination of Hiebert's centered and fuzzy sets. In my opinion, there can be and even must be centered sets with no clearly definable boundaries. Every movement that has not yet hardened into an organization is just such a centered set. Perhaps what Hiebert has in mind when he says of centered sets, *"they do have sharp boundaries"* (p. 124), is that such boundaries exist even if no human can tell exactly where they are. That makes some sense in light of the context where he describes centered sets. If he means that anyone knows for certain where those boundaries are then the whole point of defining the set by the center is lost. Then there is little or no real difference between a bounded set and a centered set. I prefer to say that at least some centered sets (perhaps all) have no sharp, definable boundaries to any human intelligence. In that sense they are like fuzzy sets, but they differ from fuzzy sets in having a strong center. This describes evangelicalism perfectly.

tion is not who is "in" and who is "out" but who is nearer the center and who is moving away from it. Authentic evangelicalism is defined by its centrifugal center of powerful gravity and not by outlying boundaries that serve as walls or fences. The center is Jesus Christ and the gospel, but it also includes the four or five common core commitments identified above: biblicism, conversionism, crucicentrism, activism in missions and social transformation, and deferential respect for historic Christian orthodoxy. People gathered around the center or moving toward it are authentically evangelical; people or institutions moving away from it or with their backs turned against it are of questionable evangelical status. But it is not a matter of being "in" or "out" as there is no evangelical magisterium to decide that. Conservatives seem to want such an evangelical magisterium, but what would it look like? There is no evangelical headquarters and no central authenticating authority.

Some conservative critics have asked rhetorically how there can be a center without a circumference. They should know better. There are many centers without circumferences in nature and in mathematics and in other realms of reality. In nature the solar system is a center (the sun) without a clear or definite circumference. Mathematicians know about "fuzzy sets" of numbers without definite limits. Sociology knows that movements are centers without boundaries; the moment a movement identifies boundaries it is no longer a movement but an organization. The two are different even if often related. An organization must have boundaries; a movement cannot have boundaries. An analogy may help. Who is an American? Any and every US citizen is an American. America is not a movement but a definite organization even if nobody knows for sure exactly how many members it has and even if at times problems arise in identifying certain people as either members or not members (e.g., children of citizens born in other countries who must be nationalized even though that is a formal process). By contrast, who is a Westerner? Not all Europeans or Americans are truly Westerners culturally and many people living in Asia are Westernized. Some people stand out as paragons of Western culture, but others are mixtures and hybrids of that and other cultures.

So it is with "evangelical." There is no office or litmus test for determining precisely who is an evangelical and yet we all know that not everyone who claims the label deserves it. There is a definite movement rightly described that way, but it has no boundaries. It only has a center and that must suffice for defining it. This won't sit well with many conservatives, but they need to answer how it can be otherwise. Who (besides themselves) do they want to have the power to decide who is in and who is out of the evangelical movement? In that sense, "evangelical" is an essentially contested concept. But at the same time, postconservatives do not intend it to be compatible with anything and everything, which is where the center comes into play. Much of this, as with other disagreements between conservatives and postconservatives, comes down to levels of comfort with ambiguity. The former are generally uncomfortable with it and the latter are generally more comfortable with it.

A fifth common feature of postconservative evangelical theology is a tendency to view the enduring essence of Christianity, and therefore the core identity of evangelical faith, as spiritual experience rather than as doctrinal belief. Here postconservatism's pietistic roots are more in evidence than anywhere else. It is also here that conservatives raise some of their sharpest criticisms because of the alleged similarity to the theology of Friedrich Schleiermacher, the father of liberal theology. No postconservative theologian has done more to explicate this vision of evangelical identity than Stanley Grenz, whose 1993 book *Revisioning Evangelical Theology* raised conservative eyebrows and provoked comparisons with Schleiermacher's method that centered around religious experience (God-consciousness) as the heart and essence of religion, including Christianity.[46] Grenz argued that evangelicalism is a vision of the Christian faith expressed primarily in a distinctive spirituality. A shared spiritual experience—"convertive piety"—rather than a doctrinal system defines authentic evangelicalism.[47]

---

46. Stanley J. Grenz, *Revisioning Evangelical Theology: A Fresh Agenda for the 21st Century* (Downers Grove, IL: InterVarsity, 1993).
47. Ibid., 35.

For Grenz, as for many if not most postconservative evangelicals, what defines evangelical faith is "conversional piety" that
manifests in a personal, transforming relationship with Jesus
Christ and is expressed communally in shared stories (testimonies), hymns, witness, and worship. Grenz advocated a move
from a "creed-based" to a "spirituality-based" identification of
authentic evangelicalism, thus making the experience of conversion and its outworking in evangelical piety the defining center
of the boundaryless broad evangelical "tent." He did not discard
or discount doctrine as unimportant but demoted it to secondary
status: "To be truly evangelical, right doctrine, as important as it
is, is not enough. The truth of the Christian faith must become
personally experienced truth" for authentic evangelical faith to
exist.[48] Furthermore, Grenz identified the doctrinal language
of the church as second-order language; it is the communal expression of the experience of God in Christians' encounter with
revelation.

Grenz's revisionist account of evangelical identity and especially his relegation of theological discourse and doctrinal formulation to the status of second-order language dependent on
spirituality provoked cries of "What about Schleiermacher?"
because many conservatives missed the clear distinction between
their two accounts of "experience."[49] When the father of liberal
theology placed spiritual experience at the center of Christian
faith and identified theology and doctrine as its second-order
expression, he was thinking of spiritual experience as a universal religious a priori—something residing in some measure in
all people. For him it was universal God-consciousness even if
for Christians it took a distinctively Christian form. For Grenz,
however, the experience that defines authentic evangelical faith
is the supernatural and uniquely Christian work of God, which

48. Ibid., 57.
49. Typical in this regard is Carson, who compares Grenz's theological method
with Schleiermacher's without noticing or acknowledging the significant differences (*The Gagging of God*, 481). Unlike the father of liberal theology, Grenz
affirms Scripture as the superior source and norming norm for theology as well
as for all Christian life and practice. He also makes clear, unlike Schleiermacher,
that the spirituality and religious experience to which theological language is
second order is conversion and not some vague, universal God-consciousness.

is called "conversion" and which results in a transformed life of commitment and devotion to Jesus Christ. It also includes acceptance of the authority of the Bible as the inspired, written revelation of God that provokes conversion and structures Christian existence.

A sixth common feature of postconservative evangelical theology is a tendency to hold relatively lightly to tradition while respecting the Great Tradition of Christian belief. While conservatives elevate tradition to a special authoritative status and treat it as incorrigible—even as they pay lip service to Scripture alone as infallible—postconservatives respect it even as they subordinate it to revelation and consider it at most a guide. For postconservatives, even the Great Tradition serves a ministerial rather than a magisterial role in theology and receives a vote but never a veto in matters of doctrinal examination and reconstruction.[50] Although Alister McGrath may not be thoroughly postconservative, he makes a postconservative move when he argues that tradition must be reconsidered from time to time in the light of Scripture. The reason, he explains, is that "we may, through weakness or sheer cussedness, get our interpretations wrong from time to time and need correction."[51] Again, McGrath sounds decidedly postconservative when he declares, "Evangelicalism is principally about being biblical not about the uncritical repetition of past evangelical beliefs."[52]

Kevin Vanhoozer agrees with McGrath and underscores the postconservative discomfort with evangelical traditionalism, whether of the biblicist or paleo-orthodox variety: "*Sola scriptura* means at least this: that the church's proclamation is always subject to potential correction from the canon. It is for this reason that we must resist simply collapsing the text into the tradition of its interpretation and performance."[53] Contrary to some conservative critics, however, postconservatives do not simply shrug off tradition as irrelevant, in particular the Great Tradition of

50. Collins, *Evangelical Moment*, 197.
51. Alister McGrath, "Evangelical Theological Method: The State of the Art," in *Evangelical Futures: A Conversation on Theological Method*, ed. John G. Stackhouse, Jr. (Grand Rapids: Baker Academic, 2000), 31.
52. Ibid., 32.
53. Vanhoozer, *Drama of Doctrine*, 152.

the early ecumenical consensus plus the common teachings of the sixteenth-century Reformation. They treat it deferentially and with great respect while regarding it as always open to correction from Scripture. Grenz, Pinnock, and John Franke all decry the "virtual elimination of tradition in much traditional Protestant theology," which results in an ironic "anti-traditional traditionalism."[54] They agree that the great creeds and confessional statements of Christian history

> are helpful as they provide insight into the faith of the church in the past and as they make us aware of the presuppositions of our own context. In addition, they stand as monuments to the community's reception and proclamation of the voice of the Spirit. Despite their great stature, such resources do not take the place of canonical Scripture as the community's constitutive authority. Moreover, they must always and continually be tested by the norm of canonical Scripture.[55]

Contrary to conservatives, who tend either implicitly or explicitly to enshrine some portion of Christian tradition as above and beyond question or reconsideration, postconservatives insist on the freedom to question and even reconstruct any part of Christian tradition in the light of deeper and better understandings of Scripture. At the same time they view the Great Tradition much as US judges view the history of superior and Supreme Court decisions—as precedent rulings to be overturned only when the full force of a reasonable interpretation of the US Constitution requires it.

These six family resemblances of postconservative evangelical theology do not exhaust the subject. Also important in understanding this style of evangelical theology are new horizons in understanding God (reconstruction and revision of classical Christian theism) and new ways of regarding and describing the task of theology in relation to Scripture (theology as directed per-

---

54. John R. Franke, *The Character of Theology: A Postconservative Evangelical Approach* (Grand Rapids: Baker Academic, 2005), 150.

55. Stanley J. Grenz and John R. Franke, *Beyond Foundationalism: Shaping Theology in a Postmodern Context* (Louisville: Westminster John Knox, 2001), 124.

formance improvising creatively and imaginatively on the text of Scripture). These and other aspects of postconservative thinking in evangelical theology will be explored in later chapters of this book. I only hope that this chapter has provided a sense of the style of theology described here as postconservative. Yale theologian Hans Frei, often considered the father of the postliberal movement in theology, coined the phrase "generous orthodoxy," which has been picked up and used by evangelical theologians Donald Bloesch and Brian McLaren. That phrase helpfully expresses the style of theology I am here calling postconservative, even if it does not exhaust it. I think it is also helpful to talk about "critical orthodoxy" in describing postconservative theology. This style of evangelical theology does not eschew correct doctrine or propositions or the Great Tradition of Christian belief but subjects all to the greater authority of divine revelation in Jesus Christ and in Scripture, which may at any time break forth in new light that corrects what has always been believed and taught by Christians. That style demands humility, generosity, and openness of spirit in conducting the work of theology and handling the cognitive content of the faith.

2

Christianity's Essence

Transformation over Information

Postconservative evangelicals believe that conservative evangelicals tend to place too much emphasis and value on facts; authentic Christianity is too often equated with correct grasp of information. That is, conservative evangelicals, in varying degrees and with some exceptions, underscore and highlight the *propositional* nature of revelation and the *cognitive* aspects of Christian discipleship. When attempting to identify whether a person or group is Christian, they often turn to examination of doctrinal beliefs.

Conservative Evangelical Theology's Identification of Christianity's Essence

Conservatives are not entirely wrong. Once again it is important to say that being postconservative does not mean rejecting everything associated with conservative evangelicalism. The prefix "post-" in front of a term does not mean total disagreement with what the term designates; it simply indicates a desire and attempt to move beyond some aspects of it while preserving the best of it. Conservative evangelicals are often called post-fundamentalist evangelicals; their movement arose out of and moved away from fundamentalism in the 1940s and 1950s. To distinguish them from fundamentalism, which tended to be anti-intellectual and separatistic, scholars called the new evangelicals neoevangelicals or postfundamentalist evangelicals. By no means did the new evangelicals reject everything associated with fundamentalism!

Two books by evangelical historians tell the story of the emergence of conservative evangelicalism out of fundamentalist ranks especially well. Joel A. Carpenter's *Revive Us Again: The Reawakening of American Fundamentalism* and George Marsden's *Reforming Fundamentalism: Fuller Seminary and the New Evangelicalism* both recount in some detail how conservative evangelicalism grew out of and away from the older fundamentalist evangelicalism without tearing itself from its roots entirely.[1] To call establishment evangelicalism "postfundamentalist" does not indicate that it totally disengages from fundamentalism and has nothing in common with it. The new conservative postfundamentalism of evangelicals such as Harold John Ockenga, E. J. Carnell, and Carl F. H. Henry simply wanted to reform fundamentalism by correcting it. Their former fundamentalist friends and colleagues, of course, accused them of going much further. That is always the way it goes.

So it is with postconservative evangelicalism; its proponents do not reject everything of conservative evangelicalism—or of fundamentalism. Rather, postconservatives simply want to continue the reform of fundamentalism begun by the generation before them. They believe that continued reform necessitates correcting even conservative evangelicalism. And, yes, they know full well that another generation will correct and reform their approach to Christianity and to theology. That's part of what

1. Joel A. Carpenter, *Revive Us Again: The Reawakening of American Fundamentalism* (New York: Oxford University Press, 1997); George Marsden, *Reforming Fundamentalism: Fuller Seminary and the New Evangelicalism* (Grand Rapids: Eerdmans, 1995).

makes them postconservative! They understand and accept that there is no final stopping place in the process of ongoing correction and reform short of the return of Jesus Christ. And who knows? Perhaps even in the consummation of redemption there will be much to keep learning and more growth to experience in understanding the gospel.

Postconservative evangelicals worry that their conservative brothers and sisters are too obsessed with the cognitive and intellectual sides of the gospel and of Christian existence. Their concern is that conservatives are one-sided about this; they do not desire to throw the baby out with the bathwater and empty Christianity of stable cognitive content. They simply want to correct this one-sidedness. The accusation that postconservative evangelicals favor unfettered theological experimentation because they have tossed aside the objective content of revelation in favor of reveling in subjective feelings is simply inaccurate; it is a vicious calumny unjustified by any fair reading of the works of postconservatives.

Millard Erickson is a fine example of a standard, conservative, establishment evangelical thinker. His *Christian Theology* is considered a standard text of conservative evangelical theology and is widely used in evangelical seminaries.[2] Most, if not all, conservative evangelical thinkers would agree with Erickson that the "locus of permanence in Christianity" is Christianity's doctrinal content. In chapter five of part one of *Christian Theology*, "Contemporizing the Christian Message," Erickson discusses this locus of permanence in Christianity. He covers a range of theological opinions about what constitutes Christianity's true essence that provides continuity and stability through change. Some theologians have identified that with an institution such as the ecclesiastical hierarchy of bishops; others have regarded it as a certain way of life based on the ethical teachings of Jesus and imitating his loving life. Without rejecting ecclesiastical structures or ethical living, Erickson expresses strong preference for doctrines as the permanent essence of authentic Christianity and acknowledges fundamentalist leader J. Gresham Machen as

2. Millard Erickson, *Christian Theology*, 2nd ed. (Grand Rapids: Baker Academic, 1998).

a forerunner in this.[3] Erickson writes, "It should be apparent, from the view of religion adopted in the first chapter, that the doctrinal content is a major component of Christianity, and is therefore to be preserved. For our purposes in this volume, it will be regarded as the most important permanent element."[4]

In all fairness to Erickson and those who agree with him, we must acknowledge that he goes on to argue for a continuous process of "contemporizing theology." That is, the doctrinal essence once identified must be expressed in new ways for each culture and each generation. Contemporary and contextually sensitive restatement of doctrine is necessary, but it must faithfully preserve the original cognitive doctrinal revelation contained in Scripture. Erickson distinguishes between those theologians who contemporize the Christian message by *translating* it into contemporary idiom from those who *transform* it by accommodating to culture. The latter are relativists while the former are not.

Contrary to what many secularists and liberal Christian thinkers assume, conservative evangelicals like Erickson do not advocate a theology that is oblivious to contemporary society and its thought forms. Many fundamentalists might object to the strong emphasis Erickson places on translating the original Christian message derived from divine revelation in Scripture into contemporary thought forms. Some might even accuse him of being a transformer himself! In fact, the line between his categories of those who transform the original message and those who translate it is difficult to pin down; it shifts and slips as one tries to grasp it. But Erickson is adamant that contemporizing Christianity is an essential part of the evangelical theologian's task. Nevertheless, together with fundamentalists and conservatives generally, he affirms the timeless nature of biblical truths and our ability to identify them and distinguish between them and their forms of expression:

> It will be seen from the foregoing that the really crucial task of theology will be to identify the timeless truths, the essence of the doctrines, and to separate them from the temporal form in which

3. Ibid., 121.
4. Ibid., 122.

they were expressed, so that a new form may be created. How can we locate and identify this permanent element or essence?[5]

Erickson finishes this thought by answering his own question. The answer is not particularly pertinent to our discussion; what is pertinent is his and other conservative evangelicals' belief that the essence of Christianity that identifies authentic Christianity and distinguishes it from counterfeit Christianity is a cognitive deposit of doctrinal content drawn from the propositions of divine revelation in Scripture.

Erickson is not alone in making this judgment about Christianity's essence. Many, if not most, other conservative theologians, both Protestant and Catholic, do the same. One can see it very much in evidence, for example, in D. A. Carson's antipluralist diatribe, *The Gagging of God: Christianity Confronts Pluralism.*[6] There the author criticizes any and every attempt to move away from identification of Christianity's true essence as doctrine intellectually communicated and intellectually grasped. He argues that such movement inevitably ends in pluralism; Christianity loses its meaning and becomes compatible with anything and everything. Our concern here, however, is not so much with Carson's argument about where other views of Christianity's essence lead as with his apparent agreement with Erickson about Christianity's essence. According to Carson, authentic communication of the gospel inevitably includes an irreducible intellectual content because "the historic gospel is unavoidably cast as intellectual content that must be taught and proclaimed."[7] He notes, "Until recently evangelicalism has tried to define itself primarily in theological categories, and that . . . emphasis seems to be changing among many who still attach themselves to that label."[8]

The context of that last quotation makes clear that for Carson the traditional self-identification of evangelicalism by means of theological categories is best, and defection from it leads to doc-

---

5. Ibid., 120.
6. D. A. Carson, *The Gagging of God: Christianity Confronts Pluralism* (Grand Rapids: Zondervan, 1996).
7. Ibid., 508.
8. Ibid., 456.

trinal pluralism and dilutes the evangelical witness. But we must be fair to Carson. Just as Erickson does not reject but advocates contemporizing the Christian message, so Carson acknowledges that propositions do not exhaust Christianity. He does not want to reduce authentic Christianity to a set of facts to be learned and given intellectual assent. Hardly any evangelical does. According to Carson, "Scripture's purpose is not simply to fill our heads with facts, but to bring us to the living God."[9] To this, postconservatives say a hearty "Amen!" However, overall and in general, the burden of Carson's book, like Erickson's and most conservative evangelicals', is to preserve and protect the cognitive doctrinal content of historic evangelicalism—evangelical orthodoxy—as its permanent, enduring, and unchanging essence.

Erickson and Carson are used here as two examples of a tendency among conservative evangelical theologians; to one degree or another they tend to elevate *cognitive knowledge and affirmation of correct doctrines* as the defining hallmarks of authentic evangelical faith. They tend to underscore and highlight the didactic side of Scripture and interpret revelation as primarily communication of information about God. They may pay lip service or more to the overarching goal of personal transformation, but their main concern is with upholding *orthodoxy* (correct doctrinal affirmation) as Christianity's and evangelicalism's permanent essence.

Common Ground between Conservative and Postconservative Evangelicals

Before considering how postconservative evangelicalism differs in regard to the matter of identifying Christianity's permanent essence, it is necessary to express hearty agreement with some aspects of the viewpoint of conservative evangelicals. By no means do postconservatives deny or even ignore the factual side of divine revelation or the content of information involved in authentic Christianity. The common ground between conservatives and postconservatives is great. In contrast to much liberal

9. Ibid., 167.

theology, both believe there is a gospel supernaturally communicated to human beings by special divine revelation and that apart from this gospel people cannot know God as they should. And they share common ground with regard to a supernaturally secured source of authority for right believing and living in divine revelation. Postconservatives agree with conservative evangelical theologian David Wells when he says,

What is most needed [today] is what the historic Christian view on biblical revelation actually secures and that is the means to authorize and prescribe what is right, not because of horizontal preferences, but because of a vertical and transcendent meaning which has been divinely given and which has the power to relativize all human thought.[10]

The difference between conservatives and postconservatives does *not* lie along the line of affirming or denying a transcendent source of authority for believing and living. As we will see, the difference lies in whether that transcendent source and the Christian identity it creates and preserves is primarily a content of information or primarily a means of transformation. Thinking readers will immediately respond, "It's both!" Indeed, it is both. But conservatives tend to overemphasize the informational content and postconservatives wish to balance that with an emphasis on the transformational and relational aspects of revelation and Christianity's essence.

Postconservative Evangelicalism's Experiential Impulse

Earlier in this book we explored the dual nature of the evangelical movement from its birth in the Great Awakenings and down through the decades and centuries in Europe and North America. On the one hand, evangelicalism has inherited from Protestant orthodoxy and Puritan Reformed theology a strongly confessional emphasis that seeks to preserve orthodoxy. Conser-

10. David Wells, "Word and World: Biblical Authority and the Quandry of Modernity," in *Evangelical Affirmations*, ed. Kenneth S. Kantzer and Carl F. H. Henry (Grand Rapids: Zondervan, 1990), 171.

vative evangelicals tend to work out of that side of the heritage. On the other hand, evangelicalism has inherited from Pietism and Revivalism a strong emphasis on the experience of the transforming power of God. Postconservatives tend to work out of that side of the heritage. Some might even argue that there are two evangelicalisms and that these two movements have been somewhat artificially pasted together by their common opposition to liberal defection from authentic Christianity. Conservatives abhor twentieth-century liberal Protestantism's defection from orthodoxy; postconservatives bemoan twentieth-century mainstream Protestantism's loss of spiritual fervor and transforming spiritual power.

Evangelicalism grew and gained respectability and even a measure of participation in the "mainstream" of American society, beginning with Jimmy Carter's presidency and a 1976 cover story about evangelicalism in *Time* magazine. Eventually evangelicalism began to take greater notice of the duality within itself. Conservatives worried that the Pietist wing of the movement was vulnerable to the relativistic ravages of liberalism; postconservatives worry that conservatives are vulnerable to dead orthodoxy and even fundamentalism. The two sides began to snipe at each other and take potshots at each other in print. The unstable compound that is evangelicalism threatens to explode, revealing the deep gulf that has always existed between evangelicalism's two parties and turning it into an unbridgeable chasm. One need only read Carson's *The Gagging of God* and Wells's *No Place for Truth* with their stern warnings against evangelical defection from truth. Context makes clear that Carson is referring to postconservative evangelical theologians when he wonders, "Is contemporary evangelicalism displaying innovative creativity as a function of evangelistic zeal, or toadish captivity to whatever is novel, now that its interest in truth has so sadly waned, in order to titillate the masses? Inevitably one can find some examples of both."[11]

Along the same lines Carson critiques postconservatives harshly for infidelity to the Scriptures: "Despite formal affirmations of Scripture's authority and even inerrancy, a great deal

11. Carson, *The Gagging of God*, 472.

of contemporary evangelicalism does not burn with zeal to be submissive to Scripture."[12] And most harsh of all is Carson's estimation of the damage being done by postconservatives to Christianity in Western culture: "I cannot escape the dreadful feeling that modern evangelicalism in the West more successfully effects the gagging of God . . . than all the post-modernists together."[13] Although Carson does not identify very many evangelicals as the targets of these stringent criticisms, astute readers are justified in believing they are aimed at postconservative evangelicals in general. The one name he does offer in connection with such critiques is Stanley J. Grenz.[14] One has to wonder if Carson is overwrought about the alleged defections of postconservative evangelicals from the historic evangelical faith. Is it possible that he is simply looking across the divide between evangelicalism's two sides and fretting far too much about their differences of emphasis and style? Certainly the final quote offered above sounds frantic and overblown insofar as it is aimed at postconservative evangelicals. But readers will have to judge for themselves as in this and later chapters I unfold what postconservatives really believe.

Similar statements about postconservative evangelicals can be found in Wells's and other conservative, confessional evangelicals' jeremiads about the contemporary state of evangelicalism.[15] One gets the feeling that they are putting the worst spin possible on the statements of some postconservative evangelicals; they seem

12. Ibid., 480.
13. Ibid., 488.
14. Ibid., 481.
15. Here I am using "confessional evangelical" as synonymous with "conservative evangelical," although I believe that all evangelicals are confessional Christians. Even postconservatives confess something; contrary to what Carson and Wells imply, their faith is not contentless. However, in the current lively discussion about these matters conservatives have arrogated to themselves the label "confessional evangelicals." I wish to affirm that I, too, am a "confessional evangelical" because I also confess the gospel. A difference lies in the fact that I, like many postconservatives, prefer to confess my own faith for myself rather than affirm or swear allegiance to a historic creed or written confessional statement. My own statement of faith is no less a confession of faith, however, than is another evangelical's signing of the Westminster Confession or the Baptist Faith and Message.

at times to be operating out of a hermeneutic of suspicion rather than a hermeneutic of charity. As we will see, postconservative evangelicals do not deny doctrine or revel in subjectivism or relativism. They do, however, regard Christianity's and evangelicalism's enduring and permanent essence as something more than knowledge of—or even assent to—information and facts. Authentic Christianity and true evangelical faith have more to do with the personal transforming power of a relationship with God through Jesus Christ than with factual knowledge or affirmation of correct ideas.

Now we will look carefully at several leading postconservative evangelical theologians who share this difference from the conservatives: without in any way rejecting or neglecting the importance of correct thinking, they regard transforming spirituality as more crucial for identifying authentic Christianity and for understanding true evangelical faith. This is perhaps the most basic difference between conservative and postconservative evangelicals. Postconservative evangelicals are not at all interested in a subjectivistic, relativistic "spirituality" accommodated to the spirit of the age. But they are interested in experiencing God. A shallow interpretation can and often does posit a link with liberal theology, which began out of the work of Friedrich Schleiermacher, the father of modern theology and the first true liberal theologian. Schleiermacher defined the essence of religion as God-consciousness and made clear that this is a universal human "religious a priori." That is, God-consciousness as a feeling of utter dependence on the infinite (*Gefühl*) is what distinguishes religion from ethics and philosophy. It is not so much about reason or ideation as about feeling. Today Schleiermacher's identification of the inner essence of all religiousness might be called "cosmic piety." What made Schleiermacher a liberal was that he tended to elevate this God-consciousness to the status of a source and norm for theology alongside, if not higher than, Scripture. It certainly functioned for him as a touchstone of truth, by means of which one might determine what within Scripture is revelatory and what is not.

Of course, there is much more to Schleiermacher than this. In his systematic theology, *The Christian Faith*, he explored the specifically Christian form of universal God-consciousness, which lies in an experience of Christ as redeemer. Insofar as Schleiermacher's theology was Christocentric it was evangelical (in the word's broadest sense), but insofar as it continued to use universal human God-consciousness as the ultimate norm for Christianity and theology it fell into and actually created liberal theology. A fair reading of Schleiermacher may lead one to believe he was attempting to adjust Christianity to modernity by disentangling it from science, broadly defined. Christianity, like religion in general, is about feeling and little more. Science is the realm of facts and knowledge. In any case, his vision of Christianity was truncated by an antisupernaturalist bias.[16]

It doesn't help matters that Schleiermacher came up through the ranks of Pietism in Germany. That was his Christian heritage and he referred to himself as a "pietist of a higher order." In other words, he considered himself an "enlightened pietist." His Pietism was qualified and adjusted by the philosophy of Kant and the Enlightenment in general. Certain surface similarities between Schleiermacher's interests and postconservative evangelicals' concerns lead many critics to suspect that postconservative evangelical theology is leading evangelicals down the primrose path to thoroughgoing liberalism. I, for one, do not think that is the case. It is certainly no more true than that conservative evangelical theology inevitably leads back to fundamentalism or dead orthodoxy.

The stark and profound differences between Schleiermacher's liberal, negotiated Christianity and postconservative evangelicalism will become apparent in the remainder of this chapter and, hopefully, throughout the rest of this book. Postconservatives have no interest in being liberal; accommodation to culture is not what postconservative evangelicalism is about. In fact, postconservatives are afraid that conservative evangelicalism is unconsciously accommodated to culture—to the very modernity conservatives so often decry. If anything, postconservative evan-

16. For a more detailed account and critique of Schleiermacher's theology, see the chapter on Schleiermacher in Stanley J. Grenz and Roger E. Olson, *20th Century Theology: God and the World in a Transitional Age* (Downers Grove, IL: InterVarsity, 1993).

gelicalism is primarily about freeing evangelical theology from captivity to Enlightenment culture's rationalism and obsession with "facts" to the exclusion of truth in experience and personal knowledge.

Postconservative evangelicals regard the essence of Christianity and evangelical faith as transformation more than information. Together with conservatives they acknowledge that information is part of the picture and that information can be transforming. But they do not believe that facts constitute the essence of authentic Christianity or true evangelicalism, both of which are primarily expressions of the transforming power of a relationship—the relationship between God in Jesus Christ manifested through the Holy Spirit and the person in community. The thrust of the biblical message is that God condescends to enter into relationship with persons in order to lift them up to a relationship with him that is both juridical (legal, declarative) and ontological (having to do with substance). Persons are forgiven by the grace of God upon repentance and faith because of what God has done in Christ and they are transformed by having a personal relationship with God through Jesus Christ in the power of the Holy Spirit. That's it in a nutshell.

Yes, of course, there's much more to it than this. Rather unfair critics have charged me and other postconservatives with promoting a minimalist account of Christianity on the basis of a brief "nutshell" summary of the main point of Christianity, which is not meant to say everything. But this is the heart of the matter. What distinguishes Christianity and therefore evangelicalism from every other religious tradition and philosophy and "gospel" is its promise and power to deliver changed legal status in relation to God (viz., forgiveness) and substantial change (viz., divinization—partial participation in the very being of God). Doctrine is secondary; it is the second-order language of the church that brings to expression this transforming experience—which is supernatural, contrary to Schleiermacher's God-consciousness. To say that *an* experience, not religious experience *in general*, is the essence of Christianity and therefore also of evangelicalism is to say what primarily distinguishes Christianity from other religions and identifies the authentic from the inauthentic among those who claim to be Christians. Of course, doctrine comes into play along with experience, but doctrine serves experience and not vice versa. One is the master and the other is the servant. The idea that transforming experience is the permanent and identifying essence of Christianity and of evangelicalism can be understood properly only by examining postconservative (and perhaps other) evangelicals who make this claim. Their views have been seriously misrepresented by some critics and perhaps unintentionally distorted by others. We must turn to their own testimonies and arguments.

Postconservative Evangelical Theologians on Christianity's Essence: Alister McGrath and Stanley J. Grenz

One evangelical theologian who works along the boundary between conservative and postconservative is Alister McGrath of Oxford University. McGrath has been very critical of the rationalistic strain of thought within evangelical theology. Anyone who knows McGrath's work knows how dedicated he is to orthodoxy, but he is even more committed to the transforming gospel that manifests in the transforming experience of God. In *A Passion for Truth: The Intellectual Coherence of Evangelicalism* he decries the tendency of many evangelical thinkers to lapse into forms of Enlightenment-inspired rationalism.[17] He also argues for a greater evangelical appreciation of experience as crucial to theology. He warns against a disdain for experience, common among conservative evangelical theologians: "This widespread disenchantment with experience as a theological resource must not allow us to reject a significant experiential component in theological reflection. . . . Theology can address experience, without becoming reduced to the level of a mere reiteration of what we experience and observe."[18] McGrath stops short of identifying experience as the essence of authentic Christianity, but he does elevate its status as a necessary component of authentic evangelicalism.

17. Alister McGrath, *A Passion for Truth: The Intellectual Coherence of Evangelicalism* (Downers Grove, IL: InterVarsity, 1996), 106.
    18. Ibid., 87.

This perspective appears, for example, in his criticism of evangelicals who reduce the gospel to facts: "It is a travesty of the biblical idea of 'truth' to equate it with the Enlightenment notion of conceptual or propositional correspondence, or the derived view of evangelism as the proclamation of the propositional correctness of Christian doctrine."[19] From the context, it is clear that he is talking about the Princeton theologian Charles Hodge and his theological disciples.

McGrath represents an ally of postconservative evangelical thought on some issues even if he is really quite conservative on other issues. Stanley J. Grenz is less equivocal about the experiential nature of the essence of Christianity and evangelicalism. His *Revisioning Evangelical Theology: A Fresh Agenda for the 21st Century* can be considered the manifesto of postconservative evangelicalism.[20] It drew severe criticism from conservatives, who called it a Schleiermachian treatise that would lead down a slippery slope to liberal theology. In this book, Grenz, who died an untimely death at age fifty-five in 2005, staked out a claim that authentic evangelicalism is defined by experience without falling into subjectivism or Schleiermachian liberalism. In other words, for Grenz and most other postconservatives, "real Christianity"—to use a term especially associated with Pietism, going back to the movement's forerunner Johann Arndt, who wrote a book by that title in the seventeenth century—is defined by a certain experience of God that is supernatural, personally transforming, and centered around the cross of Jesus Christ and the indwelling of the Holy Spirit. It may be called "convertive piety" or "conversional piety." Correct doctrine may exist without it, in which case real Christianity is not present. A person who has this experience may be a real Christian—and an evangelical—without yet being orthodox doctrinally.

According to Grenz, authentic evangelicalism—which is also Christianity at its best—is a certain vision of the true faith rather than a doctrinal system, even though doctrinal systems have their

19. Ibid., 177.
20. Stanley J. Grenz, *Revisioning Evangelical Theology: A Fresh Agenda for the 21st Century* (Downers Grove, IL: InterVarsity, 1993).

place and value.[21] That vision of true faith is a distinctive spirituality that forms evangelical Christianity's essence. For Grenz, this is not divorced from doctrine. Rather, evangelicalism is "an experiential piety cradled in a theology."[22] He asserts, "The genius of the [evangelical] movement . . . is a shared religious experience . . . couched in a shared theological language."[23] Conversion to Jesus Christ by God's grace through repentance and faith is what really defines and creates authentic Christianity and this is the message of evangelicalism: "To be truly evangelical, right doctrine, as important as it is, is not enough. The truth of the Christian faith must become personally experienced truth."[24]

Grenz acknowledges that his vision of authentic evangelicalism as a "shared experience" and "distinctive spirituality" represents a move from a "creed-based" to a "spirituality-based" identification of evangelical faith.[25] For him, what distinguishes evangelicalism from mere Christian orthodoxy—which, if divorced from the experiential dimension, is not "real Christianity"—is a personal, but not necessarily individual, relationship with Jesus Christ marked by commitment to the Lordship of Jesus Christ and prompted by a "new birth" (being "born again") by God's Spirit. The authentic Christian life is one of discipleship to Jesus Christ that cannot be reduced to adherence to propositions or confession of a creed; it is primarily a way of life marked by inward love of God and others and is a work of the Holy Spirit. Grenz concludes:

> The heart of evangelicalism, therefore, lies in its vision of the Christian life. It is a religious experience couched in theological categories. The evangelical vision of Christian spirituality attempts to maintain a balance between seemingly discordant emphases. Consequently, the creative tension we attempt is no easy matter to maintain. But just this creative balance—this vision of the spiritual life and no other—is our central [evangelical] contribution to the people of God.[26]

21. Ibid., 31.
22. Ibid., 35.
23. Ibid., 38.
24. Ibid., 57.
25. Ibid., 38.
26. Ibid., 59.

Can we make Grenz's idea of Christianity's essence and evangelicalism's "core" (inner, essential reality) more concrete? Some examples might help, but we are now moving away from Grenz into interpretation and speculation. I believe what follows is faithful to Grenz's idea; it is based on many long conversations with him about these matters. Some persons who claim to be Christians hold doctrines that seem unbiblical or very nontraditional. What if such a person is truly, undeniably converted and living a Christ-centered life in the power of the Holy Spirit? Grenz's vision of authentic Christianity at least opens the door to the possibility that such a person may be truly Christian. Many conservative evangelicals seem to slam that door shut the moment they detect heresy, even if the person is undeniably converted to Christ through repentance and faith and walking a supernaturally enabled life in the Spirit. Similarly, some persons and groups (churches, schools, publishers, etc.) claim to be evangelical but depart from historic evangelical doctrine in some areas. What if such a person is genuinely converted and exhibits a life of evangelical spirituality? What if such a group is defective in doctrine but fervent in evangelism and discipleship and displaying a genuinely Jesus-centered life of love and faithful service? Grenz's vision of authentic evangelicalism at least opens the door to the possibility that such a person or group may be truly evangelical even if unorthodox in doctrine.

Lest anyone think Grenz or any other postconservative evangelical discards doctrine we need to undertake an examination of the role it plays in his and their vision of authentic Christianity and evangelical faith. According to Grenz, "conceptual frameworks" (doctrinal systems and worldviews) inevitably arise within communities and shape individual identity and group knowledge. However, as indispensable and inevitable as they are, such systems cannot replace or stand in for spiritual experience. They are expressions of it, and their role is to govern and regulate communal communication of it. This means they represent the second-order language of faith whose first-order language is testimony, praise and worship, prayer, and proclamation. This second-order discipline of theology must be pursued "from within" the community of shared spiritual experience that, especially in the case of evangelicals, is led by the Holy Spirit to regard Scripture as uniquely inspired.[27] Grenz argues that conservative evangelicalism has reversed the order of things by placing the book (Scripture) over and above the Spirit. Instead we need to realize that the Bible is the instrument of the Holy Spirit within the community of God's people to lead and guide them in their discernment of the meaning of their common spiritual experience: "We [evangelicals] often collapse the Spirit into the Bible. We exchange the dynamic character of the ongoing movement of the Spirit speaking to the community of God's people through the pages of the Bible for the book we hold in our hands."[28]

For Grenz, the ultimate authority for developing Christian belief and life is the Spirit speaking through the Scriptures in the context of the community shaped by a common spiritual experience of convertive piety. Scripture is this unique vehicle or instrumentality that serves as the primary voice of the Holy Spirit, while doctrine is the community's attempt to express the voice of the Spirit through Scripture in concert with the experience of the transforming work of God in persons. All happens successfully only within the context of a personal relationship with Jesus Christ. Grenz has no interest in playing doctrine against experience or vice versa, but he is concerned to highlight the role of experience as evangelicalism's distinctive contribution to Christianity in the modern world and to avoid identification of authentic Christianity or evangelicalism with ideas and concepts.

To return to the examples given above, what about the individual or organization that claims to be Christian and even evangelical but is not doctrinally correct? I believe Grenz's proposal does not intend to neglect the doctrinal dimension in defining true Christianity or authentic evangelicalism but is aimed at bringing into greater focus the importance of the role of personal faith formed by the Spirit of God around Jesus Christ. A person is "Christian" insofar as he or she is genuinely converted to Christ through personal repentance and faith and is moving along a trajectory from that conversion through a personal relationship with Jesus Christ marked by commitment to his cause, growing

27. Ibid., 75.
28. Ibid., 117.

in the knowledge of biblical truth illumined by the Holy Spirit. Does he or she not yet know or fully understand the doctrine of the deity and humanity of Jesus Christ or the Trinity? That is no obstacle to considering the person *so far* genuinely Christian. Does he or she reject the deity or humanity of Christ or the doctrine of the Trinity? Then matters become less clear. I have argued that such a person or group can be considered Christian and even evangelical insofar as they are moving toward and not away from the core doctrines that are implied by the experience of Jesus Christ as Savior and the Holy Spirit as the indwelling presence of God. Doctrine matters, but can be no substitute for experience. Doctrine provides a criterion for discerning genuine faith without being a litmus test. The crucial thing is one's trajectory in relation to the gospel that Jesus Christ is Lord of all.

Perhaps the best way of putting all this together is to say that apart from transforming experience (conversional piety), authentic evangelicalism does not exist even where doctrinal correctness is present. And that where right experience (orthopathy) and right spirituality (orthopraxy) are present in Jesus-centered living, authentic Christianity and even evangelical faith may be present even if doctrinal correctness is not yet fully present—provided that movement in the right direction is clearly discernible. Of course, Christian communities inevitably form cognitive criteria for participation and leadership and there is nothing wrong with that. But too often they fall into the disease of hardening of the categories where the cognitive conditions for participation and leadership are too detailed and brittle. Doctrinal correctness should be a criterion for leadership in Christian and especially evangelical communities; being on a trajectory toward faithful belief in core Christian doctrines should be a criterion for participation in such communities. But overarching all of that should be the umbrella of right experience, the true heart of the matter.

At this point some readers may wonder if the difference between conservative and postconservative views of the essence of Christianity and evangelical faith is slipping away into obscurity. That's because both parties value both experience and doctrine. The difference lies in the emphasis each places on them and the uses to which they are put in identifying authentic Christianity and evangelical faith. Carl F. H. Henry brings us back to the central difference by expressing in nutshell form the conservative view: "If we profess to be Christian, neither our own experience nor anyone else's can be the basis of our religious affirmations."[29] Henry and many other conservatives assert that the basis of our Christian beliefs must not be experiential because experience is subjective. For Henry and many other conservative evangelicals, the basis of our Christian beliefs must be reason grasping divine revelation. The basis of our belief in divine revelation is that the system of beliefs drawn from it is rationally superior to all competing systems of belief.[30] The test of rational superiority is internal coherence. Some conservative evangelicals would say it is evidentialist correspondence. In any case, experience is relegated to a secondary status as irrelevant to the authority of divine revelation and the truth of Christianity. Henry and conservative evangelicals in general are simply too concerned to combat subjectivism in religion; that concern drives them to denigrate experience as secondary to doctrinal belief when it comes to identifying and defining authentic Christianity.

Postconservatives tend to turn matters around and argue that every belief system has a subjective component in the sense that it is based partly on a perspective about such things as evidence and logic. What counts as evidence and how logic is used in religious belief is largely a matter of personal experience as it shapes perspective. Conversion gives persons a new, shared perspective that includes what John Calvin called the "inner testimony of the Holy Spirit." Postconservative evangelicals, and other evangelicals like Alister McGrath, fear that conservatives such as Carl Henry and all those inspired by the Old Princeton School of evangelical thought are unintentionally turning evangelical faith into a philosophy and the Bible into a book of facts to be organized into a coherent system. This is what is meant by the "evangelical Enlightenment" so criticized by postconservatives. The latter prefer to say that experience is always part of the

---

29. Carl F. H. Henry, *Towards a Recovery of Christian Belief* (Wheaton: Crossway Books, 1990), 100.
30. Ibid., 111.

basis of belief and that authentic evangelicalism should never be ashamed to acknowledge the role played by the Spirit of God and faith in our doctrinal affirmations. Postconservatives trust that genuine conversion in response to real proclamation of the gospel leads people into the light of right doctrinal thinking based on Spirit-illumined reading and interpreting of Scripture.

Clark Pinnock, Kevin Vanhoozer, and Henry Knight III on Christianity's Essence

Stanley Grenz was not the only postconservative evangelical theologian to argue that the main thrust of authentic Christianity and evangelicalism is transformation rather than information. Clark Pinnock and Kevin Vanhoozer have registered their dissatisfaction with the conservative tendency to emphasize the factual, cognitive content of Christianity when it demotes or neglects experience. Pinnock brings this postconservative move to expression in his treatment of the nature of divine revelation. For him, conservative theology has emphasized too long and too much the propositional nature of revelation and has neglected its narrative side. The point here is that for Pinnock and many other theologians, narrative is meant to transform and does transform; it creates identity in a way factual statements do not. Pinnock identifies a fault line running between theological conservatives and "moderates" (essentially the same as postconservatives) this way: "For the conservative, the view of revelation that dominates is cognitive and propositional, which imperils flexibility. Whereas for moderates, the view of revelation is closer to the salvation story itself."[31] He goes on to explain that the gospel, which is the heart and soul of Christianity, is a message that takes the form of "the greatest story ever told."[32] He labels this grand narrative of divine revelation a "eucatastrophe," which means a tragedy with a happy ending. "The central message of Christianity and therefore its essence is the epic story of redemption, enshrined

31. Clark Pinnock, *Tracking the Maze: Finding Our Way through Modern Theology from an Evangelical Perspective* (San Francisco: Harper & Row, 1990), 73.
32. Ibid., 153.

in its sacred texts and liturgies, that announces the salvation and God's liberation of the human race."[33]

According to Pinnock, in concert with Grenz and postconservatives generally, the point of this announcement in story form is to transform people; it is a story that tells about salvation and brings about salvation. He contrasts this view of revelation and the theology it engenders with that promoted by conventional, conservative evangelicalism:

> In so much evangelical theology, the test is not the Christian story but orthodox doctrines and traditional paradigms. Belief in plenary inspiration, vicarious atonement, the deity of Christ, etc., is the litmus test rather than the story on which they are doctrinal reflections. . . . It is high time we became less preoccupied with rational certainty and doctrinal precision and more concerned with telling the Christian story with its rich interplay of meanings that speak to all our human needs.[34]

Pinnock and most postconservative evangelicals are convinced of the truth of the great story not by reason as much as by the fact that it does speak to all our human needs. We experience our humanity fulfilled and our ultimate questions and concerns met and answered by our encounter with the story and its author. For Pinnock the essence of Christianity and therefore of evangelical faith lies in the story and our encounter with its author through its witness. The point of the story is to announce what God has done and to do it in us.

So what about the cognitive dimension of Christianity? With Grenz, Pinnock relegates it to secondary status without discarding or neglecting it. He asserts:

> Christian doctrines are not absolute truths, free of contextual factors in formulation or infallible in and of themselves. Theology is the never-ending search for the intelligible meaning of the story so far as it can be known. Therefore, it will need to be more dynamic and flexible than can be a propositional theology.[35]

33. Ibid.
34. Ibid., 184.
35. Ibid., 186.

In other words, Pinnock, like all postconservatives, regards all doctrines and theological systems as "man-made" rather than "God-made." God sends a story that includes some propositions that help us interpret it. Theology is our attempt to interpret it further and create doctrines that do justice to it. But doctrines are our products; they are not divinely communicated. Therefore they are always open to revision as required by deeper insight into the meaning of the great story of God. We will explore Pinnock's view of revelation more fully in a later chapter. Here it will suffice to say that his view of the essence of Christianity and of evangelicalism is consistent with Grenz's and other postconservatives' insofar as it moves away from divinely delivered propositions developed into coherent doctrinal systems and focuses instead on transformation. In Pinnock's account that transformation is what God has done for us in Christ as narrated in the biblical story. It is also what God is doing in us through the Holy Spirit as we enter into that story and become part of it. The cognitive side of Christianity is secondary; doctrine is the second-order language of the church.

Pinnock's postconservative account of Christianity's essence immediately raises questions of subjectivism and relativism from conservatives. Sometimes postconservatives (and others) worry about conservatives' obsession with combating subjectivism and relativism. That's not to say subjectivism and relativism are good things; no evangelical thinks so. But it is possible to focus so one-sidedly on them that they become all-consuming to the exclusion of every other issue and concern. Subjectivism and relativism can be ruled out by establishing an absolutistic, totalizing teaching magisterium that leaves no room for reform. That happened in Luther's day; his reforming efforts were countered with accusations that he was destroying the church by questioning its absolute authority and monopoly on truth. Nevertheless, postconservatives need to hear the concerns of conservatives such as Millard Erickson, D. A. Carson, and David Wells, and not just shrug them off as unworthy of response.

Pinnock does respond to them. A fuller account of his response will be given in a later chapter, but here it is helpful to say that he does not discard the categories of orthodoxy and heresy. He

asks how one can approach the question of heresy if the essence of Christianity is understood as story.[36] Remember that
for him "story" is more or less a cipher for the larger experience
of transformation wrought by God through redeeming activity, including drawing people into the story. He says, "Sound
doctrine is the way of interpretation that preserves the story in
its integrity, while unsound doctrine will be that which spoils
the story for its hearers."[37] In other words, not every account of
the story and its meaning is equal; some articulate its meaning
and significance in a way that respects its original integrity and
some are actually working out of another story and corrupting
the canonical narrative by subjecting it to a different universe
of meaning.[38]

Of course, the question will inevitably arise, "Who decides
such matters, and how?" But even conservatives cannot assure
that doctrine is correct if one sets the standard of assurance high
enough. In fact, that is what some of them seem to do. They set
the standard of certainty that doctrine is right very high and
then claim to have met it without actually doing so. Doubts and
questions still arise and there is no absolute guarantee that this
way of expressing truth is the one and only possible way—unless, of course, a magisterium is established that has the power
to exclude persons and groups who disagree. Some postconservatives fear that this is exactly what some conservatives try to
do when their orthodoxy is challenged by someone within the
evangelical movement.

What it really comes down to is that postconservatives are
more comfortable with uncertainty and ambiguity than conservatives. But that does not mean they are relativists. It is one thing
to admit a measure of perspective that influences every belief
and a lack of absolute proof that a belief or system is correct; it
is another thing to deny the very existence of truth itself. Postconservatives are critical realists, not relativists. Absolute truth
is what God knows; our grasp of truth is always from a certain
finite perspective and infected with finitude and fallenness. Some

36. Ibid., 189.
37. Ibid., 213.
38. Ibid., 189–90.

conservatives mistake intellectual humility for relativism. That's a profound category mistake and unworthy of serious thinkers.

Another postconservative evangelical theologian who identifies the essence of Christianity and of evangelicalism as transformation over information is Kevin Vanhoozer. So far he has not been the subject of much conservative criticism, but one has to wonder why when he says,

> The postmodern condition has awakened theologians from their dogmatic slumbers—to be precise, from the dream that doctrine or system is the be-all and end-all of theology. I have argued that the Bible is much more than a book of information, more even than divinely revealed information. It is a collection of divine communicative actions that continue to work their effects in those who read in Spirit and in truth.[39]

In other words, divine revelation takes many forms, all of which can be included under the general heading of divine communicative actions, and all are for the purpose of changing people's lives more than delivering information.

Vanhoozer's postconservative view of theology will be discussed in more detail later, but for now it is important to know that, along with Grenz and Pinnock and most postconservatives, he is interested in affirming that the main goal of revelation is establishing a covenant relationship between God and humans such that the latter are transformed. About the Bible he says, "Viewing texts as doing things other than representing states of affairs opens up possibilities for transformative reading that the modern obsession with information has eclipsed."[40] This is an implicit criticism of conservative theology insofar as it views the Bible as primarily a vehicle of information communication. For Vanhoozer the Bible is literature and literature is meant to transform readers. The Bible identifies God for us and communicates God's speech acts that affect our very identities.

Vanhoozer argues that although revelation contains propositions it transcends communication of information; it is a drama

---

39. Kevin J. Vanhoozer, *First Theology: God, Scripture and Hermeneutics* (Downers Grove, IL: InterVarsity, 2002), 39.

40. Ibid., 164.

that shows more than tells.[41] And by showing it enacts; revelation transforms by extending the action of God it records into the lives of those drawn into it by faithful reading. This carries through into Vanhoozer's vision of the Christian faith, which is not so much about knowledge of facts as about acting out the unfinished part of the drama of divine revelation: "The Christian faith is not a system of ideas or moral values but a five-act theo-drama in which God's speech and action play the decisive parts."[42] The first three acts of the drama are contained in Scripture, but the drama is unfinished. "The church continues to play out the final scenes of act 4."[43] Theology is about guiding the continuing action of the play, which will only be finished by God himself in the consummation (return of Christ): "The task of theology is to ensure that we fit into the action so that we are following rather than opposing Jesus Christ."[44] In other words, for Vanhoozer, the whole point of Christianity (and inevitably also, therefore, of evangelicalism) is faithfully and creatively to continue the action of the divine drama begun in the history Scripture records, and that means being transformed both by the play and by the contemporary action. In sum, "The words of the Bible are not simply carriers of information but *means of transformation*."[45]

Implicit, if not explicit, in Vanhoozer's postconservative theology is the idea that Christianity's essence, the main point of it all, is establishing covenantal relationship between God and humans that transforms and equips humans to take up and continue the activity of God. The emphasis is on action and practice. Underlying that is the necessity of transformation. For Vanhoozer and most postconservatives, communication of information and development of correct belief is only one part of the larger picture of the divine drama into which we are drawn by God's Spirit working through the drama. The larger picture is the unfolding drama and our participation in it, which means our

41. Kevin J. Vanhoozer, *The Drama of Doctrine: A Canonical-Linguistic Approach to Christian Theology* (Louisville: Westminster John Knox, 2005), 48.
42. Ibid., 57.
43. Ibid.
44. Ibid.
45. Ibid., 70.

continuing it together with God. The decisive acts are finished; God did them in Christ but wrote a script that is unfinished and invited us to participate. We join in the action and become actors and players in the continuing drama. We are not merely learners—even ones who are changed by the learning. We are actors and practitioners who are transformed by the action and by our participation in it.

Another postconservative evangelical theologian who argues that Christianity's essence is transformation more than information is Henry H. Knight III. In *A Future for Truth: Evangelical Theology in a Postmodern World* the Methodist theologian expresses a preference for understanding revelation as narrative over proposition, story over fact. Without in any way denying the truth of Scripture, Knight defines its purpose more as transformational than informational:

> This is the reason scripture is the way it is—the divine Author has inspired it in such a way that it enables the Holy Spirit to use it to illumine our hearts and transform our lives. It is no accident that so much of scripture is narrative, metaphor, and the like—God is not simply sending us a memorandum but preparing a medium through which we can have true relationship with God, one in which we come to know God as God actually is.[46]

Knight characterizes the purpose of the biblical narrative in transformational terms: "By dwelling in the biblical narrative the Christian life receives its particular shape and the Christian believer is enabled to see the world as it truly is."[47] In other words, the effect of reading Scripture faithfully and thus of being a Christian is not so much to receive new information as to receive a new perspective that shapes life. Thus, in the inimitable words of Hans Frei, founder of the postliberal school of theology, the Bible comes to absorb the world for the believing reader. The result is that the Christian is changed from a person who sees the world one way to a person who sees the world another way. That is a greater change than merely knowing something one did not know

46. Henry H. Knight III, *A Future for Truth: Evangelical Theology in a Postmodern World* (Nashville: Abingdon, 1997), 116.
47. Ibid., 180.

before. All of life is changed; one's identity is transformed through encounter with the God-identifying narrative of Scripture. And that is what being Christian and evangelical is all about.

All the theologians we have been discussing here, beginning with McGrath, have one thing in common: they either explicitly or implicitly regard the essence of Christianity and the heartbeat of authentic evangelicalism as transformation rather than information without in any way denying that information is part of the package. That is part of what makes them postconservatives; they disagree with Millard Erickson and other conservative evangelical thinkers who identify Christianity's essence as doctrine. Each makes room for doctrine as second-order reflection on the larger phenomenon of experience and/or drama. In fact, for them drama and experience cannot be separated, for the drama is experience creating and identity forming. Each of these theologians acknowledges that doctrine is inevitable and essential, but each also acknowledges that doctrine plays a servant role in relation to the transformational aspect of revelation and the gospel.

Inevitably the question will arise why information and transformation must be separated in this way. Why can't both be essential to authentic Christianity and evangelical faith? Why isn't it "both/and" rather than "either/or"? That's a valid question, but the fact of the matter is that when certain dualities are posed over against each other they tend to move above or below each other. Law and grace, divine goodness and power, justification and sanctification, all good Christians affirm both sides of each duality. But inevitably people place one over the other in each duality. One side qualifies the other side because of a certain tension in their juxtaposition. So it is with transformation and information. Both are important and information can be transforming. But information alone does not transform; everyone knows it is possible to receive and absorb facts without being changed by them. What is the essence of a marital relationship? The inevitable factual knowledge about the other person or the desirable personally transforming relationship of love? Surely most people would say the relationship's the thing. And the relationship is transformative; in marriage both persons change in relationship to the other. But what would a marital relationship be without facts? And yet the facts one knows about one's spouse are secondary to the love relationship. They play a role but they are not "of the essence."

Postconservative evangelicals simply want to register their complaint about conservative evangelicalism: it tends to specialize too much in the propositional, factual dimension of Christianity and evangelicalism. Doctrine is made too large by conservatives. They tend to forget that there was authentic Christianity before there was orthodoxy. And orthodoxy changes; one can deny it but one cannot escape it. What does not change about authentic Christianity is the experience of being transformed by the Holy Spirit in relationship with Jesus Christ as Savior and Lord.

3

The Word Made Fresh

Theology's Revisioning Task

One of the most fundamental differences between conservative and postconservative evangelical theologies has to do with their visions of theology's tasks. Put most simply, conservative evangelical theology tends to regard the constructive task of theology as completed whereas postconservative theology tends to regard it as always incomplete.

Theology's Tasks

Most evangelicals would agree that theology has four main tasks grouped under two headings. First are the two critical tasks of theology: to examine teachings about God that someone claims are Christian to determine whether they deserve that label. Not everything that wears the label "Christian" is worthy of it. In the earliest stages of Christian theology this was its main task, and it gave rise to the discipline of Christian theology. During the first centuries after Christ and the apostles, heresies such as Gnosticism and Montanism arose and challenged the church's faith and proclamation. Later, Arianism, Apollinarianism, Nestorianism, and Eutychianism challenged the church's collective faith in Christ as truly God and truly human yet one person. The church began its theological endeavors with the critical task by carefully examining and then rejecting these false gospels.

The second part of the critical task is to determine which truly Christian beliefs are crucial to the gospel and which are secondary, and to put them in their proper orders by level of importance. One way to describe this is to say that true Christian beliefs are either dogmas, doctrines, or opinions. In common language "dogma" and "doctrine" are barely distinguishable, but here, for our purposes, we will distinguish between them. A dogma is a belief considered essential to Christian faith; where it is denied, Christianity can hardly be recognized as present. Doctrines are beliefs that are not essential to Christianity but are important to some particular group of Christians. For example, a dogma might be that Jesus Christ is both truly God and truly human and yet one unified person. Christians believed this long before it was spelled out at the Council of Chalcedon in 451. A doctrine might be that only persons mature enough to express their faith for themselves should be baptized. Not all Christians believe it and hardly anyone thinks Christianity is absent where infants are baptized. For Baptists and some others, however, this belief and practice are important.

An opinion is a belief that may be interesting and worthy of discussion but is not crucial for fellowship. Most branches of Christianity would say that specific views of the "end times" (eschatology) lie in this category. That Christ will return before a millennial reign on earth (Revelation 20) is an opinion strongly held by many conservative Christians, but most would not insist that it be made a test of fellowship in any church.

These three categories seem inescapable; every thinking Christian works with them even if under other labels. Hardly anyone thinks everything he or she believes as a Christian is equally important. Churches almost always have to develop something like these three categories even if they are not formalized. One theological difference between conservatives and liberals relates to how beliefs are distributed over these three categories. Conservatives tend to locate many beliefs in the dogma and doctrine category, leaving fewer to the opinion category. Fundamentalists especially tend to empty the opinion category of most of its content and fill up the dogma category. Some even place premillennialism (belief that Jesus Christ will return before the millennial reign on earth) in the dogma category. Liberals tend to empty the dogma category and fill up the opinion category. Unitarians, for example, often claim to have no dogmas. However, even the strictest, most conservative fundamentalist Christians acknowledge some beliefs as opinion and allow diversity about them. And even the most liberal Christians admit that some things (such as justice for all) are dogmas.

I argue that the two steps or stages of theology's critical task are inevitable and necessary; they are always being carried out even where they are not recognized formally as theology or acknowledged as essential tasks of the church. No Christian church accepts anything and everything. Even the most tolerant and inclusive Christian groups have some standards by which they judge the soundness of beliefs. On the critical tasks of theology, conservative and postconservative evangelicals do not disagree in principle. They may disagree somewhat about the contents of the three categories of dogma, doctrine, and opinion, but they do not disagree about the importance of having these categories and rightly placing true Christian beliefs in them appropriately.

The constructive tasks of theology include developing properly Christian doctrines out of the materials of divine revelation and relating them to the contemporary context in faithful and relevant ways. Here is where conservatives and postconservatives tend to go their separate ways. Overall and in general, conservative evangelical theologians are suspicious of theology's constructive tasks—especially development of properly Christian beliefs—and hesitant to practice them. Some, such as Millard Erickson, heartily endorse the task of "contemporizing the Christian message,"[1] but many are wary of any evangelical effort to be culturally relevant, and most neglect or reject outright the project of developing

---

1. Millard Erickson, *Christian Theology*, 2nd ed. (Grand Rapids: Baker Academic, 1998), 115–34.

new or reconstructed Christian doctrines. Another way of putting this is that conservative evangelicals tend to treat the first step of theology's constructive task—developing or reconstructing properly Christian beliefs—as finished. Postconservatives, however, tend to regard this constructive task as always unfinished and doctrines as always open to correction and revision.

The Conservative Habit of Traditionalism

This is a difficult thesis to prove. Some who regard themselves as conservative evangelicals may disagree and argue that they do remain open to new developments in doctrine. Few blatantly close the door on this issue. Therefore, my characterization of conservative evangelical theology is admittedly impressionistic; it is based on my own reading of conservative evangelical theologies. Over the approximately twenty-five years of my career as an evangelical theologian, I have noticed this basic difference that remains unacknowledged by most conservatives. A habit of the conservative theological mind is to specialize in reiterating traditional doctrinal formulations and criticizing reconstructions and reformulations of doctrine. I can think of few exceptions. Almost all evangelical theologians who call themselves conservative treat the constructive task of theology, especially the first step (revision and reconstruction of doctrines), as finished and closed. Almost all of them treat revisionist or reformist theologies that believe in and practice ongoing doctrinal development as dangerous.

Throughout this book we will occasionally refer to a relatively new movement among conservative evangelicals that is sometimes called "paleo-orthodoxy." This is a term coined by the movement's best-known proponent, Thomas Oden. Along with Oden, the movement includes D. H. Williams and many other, lesser known evangelical thinkers. Paleo-orthodoxy is the idea that all truly important doctrinal issues were settled by the early church fathers and that modern and contemporary Christians should return to the patristic sources, including the first several councils, their decrees, canons, creeds, and definitions of faith, and should regard them as authoritative. While Oden and Williams do not close the door entirely on doctrinal development, they do not practice it and tend to be critical of those who do. Williams speaks for all paleo-orthodox conservative evangelicals when he says, "When a local church makes a theological statement, it needs to see itself standing under the authority of the confessional and doctrinal umbrella of the early church, which assumes the primacy of Scripture and the apostolic faith."[2] This is a somewhat ambiguous prescription. It might be interpreted as simply arguing for a general respect for early church tradition and especially for emulation of the early church's embrace of the authority of Scripture and the gospel proclaimed by the apostles. However, the entire context makes clear that Williams is arguing against any movement away from the teachings of the early church. Throughout his writings, Williams, like Oden and other paleo-orthodox conservative evangelicals and like Eastern Orthodox theologians, appeals to a consensus of early Christian doctrinal teachings as normative. He refers to "the normative value of the truths housed in the great confessions of the late patristic era."[3] For him, contemporary reformation of the church and its beliefs can properly be carried out only by a restoration of the "ancient catholicity of the church"[4] because that early church doctrinal consensus forms the "baseline for our Christian identity."[5]

Neither Oden nor Williams nor any other paleo-orthodox evangelical thinker absolutely rejects contemporary doctrinal development in the church, but they express themselves in an ambiguous manner leaving one wondering where they really stand on the issue of possible criticism and reconstruction of ancient or traditional formulations of faith. For example, Williams admits, "The Christian tradition was and always is in the process of development."[6] However, he also insists, "Development . . . is

2. D. H. Williams, *Retrieving the Tradition and Renewing Evangelicalism: A Primer for Suspicious Protestants* (Grand Rapids: Eerdmans, 1999), 203–4.

3. Ibid., 171–72.

4. Ibid., 201.

5. Ibid., 207.

6. D. H. Williams, *Evangelicals and Tradition: The Formative Influence of the Early Church* (Grand Rapids: Baker Academic, 2005), 35.

not the introduction of changes but a response to discovering how the deposit of faith should function as a resource for the needs of the present."[7] Williams makes abundantly clear that the mentioned "deposit of faith" is the ancient ecumenical doctrinal consensus of the early church, which should always function as the normative interpretive lens through which Christians read and interpret the Bible. For him, "it is fair to say that we will rightly hear God's Word only as we hear it in the corporate and historical voice of the church."[8]

Oden echoes much of what Williams says (or vice versa). On the one hand, like Williams, he affirms the supreme authority of Scripture in theology and argues that even the early church fathers did the same. On the other hand, he belittles or even rejects any attempt to use Scripture to correct or reconstruct the ancient ecumenical consensus of the church: "Interpreters who pretend to improve upon apostolic testimony are tampering with the evidence."[9] Like Williams, Oden is somewhat ambiguous about all this. Immediately following that stringent statement, which seems to outlaw all doctrinal reconstruction, he says, "This does not imply that there can be no progress in our ever-inadequate attempts to grasp and articulate ancient ecumenical teaching."[10] However, that does not give any license to diverge significantly from ancient ecumenical doctrinal teaching even if compelled to do so by Scripture itself. The "progress" Oden allows lies only in our understanding of ancient teaching; it does not allow for significant divergence from it. Like Williams, Oden recommends that all Christians, including evangelicals, adhere to the ancient Vincentian Canon (named after Vincent of Leríns), which says that Christians ought to believe what has always been believed by Christians everywhere. His own version of it is, "Classic Christian teaching holds fast to what has been believed and consented to around the world by Christians of all times and places. Individuals who likewise hold fast to

7. Ibid.

8. Ibid., 101.

9. Thomas C. Oden, *The Rebirth of Orthodoxy: Signs of New Life in Christianity* (San Francisco: HarperSanFrancisco, 2003), 123.

10. Ibid.

that consensual belief can rest assured that they are following orthodox faith."[11]

Oden lays down three tests for any assertion of Christian faith, which seem to rule out from the beginning any possibility of faithful practice of theology's constructive task: universality, apostolic antiquity, and conciliar consent. He claims, "If an assertion passes these three tests, it may be said to express the mind of the believing church, and thus be accepted as trustworthy. If an assertion fails any of these tests, it cannot be confidently termed classic Christianity (though it may still be open to ecumenical debate)."[12] Later in the same context Oden poses the question of a new formulation of doctrine that goes against the ancient consensus and says such must be judged by faithfulness to the consensual tradition.[13] "Local views that inveigh against the consensual memory must be tested against that memory."[14] He also insists, "Apostolicity trumps contemporaneity."[15]

Even though both Williams and Oden pay homage to the superior authority of Scripture over every other source and norm of theology, both seem to undermine that by insisting that Scripture can rightly be interpreted only by means of faithful adherence to the patristic and conciliar consensus of teaching. The latter becomes the litmus test for determining whether any new teaching or revision of old teaching is orthodox. The question of possible error in ancient tradition remains unanswered, however. Both Williams and Oden deny the infallibility of the church fathers, but both also treat the ancient ecumenical consensus as functionally inerrant for faithful biblical interpretation and doctrinal development.

I do not think Williams and Oden are aware of this ambiguity in their paleo-orthodoxy, but I cannot escape noticing it. On the one hand, they affirm Scripture's superiority over tradition, leaving the door open to doctrinal correction and development. On the other hand, they also affirm tradition's authority for in-

---

11. Ibid., 162.
12. Ibid.
13. Ibid., 165–66.
14. Ibid., 166.
15. Ibid., 167.

terpreting Scripture, closing the door to doctrinal correction and development. Of course, both affirm doctrinal correction where contemporary teaching strays away from the ancient ecumenical consensus. The upshot seems to be that theology's constructive task is finished; it was finished in the patristic age with the doctors and teachers of the undivided church and with the ecumenical councils. Neither one of them encourages doctrinal revision unless that means returning to the ancient sources.

Conservative Appeal to an Established Evangelical Tradition

Very different from Williams and Oden is Wayne Grudem, although Grudem is no less conservative than they are. Instead of appealing to the ancient ecumenical consensus Grudem appeals to a "conservative evangelical tradition" collectively represented by thirty-four systems of theology, all of which allegedly hold to the inerrancy of the Bible. Grudem says little about the church fathers and rarely appeals to their authority, even though he does support some ancient doctrinal formulations as biblical. His formal authority is Scripture alone and he nowhere closes the door absolutely on doctrinal correction and revision. For him, as for many conservative evangelicals influenced by Charles Hodge and the Old Princeton School of Reformed theology, "systematic theology involves collecting and understanding all the relevant passages in the Bible on various topics and then summarizing their teachings clearly so that we know what to believe about each topic."[16] There is no mention of ancient tradition as an authority for theology. However, informally Grudem uses the "conservative evangelical tradition" as a guide for, if not guardian of, orthodoxy. Functionally, in other words, Grudem's approach parallels that of Williams and Oden insofar as all of them anchor theological reflection to a tradition from which one should not stray.

Like Williams and Oden, however, Grudem is not entirely clear or consistent. Even though the conservative evangelical tradition

16. Wayne Grudem, *Systematic Theology: An Introduction to Biblical Doctrine* (Grand Rapids: Zondervan, 1994), 21.

functions as a limit to doctrinal development Scripture alone is normative and authoritative for what should be believed: "It is Scripture alone, not 'conservative evangelical tradition' or any other human authority, that must function as the normative authority for the definition of what we should believe."[17] Nevertheless, by beginning his systematic theology by appealing to the thirty-four systematic theologies that he regards as a kind of canon outside the Scriptural canon—at least for developing a truly evangelical systematic theology—Grudem betrays a preference for the use of tradition to limit doctrinal progress and development. Throughout his *Systematic Theology* he neglects or rejects significant doctrinal reconstruction; his only goal seems to be to restate in contemporary language what evangelicals have always believed the Bible says.

Millard Erickson is by all accounts one of the leading conservative evangelical theologians; his *Christian Theology* is for many evangelicals the gold standard for establishment, mainline, conservative evangelical thought.[18] And he has expressed his own views about doctrinal revision and reconstruction in *The Evangelical Left: Encountering Postconservative Evangelical Theology*.[19] In all his writings Erickson affirms the sole supreme authority of the Bible and rejects any equal authority of tradition or culture (e.g., philosophy or science) while acknowledging that tradition and culture can be helpful tools for theological interpretation and expression. His basic approach to theology differs little from Grudem's, except that Erickson values "contemporizing the Christian message" so long as its essence is unchanged.

In both *Christian Theology* and *The Evangelical Left*, Erickson appeals to "the established evangelical position"—a phrase drawn from the latter book but an idea also represented in the former—as a criterion and norm for what can be considered valid in evangelical theology.[20] Nowhere does he explicitly or overtly reject any and every attempt at doctrinal revision or reconstruc-

---

17. Ibid., 25.
18. Millard Erickson, *Christian Theology*, 2nd ed. (Grand Rapids: Baker Academic, 1998).
19. Millard Erickson, *The Evangelical Left: Encountering Postconservative Evangelical Theology* (Grand Rapids: Baker Academic, 1997).
20. Ibid., 61.

tion, but his habit of mind is to criticize such attempts insofar as they deviate from the evangelical tradition. He seems to assume that the established or received evangelical tradition has captured the totality of biblical doctrine and admits of no significant correction or revision. His own exposition of doctrines in *Christian Theology* seems to be intended as a restatement of earlier evangelical doctrinal systems such as one finds in Augustus Hopkins Strong (a Baptist theologian in the early twentieth century) and Carl F. H. Henry. Doctrinal creativity is not what Erickson is about and he does not seem to appreciate it in others.

The same can be said of D. A. Carson and the team that produced the Evangelical Affirmations in 1989 and 1990 as represented in the book *Evangelical Affirmations*.[21] Both affirm that the Bible alone stands as the supreme authority for theology and that, in principle, any human doctrine or system of thought is open to correction by Scripture.[22] However, both also criticize attempts to construct doctrines anew or revise traditional doctrines even by appeal to Scripture. Carson argues that evangelicalism has traditionally defined itself by means of theological categories and he criticizes contemporary evangelicals who attempt to display innovative creativity.[23] He even compares them with rebellious adolescents! Throughout the *Evangelical Affirmations* volume, the authors decry proposed revisions of historic evangelical doctrines and argue for strict adherence to traditional evangelical interpretations.[24]

All this is to say that one hallmark of conservative evangelical theology is explicit or implicit closure to the constructive task of theology and especially that part of the constructive task that seeks to construct new doctrines or reconstruct old ones. Doctrinal "revisionism" is a bad word to conservatives, for whom it has become a technical term for liberal theology since its adop-

21. Kenneth Kantzer and Carl F. H. Henry, eds., *Evangelical Affirmations* (Grand Rapids: Zondervan, 1990).

22. D. A. Carson, *The Gagging of God: Christianity Confronts Pluralism* (Grand Rapids: Zondervan, 1996), 449.

23. Ibid., 472.

24. See, for example, J. I. Packer, "Evangelicals and the Way of Salvation: New Challenges to the Gospel—Universalism, and Justification by Faith," in *Evangelical Affirmations*, ed. Kantzer and Henry, 114.

tion for that purpose by David Tracy in *Blessed Rage for Order: The New Pluralism in Theology*.[25] Consequently, postconservatives seem to prefer to speak of doctrinal "reform." Postconservatives do not believe that all doctrinal revision is evidence of liberal theology at work. Liberal theology is that approach to doctrinal reconstruction that gives maximal acknowledgment to the claims of modernity and rejects any absolute authority outside the self.[26] Postconservative evangelicals make neither of those moves in theology. However, postconservatives are critical realists as opposed to naive or uncritical realists; they recognize that truth and reality *as known by God* lies beyond human grasp. At best we always "see through a glass darkly" and all our interpretations and formulations about truth and reality are open to correction by further light from God's Word.

Open Theology in Postconservative Evangelicalism

One hallmark of postconservative evangelical theology that functionally sets it apart from conservative evangelical theology, then, is *openness to doctrinal correction and revision in light of God's Word*. In other words, the constructive task of theology is always unfinished and theologians are called to faithful and free reconsideration of traditional doctrinal formulations tethered absolutely only to God's revelation in Jesus Christ and in Scripture. That is, postconservative evangelical theologians adhere to the "scripture principle": only the canonical Scriptures serve a constitutional role in theology. Tradition, whether ancient and ecumenical or established evangelical, always gets only a vote—never a veto—in doctrinal controversies. One thing that makes postconservatives *postconservative*, as opposed to conservative,

25. David Tracy, *Blessed Rage for Order: The New Pluralism in Theology* (New York: Seabury, 1975; repr., Chicago: The University of Chicago Press, 1996).

26. These characterizations of liberal theology are drawn from the works of two scholars: Claude Welch, *Protestant Thought in the Nineteenth Century*, 2 vols. (New Haven and London: Yale University Press, 1972–85); Gary Dorrien, *The Making of American Liberal Theology: Imagining Progressive Religion* (Louisville: Westminster John Knox, 2000); Dorrien, *The Making of American Liberal Theology: Idealism, Realism, and Modernity* (Louisville: Westminster John Knox, 2003).

is their suspicion of closure to doctrinal development by appeal to tradition; they do not reject tradition as something pernicious, but they consider it relative in authority compared with revelation itself. Thus they are ever aware of the possible need to reformulate traditional dogmas and doctrines and express them in ways that are more biblical and intelligible than before. Critics may charge them with "cultural relativism," but this is simply vicious calumny. Postconservative evangelicals are not relativists but critical realists. They agree with Alfred Lord Tennyson, who wrote, "Our little systems have their day; they have their day and cease to be. They are but broken lights of Thee, and Thou, O God, art more than they."[27]

One of the first manifestos of postconservative evangelical theology was an article by Clark Pinnock, "An Evangelical Theology: Conservative and Contemporary."[28] While affirming evangelical fidelity to classical Christian orthodoxy, Pinnock criticized conservative theology for failing to update doctrines for modern (and now postmodern) hearers:

> Conservative Christianity needs to work much harder at formulating creative proposals of the biblical message for today. It is not enough to expose the un-Christian assumptions of modernity unless we are prepared to do this task, too. Somehow, the classical doctrines have to be reappropriated in terms of modern experience, and this can be done without compromise with the help of the God who rules over every age and generation.[29]

Much of Pinnock's article can be read as little different from Erickson's call for "contemporizing the Christian message," but near its end the author steps out of the conservative box and suggests something very postconservative—doctrinal creativity and innovation:

> It would be a sad picture if Scripture were seen to be a limit and restriction, without any room left for freedom and creativity. In-

27. Alfred Lord Tennyson, *In Memorium*, "Prelude," lines 17–18.
28. Clark Pinnock, "An Evangelical Theology: Conservative and Contemporary," *Christianity Today*, January 5, 1979, 23–29.
29. Ibid., 408–9.

deed there is a liberating factor, the reality of the living God who leads and guides his people who are involved in struggles and changes. We have hope in the Spirit of God who abides with the church, and leads us further into all truth. Scripture is normative, but it always needs to be read afresh and applied in new ways. And because it is God's Word, it is new in each situation and fresh to every person. . . . Fidelity does not consist in simply repeating old formulas drafted in an earlier time. It includes the creative thinking required to make the old message fresh and new.[30]

Pinnock's style or strategy in this article is moving toward postconservatism even as he expresses high regard for classical Christian orthodoxy. Toward the end of the article, the surrounding context of the quote above, he definitely moves in the direction he would later go with doctrinal revision and reconstruction. Clearly the approach expressed by Pinnock in this 1979 article is away from conservative theology and toward what I am calling postconservative, in that he opens the door to doctrinal revision in light of improved Scriptural understanding and cultural needs.

By all accounts Bernard Ramm is an evangelical theologian who set the course for postconservative thinking in evangelical theology. To call him a postconservative would be anachronistic; he belongs to an earlier generation and always had one foot firmly planted in conservative, if not traditionalist, thinking. However, toward the end of his career he wrote a volume that garnered critical attention from conservative evangelicals: *After Fundamentalism: The Future of Evangelical Theology*.[31] The title was not his preference; he wanted the subtitle to be the title of the book and he was dismayed by the publisher's choice.[32] However, I think the title aptly describes his trajectory—farther away from fundamentalism while remaining faithfully evangelical. Ramm argues that the Enlightenment brought about some changes in culture that cannot be rejected and with which all

30. Ibid., 28.
31. Bernard Ramm, *After Fundamentalism: The Future of Evangelical Theology* (San Francisco: Harper & Row, 1983).
32. Ramm told me this in personal conversation when I studied under him in a DMin seminar at Bethel Theological Seminary during the summer of 1985.

thinking people—including evangelicals—must come to terms. He accused some conservative theologians of obscurantism because they refuse to acknowledge the good resulting from the Enlightenment.[33]

Ramm argues that because of the Enlightenment evangelical theology needs a new paradigm:

> If an evangelical feels that the Enlightenment and modern learning have ushered in a new cultural epoch, which in turn has precipitated into existence a new and radical set of issues for evangelical theology, then such a person will feel the need of a new paradigm. If an evangelical feels that the Enlightenment is but one more chapter in the history of unbelief, then he or she will not feel that a new paradigm is necessary.[34]

Ramm makes crystal clear that he believes evangelical theology needs a new paradigm and that Swiss theologian Karl Barth offers the best avenue toward it. He criticizes Charles Hodge, who offered the paradigm in which most conservative evangelical scholars work. Ironically, of course, many critics argue that Hodge's paradigm, which Ramm labels "inerrant propositionalism," is inspired by the Enlightenment. Ramm does not seem to notice this, although he does critique Hodge's manner of attempting to relate inspired Scripture with modern knowledge.[35]

According to Ramm, the traditional evangelical doctrine of Scripture stemming from the Old Princeton School of theology (Hodge, Alexander, Warfield, and Machen) is not viable anymore. Its unnuanced equation of Scripture with God's Word and its deductive argument from that to strict verbal inerrancy ends with all kinds of contortions to explain the phenomena of Scripture, which simply does not seem to be inerrant. Barth provided the way forward by distinguishing between the Word of God and Scripture while keeping them in close relation. "Barth believed that the Word of God is in Scripture as the *Sache* [subject matter] of Scripture."[36] Scripture is "witness" to the Word of God and not

33. Ramm, *After Fundamentalism*, 19.
34. Ibid., 25–26.
35. Ibid., 44.
36. Ibid., 93.

identical with the Word of God. Rather, the relation between them is dialectical and involves a "diastasis." "The Word of God exists 'in, with, and under' the culturally conditioned text."[37] This is a sacramental view of the Word of God and Scripture; the former indwells and shines through the latter without the latter being identical with the former. According to Ramm, "Barth's concept of the diastasis [of Scripture and Word of God] enables a theologian to come to terms with modern learning and at the same time retain the theological integrity of Holy Scripture—which the doctrines of inspiration and revelation are really all about."[38] Ramm believed that Barth's approach provided a solution to a problem in the traditional evangelical doctrine of Scripture as the Word of God, for in the latter "there is no genuine, valid working hypothesis for most evangelicals to interact with the humanity of Scripture in general and biblical criticism in particular."[39]

Not all postconservative evangelicals are going to agree with Ramm's endorsement of Barth's paradigm for understanding Scripture. One who is not usually considered postconservative, however, does: Donald G. Bloesch. In *Holy Scripture: Revelation, Inspiration and Interpretation*, this confessional evangelical adopts a similar position to Ramm's and acknowledges Barth's influences.[40] The point, however, is not this particular reconstruction of the doctrine of Scripture; the point is the style and strategy of opening up the traditional evangelical doctrine of Scripture and subjecting it to criticism and pointing toward a different model that is more biblical and culturally relevant. For Ramm and Bloesch it is more biblical because it avoids the tendency toward bibliolatry implicit in the identification of the words of the Bible with God's Word.

In *Tracking the Maze: Finding Our Way through Modern Theology from an Evangelical Perspective*, Clark Pinnock moved further along the trajectory he set in his *Christianity Today* article and advocated fresh and creative theological construction or recon-

37. Ibid., 47.
38. Ibid., 95.
39. Ibid., 114.
40. Donald G. Bloesch, *Holy Scripture: Revelation, Inspiration and Interpretation* (Downers Grove, IL: InterVarsity, 1984).

struction.[41] He declared his break from conservative theology
by asserting, "Conservative theology offers a thunderous reaf-
firmation of tradition in the face of so many modern doubts, an
apparently safe refuge from the relativizing effects of history."[42]
He asks, "Why do conservatives assume that the received doctrinal paradigms created by human beings like ourselves are
incapable of improvement?" Rather, he insists, "Respect for the
past does not require closed-mindedness" to future corrections
and reformulations.[43] Far from tossing aside tradition, Pinnock
affirms its value as one of theology's sources and norms, but
insists, "The achievements of the past can be respected while
the ongoing work of reformation can proceed."[44]

In the last chapter we explored Pinnock's ideas of revelation
as story and theology as the ongoing search or pilgrimage for
an intelligible expression of the grand story of redemption in
culturally sensitive ways. One case study of this is Pinnock's own
arrival at what is known as open theism—the belief that Scripture
reveals a God who limits himself so that part of the future is unknown even to him. His book *Most Moved Mover: A Theology of
God's Openness* is a fine example of postconservative evangelical
thinking about God, even if some postconservatives do not agree
with its central thesis about God's foreknowledge. There Pinnock
argues that God voluntarily chooses to be affected by creation
and especially free agents such as humans for the sake of love
so that he does not know the future exhaustively and infallibly.
He argues this on biblical as well as metaphysical grounds. We
will examine open theism more fully in a later chapter. The point
of mentioning it here is simply to say it is a product of the postconservative style of doing evangelical theology in that it has the
courage to challenge traditional ways of thinking out of biblical
fidelity and not cultural accommodation or philosophy.[45]

41. Clark Pinnock, *Tracking the Maze: Finding Our Way through Modern Theology from an Evangelical Perspective* (San Francisco: Harper & Row, 1990).
42. Ibid., 48.
43. Ibid., 51.
44. Ibid., 72.
45. "It is not the open view of God that is philosophy-driven so much as conventional theism itself." Clark Pinnock, *Most Moved Mover: A Theology of God's
Openness* (Grand Rapids: Baker Academic, 2001), 115.

A theologian not always considered evangelical but who embodies the postconservative approach without being liberal is the late James William McClendon Jr., who taught at Fuller Theological Seminary in his later years. His discussion of religious authority, doctrine, and tradition in *Doctrine: Systematic Theology, Volume II* is a stellar expression of the postconservative view of theology as a never-ending constructive project.[46] McClendon questions "whether tradition must monopolize the voice of God in Scripture"[47] and yet also affirms the importance of tradition as the handing down of the gospel from generation to generation. Like any good postconservative, he gives tradition a large role in theology without embracing traditionalism: "The theological task is to recognize and honor this conservative tendency [to preserve and conserve what has been believed] . . . while forever guarding against its fertile and poisonous excesses."[48] The context makes clear that by "its fertile and poisonous excesses" he means the refusal to acknowledge tradition's fallibility and need for reform in light of better insights into Scripture.

Of creeds and confessions of faith McClendon says they have a supplementary authority to Scripture, but they cannot be granted equal authority with Scripture even implicitly. They are at best "hermeneutical aids subordinate to Scripture."[49] McClendon locates religious authority in God and then subordinates to God's authority God-designated authorities, beginning especially with Jesus Christ and Scripture. Scripture derives its authority from Jesus Christ. The church also shares in authority, as does tradition, but neither can be recognized as absolute. All subordinate authorities (after Jesus Christ and Scripture) require "assessment, discernment, judgment."[50]

In summary, when full authority is assigned to God alone, the result is the subordination of every human locus of authority. The *disciple* whose soul is competent, the *book* whose word is

46. James W. McClendon Jr., *Systematic Theology*, vol. 2, *Doctrine* (Nashville: Abingdon, 1994).
47. Ibid., 468.
48. Ibid., 470.
49. Ibid., 471.
50. Ibid., 478.

divine, the *church* whose fellowship is spiritual can make their claims only as *proximate* authorities, each beneath the sovereign authority of God.[51]

McClendon's vision of authority for Christian theology is consistent with that of other postconservative evangelicals even if they do not spell it out so explicitly. This is why doctrine must remain open to reconstruction and revision: only God and his Word are absolutely authoritative. To elevate any lesser being to inviolable authority even in practice and not in statement is to flirt with idolatry and close the door to reform of that which is finite, fallible, and fallen.

Certainly Stanley J. Grenz was one of the consummate postconservative evangelical thinkers; his death removed from them one of their two or three leading lights. According to Grenz, theology is a conversation between three sources and norms: the Spirit speaking through Scripture, the theological tradition of Christianity, and the contemporary cultural context. This "trialogue" is stated in virtually all of his books. In *Revisioning Evangelical Theology*, he calls these the "three pillars of theology" and places highest authority in Scripture.[52] His postconservative side comes out when he says, "But theology is not merely the systematic repetition of the content of the Bible."[53] This is how he viewed conservative evangelical theology as practiced by thinkers such as Wayne Grudem. Instead, he argues, "A truly helpful theology must articulate the biblical kerygma, in a way understandable by contemporary culture, while maintaining a fundamental unity with the one people of God throughout history."[54] This may not seem particularly controversial until and unless one recognizes that for Grenz contemporary culture is a partner with Scripture and tradition in the ongoing and never-ending conversation that constitutes theology.

In spite of his paradigm of theology as trialogue among Scripture, tradition, and culture, Grenz never tires of saying

51. Ibid., 481.
52. Stanley J. Grenz, *Revisioning Evangelical Theology* (Downers Grove, IL: InterVarsity, 1993).
53. Ibid., 94.
54. Ibid., 104.

that Scripture is the primary voice in the conversation.[55] His postconservatism appears as he critiques a traditionalism that hardens traditional categories so that they are above question or reform. Instead, Grenz asserts, "Theology is progressive in that it is an ongoing discipline that repeatedly gives rise to new ways of looking at old questions, brings into view previously undervalued aspects of the Christian belief-mosaic, and occasionally even advances the church's knowledge of theological truth."[56] This statement perfectly expresses the postconservative spirit; few if any conservatives would agree. They especially disagree when Grenz insists, "A renewal of the center [of evangelical faith] . . . calls the church to the ongoing task of doctrinal retrieval and reformation."[57] Conservatives affirm the task of doctrinal retrieval, but they run from the "ongoing task of doctrinal . . . reformation" because it opens the door to ideas like open theism and inclusivism of salvation, the idea (advanced by many postconservatives) that salvation may be found by God's grace even where the gospel has not yet been explicitly proclaimed.

A younger postconservative evangelical theologian who picks up where Grenz left off is John Franke. His book, *The Character of Theology: A Postconservative Evangelical Approach*, continues themes explored by Grenz. Contrary to some critics who have accused Grenz and Franke of relativism and placing culture on a par with Scripture in terms of authority, Franke makes abundantly clear that Scripture is theology's "norming norm," whereas all other sources and norms are at best "normed norms."[58] Like Grenz, Franke affirms, "Culture can be a means through which we gain theological insight,"[59] but he does not view culture as equal with Scripture in authority.

Franke's description of theology's task is a model of clarity for expressing the postconservative style:

55. Stanley J. Grenz, *Renewing the Center: Evangelical Theology in a Post-Theological Era*, 2nd ed. (Grand Rapids: Baker Academic, 2006), 206, 211.

56. Ibid., 343.

57. Ibid., 345.

58. John R. Franke, *The Character of Theology: A Postconservative Evangelical Approach* (Grand Rapids: Baker Academic, 2005), 130–34.

59. Ibid., 140.

> The task of theology is not an attempt to identify and codify the true meaning of the text in a series of systematically arranged assertions that then function as the only proper interpretive grid through which to read the Bible. Such an approach is characteristic among those who hold confessional statements in an absolutist fashion and claim that such statements teach the "system" of doctrine contained in Scripture. The danger here is that such a procedure can hinder the ability to read the text and to listen to the Spirit in new ways. Theology should always lead us back to the Bible. Its goal is to place the Christian community in a position to be receptive to the voice of the Spirit speaking in and through the biblical text to refashion the world after the eschatological mission and purposes of God.[60]

In other words, truth cannot be captured and kept in a humanly derived doctrinal expression or system closed to revision and reform. The constructive task of theology is made necessary by the fact that doctrines, and especially systems, are human and not divine, together with the fact that God alone (including the Spirit speaking through Scripture) is absolute in authority.

One claim by Franke—and to a lesser extent perhaps by Grenz—with which many postconservatives will disagree is that the "voice of the Spirit" can also be heard speaking through culture. In my opinion, and no doubt in the opinions of many postconservative evangelicals, culture is a tool of theological construction insofar as it provides the questions and means for intelligible expression, but it cannot be viewed as a vehicle of the Spirit's voice. The Spirit speaks through Scripture and possibly through ongoing prophecy and illumination of Spirit-filled people of God—although the latter form of "speaking" would be subordinate to the voice of the Spirit through Scripture. Franke opens the door to criticism of his theological proposal when he says, "In addition to listening for the voice of the Spirit speaking through Scripture, theology must be attentive to the voice of the Spirit speaking through culture."[61] This does open the door, however unintentionally, to a kind of relativism. Fortunately, Franke does not walk through that door. One thing that keeps

60. Ibid., 135.
61. Ibid., 141.

him from doing so is his ironic view of tradition. In spite of his very postconservative view of the "character of theology," Franke explains that Christian tradition is an extension of the authority of Scripture and argues for a coinherence of Scripture and tradition similar to Williams and Oden.[62] His privileging of tradition in theology anchors his theology to the ground even as his acknowledgment of the voice of the Spirit through culture gives it wind to fly. Many postconservatives will disagree with both of these elements in Franke's proposal even as they appreciate his overall vision of doctrine as dynamic under the guidance of the Spirit speaking through Scripture.

Kevin Vanhoozer's Vision of Theology as Performance

No postconservative evangelical thinker has been more forthright and adamant about the ongoing nature of the constructive task of theology than Kevin Vanhoozer, who views theology as the faithful but also creative continuation of the drama begun by God in Scripture and carried forward by the church throughout the centuries. He observes, "The Bible is not a theological dictionary but a theological drama."[63] In other words, it is better to understand the Bible as dramatic story or play than as storehouse of information. Vanhoozer chides evangelicals who regard the Bible primarily in that way: "Nor is it of the essence of evangelicalism to believe that revelation is solely propositional or only the conveying of information."[64] His postconservative colors show most clearly in this programmatic statement that contradicts a basic conservative theological habit of the mind: "Evangelicals ought not presume that a final statement of theology has already been achieved."[65] The context makes clear that Vanhoozer is not merely talking about the need to contextualize or contemporize the

62. Ibid., 155–60.

63. Kevin J. Vanhoozer, "The Voice and the Actor: A Dramatic Proposal about the Ministry and Minstrelsy of Theology," in *Evangelical Futures: A Conversation on Theological Method*, ed. John G. Stackhouse, Jr. (Grand Rapids: Baker Academic, 2000), 64.

64. Ibid., 67.

65. Ibid.

Christian message by expressing old ideas in new idioms. Rather, he is talking about theology as dynamic and unfolding: "'Final' or absolute biblical interpretations are properly eschatological. For the moment, we must cast our doctrines not in the language of heaven but in the time-bound, culture-bound languages of earth, governed, of course, by the dialogue we find in Scripture itself."[66] Vanhoozer echoes the other postconservative thinkers we have examined so far in this chapter by valuing tradition while eschewing a traditionalism that binds theology and doctrine to the past: "Tradition is an important source for theology, but traditionalism—the excessive regard for tradition—is the enemy of vital theology."[67]

Vanhoozer has laid out his program for a postconservative evangelical approach to theology in two books: *First Theology: God, Scripture and Hermeneutics* and *The Drama of Doctrine: A Canonical-Linguistic Approach to Christian Theology*.[68] The two books echo each other, although the latter constitutes a more comprehensive treatment of theological methodology. In both volumes Vanhoozer is concerned to present an alternative to postliberal theologian George Lindbeck's three models of doctrine as laid out in *The Nature of Doctrine: Religion and Theology in a Postliberal Age*.[69] Lindbeck proposed a "cultural-linguistic" understanding of doctrine to replace the dominant conservative and liberal models, which he labeled "cognitive-propositionalist" and "experiential-expressivist," respectively. Vanhoozer finds problems with all three and seeks to develop a fourth that he calls "canonical-linguistic." Our purpose here will not be to examine Vanhoozer's theory of Christian doctrine and religious language so much as to understand his view of the constructive task of theology (although they are inseparably related).

66. Ibid., 80.
67. Ibid., 102.
68. Kevin J. Vanhoozer, *First Theology: God, Scripture and Hermeneutics* (Downers Grove, IL: InterVarsity, 2002); Vanhoozer, *The Drama of Doctrine: A Canonical-Linguistic Approach to Christian Theology* (Louisville: Westminster John Knox, 2005).
69. George Lindbeck, *The Nature of Doctrine: Religion and Theology in a Postliberal Age* (Philadelphia: Westminster, 1984).

First, it is important to know that Vanhoozer believes that "the two-party system of conservative and liberal [theologies] no longer seems adequate to describe what is taking place [in theology]."[70] His proof lies in the rise of postliberal and postconservative theologies that cannot be located on the left-right spectrum of theologies tied inextricably to modernity. Both postliberalism, inspired by the work of Yale theologian Hans Frei, and postconservatism, inspired by evangelical theologian Bernard Ramm, seek to work apart from the dominating influence of modernity. For Vanhoozer, the "postmodern condition" has awakened theologians from their dogmatic slumbers and forced them to look beyond propositions, logic, and systems to poetry, imagery, drama, and imagination as tools for theological work. Above all, it has shown that language is not primarily about stating facts; language is also and even more "communicative action." Words and phrases do things, they do not merely represent things.

For Vanhoozer, the Bible should be understood as more than a set of facts to be arranged into logical order or a doctrinal system because "Scripture contains a wide repertoire of what God does with human words."[71] "It is a collection of divine communicative actions that continue to work their effects in those who read in Spirit and in truth."[72] The Bible's aim is not so much to convey authoritative information in order to inculcate theological knowledge about God as to instill wisdom through "performance knowledge."[73] The purpose of Scripture is for God to identify himself by means of speech acts that communicate God himself to faithful readers and involve them in God's drama of redemption. Vanhoozer explicitly labels his view of Scripture and theology as postconservative and contrasts it with evangelicalism's "received view," stemming from the works of Benjamin B. Warfield of the Old Princeton School of theology, that engendered the idea of Scripture as primarily propositional and verbally inspired as well as verbally infallible. The focus

70. Vanhoozer, *Drama of Doctrine*, xiii.
71. Vanhoozer, *First Theology*, 34–35.
72. Ibid., 39.
73. Ibid., 39–40.

there was on facts and information leading to correct doctrine in a logical system. Without rejecting propositional revelation Vanhoozer criticizes an undue emphasis on these aspects of revelation. "God does many things with human language besides assert truths."[74]

When it comes to theology Vanhoozer clearly values the ongoing work of unfolding the meaning of divine revelation. Traditional interpretations must not be privileged in such a way that fresh, creative, and even imaginative proposals and performances are stifled. Theology's primary task is to continue the action of the divine drama begun in Scripture and continued in tradition. That requires both "canonical competence" and creative improvisation on the part of the theologian.[75] On the basis of a divinely delivered and authoritative script (Scripture), which comprises only the first three acts of the drama of redemption, theologians are called to improvise the rest of the dramatic action in faithfulness to the script and in anticipation of the divine conclusion of the drama in the eschaton. This requires more than repetition of repeated formulas; it requires continuity of character combined with imaginative improvisation.[76]

Vanhoozer has strong words for theological traditionalists who view theology's task as repetition of past performances. "The church is not called to play the same scene over and over but to take the gospel into new situations. To be faithful in its witness, the church must constantly be different. Indeed, at times it must even *improvise*."[77] Against brittle traditionalists he says, "What those who defend the literal sense of tradition fail to consider is that faithfulness sometimes requires change, not sameness. A living tradition requires both constancy and renewal. Tradition develops in ways that are sometimes continuous, sometimes discontinuous with what went before."[78] Vanhoozer adds, "*Sola scriptura* means at least this: that the church's performance is always subject to potential correction from the canon. It is for

74. Ibid., 153.
75. Vanhoozer, *Drama of Doctrine*, 129.
76. Ibid., 128.
77. Ibid.
78. Ibid., 126.

this reason that we must resist simply collapsing the text into the tradition of its interpretation and performance."[79] Clearly, then, Vanhoozer stands with postconservatives, who regard theology's constructive task as ever incomplete and worthy of further practice.

Vanhoozer also stands with postconservatives in rejecting liberal unfettered theological experimentation cut loose from the canon of divinely inspired Scripture. For him, as for all postconservative evangelicals, Scripture functions as the constitution for covenantal relationships between God and people; it governs and regulates the ongoing performance of the play.[80] "The norm with which the church is to assess ongoing developments in its language, thought, and life is the Spirit speaking in the Scriptures."[81] Scripture is more than norm, however; it is also the instrument by means of which the Spirit administers the covenant between God and his people today.[82] Because it is norm and instrument of covenant the canon rules the church and not vice versa.[83] This means that the imaginative, creative, and even improvisational practice of the church (including theologians) in continuing the action of the redemption drama begun in Scripture cannot be determined by the cultural or personal preferences of the actors; it must be faithful to the script even as it goes beyond it.

Thus, for Vanhoozer, the constructive task of theology may be called "faithful improvisation."[84] This involves being both properly textual and contextual in theological performance.[85] Good theology "takes account of both the script and the contemporary situation: doctrines help us to improvise judgments about what new things to say and do that are nevertheless consistent with our canonical script."[86] And doctrines are human constructions that serve as director's notes or prompts to guide

79. Ibid., 152.
80. Ibid., 133.
81. Ibid.
82. Ibid., 139.
83. Ibid., 150.
84. Ibid., 335.
85. Ibid., 311.
86. Ibid., 335.

the church's continuing performance.[87] The theologian's task is to develop these prompts in faithfulness to the script and with an eye to creative, contextual performance of the drama. But Vanhoozer cautions that theologians must not engage in "theological scriptwriting" or individualized ad-libbing, which he labels "the theatrical equivalent of heresy."[88] A good theologian is steeped in canonical competence; he or she knows the drama well and dwells in it. The script (canon) must never be viewed as a launching pad for egocentric or eccentric performance that departs from the script by developing a new story line.

Vanhoozer's idea of the constructive task of theology is best expressed by his phrase "improvising with a script." He describes it this way:

> Faithful performance and creative improvisation need not be at odds with one another; the biblical script itself is a record of previous improvisations—of God, of the prophets, and of the apostles—that display creative fidelity. The best improvisation, like the best translation, is precisely the one that diplays narrative continuity (*ipse*-identity) with what went on before. Theology is no different.[89]

Vanhoozer views the canon of Scripture as theology's primary authority, which limits the possibilities of improvisation at the same time it prompts and empowers improvisation. But just because it has an authoritative script to work with does not mean theology must be confined to the past. New situations call for new steps and dialogue and action. Vanhoozer's postconservative leanings appear nowhere more clearly than when he states, "Christian doctrine is the realization of canonical potential." Similarly, he avers, "A good performance *discovers* potential meaning that is really there, in the text, though previously hidden."[90] This is as much as to say, with all postconservative evangelicals, that God always has more light to break forth from his Word and that our task is to discover that previously undiscovered and hidden

87. Ibid., 107.
88. Ibid., 338.
89. Ibid., 344.
90. Ibid., 352.

light and improve on the accounts so far given of who God is and what God wants with us.

An interesting sidebar or footnote to this discussion of post-conservative evangelical thinkers and their visions of theology's constructive task is how faulty the criticisms of some conservative critics have been. Some of them have expressed harsh criticism, if not condemnation, for example, of Grenz's theological project while embracing and applauding Vanhoozer's. The fact is they are very similar. Both are postfoundationalist (as we will see in a later chapter) and postpropositionalist with regard to revelation and doctrine. Both view theology as ongoing conversation or dramatic performance—two ways of saying something very similar—that can and must at times break away from tradition and express new interpretations of divine revelation. Both regard Scripture as theology's primary source and norm while acknowledging other sources and norms as playing roles in theological work and play. One has to wonder what is going on when some conservative guardians of the received evangelical tradition praise Vanhoozer and criticize Grenz. Both are equally postconservative in their approaches to and styles of doing theology.

Postconservative Theology and Theology's Constructive Task

A hallmark of postconservative evangelical theology, then, that distinguishes it from conservative evangelical theology, is a willingness to continue the constructive task of theology with reconstruction of old doctrines as prompted by the Spirit speaking through the Scriptures and in full light of the Great Tradition of Christian thinking throughout the centuries. No postconservative evangelical wishes to discard tradition; every one expresses great respect and high regard for the Christian heritage of theology and especially the consensus of the early church fathers and the Protestant Reformers. Each one in some way also expresses the need for theologians, including evangelicals, to emulate the great Protestant Reformers of the sixteenth century by breaking free of tradition insofar as it is less than fully consistent with biblical revelation or flies in the face of what Bernard Ramm called the material facts of reality, and to have the courage to reconstruct doctrine so that it is more biblical and real, even if that means less traditional.[91]

So far we have remained in the abstract, but what are some doctrines under reconstruction by postconservative evangelicals? When it comes to specific doctrines and their revision, postconservatives are not marching in lockstep; that should not be expected. However, some new developments among them worry conservative theologians, who spend most of their time and energy criticizing them. Parenthetically, one way I identify conservative evangelical theologians is by their tendency to expend their theological efforts attacking other theologians' sincere efforts to reconstruct doctrines in light of God's Word.

One area where postconservatives are revising traditional Christian teaching is the doctrine of God. This project (or projects) will be examined in a later chapter. Another area of revision and reconstruction is the doctrine of salvation. Many evangelicals are working on new models of the atonement, as demonstrated in the book *Recovering the Scandal of the Cross: Atonement in New Testament and Contemporary Contexts* by Joel B. Green and

---

91. Bernard Ramm, *The Christian View of Science and Scripture* (Grand Rapids: Eerdmans, 1954), 29–30. I am aware that some readers may question this statement about changing theology in light of the material facts of reality. Neither I nor any other postconservative evangelical theologians advocate relevance at the expense of biblical fidelity. The point is simply that theology must avoid sheer obscurantism—which is well expressed in the old saying, "Don't confuse me with the facts; my mind is already made up." An obvious example from the past is theology's slow adjustment to the Copernican model of the solar system; more recently fundamentalists have refused to acknowledge the manifest ancient origins of the universe. Even Luther declared at the Diet of Worms that he would not recant his teaching unless convinced by Scripture and reason. The accusation that concern for theological revision in light of scientific and historical facts leads to relativism and away from biblical fidelity is simply false. Every theologian eventually comes to terms with material facts because it is impossible to deny that all truth is God's truth. The question is, What are the material facts? Here I only mean that once a person is convinced that something is factual, his or her theology cannot remain immune to it; there is no going back to a theology dominated by Ptolemaic cosmology or Aristotelian physics. In the same way, for example, it will be nearly impossible for theologians to ignore cloning. Cloning of humans in laboratories will require some rethinking of theories about how the soul is inherited.

Mark D. Baker.[92] Also, many evangelical thinkers are giving fresh examination and constructive reconsideration to the doctrine of justification by faith based on the insights of New Testament scholar N. T. Wright, who argues that a purely forensic, declarative doctrine of justification typical of Reformed theology is foreign to the New Testament. No postconservative evangelical theologian is at all interested in undermining the full deity and humanity of Jesus Christ or his unitary personality, but some are interested in revisiting the theme of kenosis or Kenotic Christology as taught by P. T. Forsyth and other late nineteenth- and early twentieth-century theologians to explain the incarnation so as to do justice to Jesus's humanity. The fate of the unevangelized and a possibly wider mercy of God in an inclusivistic doctrine of salvation is being considered by other postconservative evangelicals. God's work in and through world religions is of special interest to Amos Yong, among others.[93]

In these and many other ways, postconservative evangelical theologians are willing to take risks in new theological reflection in order to be more faithful to the Spirit speaking through the Scriptures and to the reality of God present and active in the world of cultures. But none of them are unfettered theological experimenters or worshipers of the goddess of novelty, as some conservative critics have charged. In each and every case the main concern is to be more biblical and less tied to tradition insofar as tradition has fallen short of the fullness of biblical fidelity.

92. Joel B. Green and Mark D. Baker, *Recovering the Scandal of the Cross: Atonement in New Testament and Contemporary Contexts* (Downers Grove, IL: InterVarsity, 2000).

93. Amos Yong, *The Spirit Poured Out on All Flesh: Pentecostalism and the Possibility of Global Theology* (Grand Rapids: Baker Academic, 2005).

4

The Postmodern Impulse in Postconservative Evangelical Theology

In order to avoid confusion it is important to distinguish between postmodernity, postmodernism, and postfoundationalism. In this chapter we will explore the preference of postconservative evangelical theologians for a postfoundationalist theological method. Because postfoundationalism is often associated with postmodernity and postmodernism, many critics have accused postconservatives of being postmodernist, but postmodernism implies much more than only a postfoundationalist epistemology (theory of knowledge). Before plunging into postconservatives' use of postfoundationalist thought, then, it is important to disentangle that from much that goes under the label "postmodern."

Postmodernity, Postmodernism, and Postfoundationalism

Hardly anyone knows what postmodernity is; the same can be said of postmodernism. One thing is clear, however: postmodernity is a cultural condition and postmodernism is its intellectual expression. Or perhaps it is better to say that postmodernism is any attempt to express the postmodern cultural condition intellectually. Beyond that, things get fuzzy. Postfoundationalism, however, is susceptible of clearer definition and description. It does relate to postmodernity and postmodernism, if only loosely.

One famous definition of postmodernity—although sometimes said of postmodernism—is "incredulity toward metanarrative."[1] This definition by philosopher Jean François Lyotard is as good a place to start as any. But unpacking it is notoriously difficult—as is any unpacking of postmodernity. A great deal of discussion and debate surrounds not only this definition but the entirety of the subject. It seems that Lyotard meant that postmoderns tend to question the veracity and authority of all comprehensive, totalizing schemes of explanation. Such metanarratives include political and social ideologies, religious worldviews, metaphysical philosophies, and scientific grand unifying theories. We must ascertain what is meant by "incredulity." A soft approach to postmodernity would say it merely means skepticism toward; a hard approach would say it includes rejection and deconstruction. In any case, a consensus is developing that the postmodern condition is skeptical with regard to grand narratives that attempt to ignore or absorb local narratives. Overarching schemes of thought that claim universal truth have a tendency to marginalize and even oppress groups not considered "mainstream." Another way of expressing the postmodern condition is that for it there is no "mainstream" anything. Everything is local and particular.

Postmodernism is any thought that attempts to draw out and do justice to the postmodern condition. It comes in at least two main varieties. On the one hand is deconstructive thought that seeks to expose the oppressive power of truth claims and especially of metanarratives. Philosophers such as Jacques Derrida, Michael Foucault, and Richard Rorty engage in this hard kind of postmodern philosophy, which seems inevitably relativistic.

1. Jean François Lyotard, *The Postmodern Condition: A Report on Knowledge*, trans. G. Bennington and B. Massumi (Manchester, UK: Manchester University Press, 1986), xxiv.

For them, all truth claims are but masks for will to power. Some critics have described this hard type of postmodern philosophy as "cognitive nihilism." Its main purpose is to relativize truth. On the other hand is a softer kind of postmodern philosophy found in thinkers such as Alasdair MacIntyre, who does not deny ontological reality or objective truth but seeks to show that even reason always operates within a narrative context. In other words, knowledge may be relative even if truth is not. For MacIntyre and his disciples—and one might add Michael Polanyi and his disciples—"reason is narrative-dependent" and "right and wrong can thus only be discerned from *within* a particular tradition."[2] "I can only answer the question 'What am I to do?' if I can answer the prior question 'Of what story or stories do I find myself a part?'"[3] This is not relativism but recognition of the relativity of perspective inherent in all human thinking. All reasoning and judging takes place from within some local context shaped by a narrative about reality and carried forward within a community of tradition created by that narrative. Thus there are no value-neutral judgments of any kind; all theories and judgments are value-laden. Truth may be objective, but knowledge never is.

It is this second, softer kind of postmodernism that influences some and perhaps most postconservative evangelicals to one extent or another. It flies in the face of the modern story that, since the Enlightenment, holds forth the ideal of pure neutrality and objectivity of thought guided solely by reason free of the stain of local perspective. The postmodern condition (postmodernity) has left that myth behind. But one does not have to go with the hard core deconstructionists to come to terms with this aspect of postmodernity; the critical realism of MacIntyre and Polanyi and other "soft postmoderns" provides a way to combine belief in absolute, transcendent reality and truth with skepticism toward grand explanatory schemes allegedly free of bias or faith.

One Christian thinker who has influenced postconservative evangelicals toward soft postmodern thinking is British mission-

2. J. Richard Middleton and Brian J. Walsh, *Truth Is Stranger than It Used to Be: Biblical Faith in a Postmodern Age* (Downers Grove, IL: InterVarsity, 1995), 68.
3. Quoted in ibid.

ary and theologian Lesslie Newbigin, whose books, including *The Gospel in a Pluralist Society* and *Proper Confidence: Faith, Doubt and Certainty in Christian Discipleship*, have especially appealed to postconservative evangelical thinkers.[4] Newbigin is a master interpreter and applier of MacIntyre's and Polanyi's soft postmodernism to theology.

Newbigin is also a postfoundationalist, as are all postmodern thinkers. Like "postmodern," "postfoundationalist" is susceptible to several meanings. Postconservatives tend to be influenced by and accept the kind of postfoundationalist epistemology practiced by soft postmodern thinkers. All this means is that they wish to move away from classical Enlightenment-inspired rationalism in philosophy and free theology from its chains so that it can be itself—theology and not philosophy. So what is postfoundationalism in this sense? At the most basic level it is any theory of knowledge that rejects the requirement that all valid knowledge be linked logically to indubitable, self-evident facts. Classical foundationalism arose during the Enlightenment in Europe with the rationalism of René Descartes and John Locke. The idea was to distinguish between "knowledge" and "opinion" (or faith or superstition) by limiting "knowledge" to what can be proven. The only way to do that, foundationalists claim, is to find self-evident truths of reason—such as, "I think, therefore I am" (Descartes' dictum)—and build a system of ideas on them. Ideas are true and constitute knowledge only to the extent they can be shown to follow ineluctably from the indubitable foundations. Empiricists such as Locke regarded proper foundations as sense experiences rather than self-evident truths of reason.

Foundationalism appears wherever systems of thought claim to constitute knowledge because the details are based on bedrock facts that cannot be seriously questioned or denied. The analogy is to a building on a foundation: only that which is solidly based on the unshakable foundation "fits" (constitutes knowledge). Evangelical theologian Nancey Murphy expresses the foundationalist view of knowledge well:

4. Lesslie Newbigin, *The Gospel in a Pluralist Society* (Grand Rapids: Eerdmans, 1989); Newbigin, *Proper Confidence: Faith, Doubt and Certainty in Christian Discipleship* (Grand Rapids: Eerdmans, 1995).

Science and religion stood for two paths to knowledge: pure reason versus traditional authority. If human reason was a faculty shared universally, then a new structure built on the deliverances of human reason must garner universal assent. So, from Descartes' time, the ideal of human knowledge focused on the general, the universal, the timeless, the theoretical—in contrast to the local, the particular, the timely, the practical. In short, it is the quest for *universal* knowledge that drives the modern quest for *indubitable* foundations.[5]

The upshot for religion has been that foundationalism required it to follow its epistemology in order to claim possession of knowledge. Whatever religion could not connect with indubitable foundations in a rational manner could not be called knowledge. So much for Calvin's "internal testimony of the Holy Spirit." So much for faith except as bending the will to conform to reason.

The result was a religion of reason that slowly sloughed off special revelation. But evangelicals were not immune to foundationalism's ravages. The Evangelical Enlightenment was conservative Protestantism's rationalist response to foundationalism; it adopted much of its ethos if not every shred of its method. Like other astute observers of evangelical history, Murphy exposes conservative theology's capitulation to foundationalism in the nineteenth century. She pins much of the blame on two theologians who especially influenced twentieth-century fundamentalism and conservative evangelical theology: Augustus Hopkins Strong and Charles Hodge. Both used foundationalist metaphors for theological method and focused on the importance of objective facts, absolute certainty, inerrancy, and solid foundations.[6] Evidence of this foundationalist approach to theology, according to Murphy and other critics of conservative theology, was and is to be found in its picture of theology as a building; without solid foundations beliefs would simply hang in midair without any support, something Strong abhorred.[7]

5. Nancey Murphy, *Beyond Liberalism and Fundamentalism: How Modern and Postmodern Philosophy Set the Theological Agenda* (Valley Forge, PA: Trinity International, 1996), 13.
6. Ibid., 15–16.
7. Ibid.

Stanley Grenz and John Franke maintain that conservative evangelical theology has continued to work from a foundationalist methodology in the twentieth century and beyond:

Evangelicals in the twentieth century, buoyed by the assumptions of modernity, have continued, with some modifications, to follow the theological paradigm of scholasticism as exemplified in the works of Charles Hodge (as well as that of others from the Old Princeton tradition such as B. B. Warfield and J. Gresham Machen).[8]

Grenz and Franke point to the theological method of the most influential postfundamentalist conservative theologian, Carl F. H. Henry, as an example of foundationalism in evangelical theology. Although Henry was not a classical rationalist in the Cartesian sense (following the thought of Descartes), he did tend to elevate reason to a special governing role in Christian theology and he regarded revelation as primarily an intellectual phenomenon. According to Henry, "Divine revelation is a mental activity."[9] For him, God's self-revelation is an "intelligible disclosure" that possesses "propositional expressibility," which makes it amenable to rational systematization. He eschewed any probabilistic approach to theology and sought for certainty for theology's conclusions (doctrines) based on logical deduction from foundational axioms. The Holy Spirit and faith played minor roles in Henry's theological epistemology. The foundational axioms, including Scripture as God's Word in rational, propositional form, were believed to be logically supported if not self-evident. Only they yield a systematic vision of reality that is comprehensive and coherent both internally and externally with the whole of experience.

Grenz and Franke explain why this conservative evangelical adoption of foundationalism is problematic:

The traditional evangelical commitment to objectivism and rational propositionalism has worked against an adequate understand-

8. Stanley J. Grenz and John R. Franke, *Beyond Foundationalism: Shaping Theology in a Postmodern Context* (Louisville: Westminster John Knox, 2001), 14.
9. Carl F. H. Henry, *Towards a Recovery of Christian Belief* (Wheaton: Crossway Books, 1990), 55.

ing of the relationship between theology and culture even among those, such as [Millard] Erickson, who have called for contextualization as part of the theological process. One of the significant results of this failure has been the relatively uncritical acceptance of modernist assumptions by most evangelical theologians.[10]

In other words, foundationalism in evangelical theology represents an accommodation to a passing cultural phase—modernity—and a stumbling block to relating theology to postmodernity. Even more serious, however, is the rationalistic hubris implicit in foundationalism that leads inevitably to doubt when people see that the foundations are not as certain as the practitioners claim. Grenz and Franke argue for a "chastened rationality" to replace the overly assured rationalism of much conservative evangelical theology influenced by Enlightenment foundationalism. Such chastened rationality leads to a "servant theology" and a "pilgrim theology" that does not claim greater certainty and totalizing power than is possible.[11]

Murphy also exposes problems with all forms of foundationalism in philosophy and theology. She argues that the claimed indubitable foundations always turn out to be either useless for yielding real knowledge of the world or not really indubitable at all. In fact, she says, postmodernity has shown that there are no objectively knowable foundations; all knowledge is value- and theory-laden. All foundations are suspended from a balcony rather than laid on solid ground. Foundationalism simply cannot be sustained in light of the postmodern awareness of pluralism of perspectives. Every foundation turns out to be a local belief more or less justified rationally but always possessing less than purely objective certainty:

> There is good reason for abandoning the foundationalist picture altogether. There is no way, using this model [of knowledge], to represent the fact that the "foundations" are partially supported from above, as in the case of theory-laden data in science or presupposition-laden intuitions in philosophical arguments. For this reason, if for no other, we need a new picture, a new model, that

10. Grenz and Franke, *Beyond Foundationalism*, 15.
11. Ibid., 16–23.

will more adequately represent what we now know to be the case about knowledge.[12]

Murphy is almost caustic in her criticism of conservative theological appropriations of foundationalism and the dead ends into which they lead:

> The foundationalist quest among modern theologians shows striking parallels to those in science and philosophy. When conservative theologians were forced to admit that the biblical texts contained contradictions, a common move was to argue that only the original autographs were inerrant. This claim is incorrigible (since all of these are lost) but the incorrigibility comes at the cost of needing to ground theology on something inaccessible to contemporary theologians; the lost autographs are inerrant but useless. This parallels the empiricists [Lockean] move to (inaccessible) sense-data in the observer's mind. And parallel to the recognition of the theory-ladenness of scientific data is the recognition of the theory-ladenness of biblical interpretations—the hermeneutical circle.[13]

In other words, even the Bible cannot function as foundation for theology in the sense that foundationalist theology desires; certainty of its truth is always embedded with faith and is never a purely objective intuition. The only way to treat the Bible as a foundation for theology in the classical foundationalist sense is to assert its inerrancy and base its authority on reason and then relegate it to a transcendental realm (the nonexistent original autographs) because its empirical form cannot fit the foundationalist criteria for foundations.

In concert with Grenz and Franke and many other postfoundationalist, postconservative theologians (a term Murphy does

12. Murphy, *Beyond Liberalism and Fundamentalism*, 93. Murphy also undermines foundationalism by appealing to "Murphy's Law" as applied to it: "Whenever one finds suitably indubitable beliefs to serve as a foundation, they will always turn out to be useless for justifying any interesting claims; beliefs that are useful for justifying other claims will always turn out not to be indubitable, and in fact, will be found to be dependent upon the structure they are intended to justify" (p. 90).

13. Ibid.

not particularly like), Murphy argues for replacing rationalist foundationalism in theology with "modest reasonableness," a "reasonableness that is modest about its own powers."[14] How she works that out in a postfoundationalist epistemology for postconservative theology will be examined later in this chapter.

Another postconservative theologian who is critical of latent and implicit foundationalism in conservative evangelical theology is Rodney Clapp. He asserts, "Foundationalists need to admit that there is no such thing as safely and absolutely secured knowledge."[15] Clapp bases this claim on the philosophy of Alasdair MacIntyre, although he could also appeal to Michael Polanyi and Lesslie Newbigin. One of Clapp's most helpful insights is that many conservative evangelicals try to combine foundationalism and nonfoundationalism. Two examples he cites are Gordon Clark and Ronald Nash, although he clearly thinks this unstable mixture is characteristic of much contemporary conservative evangelical apologetics and theology. Such theologians may not explicitly affirm classical Cartesian foundationalism and may use the language of coherentism in laying out their epistemologies (e.g., in rational presuppositionalism), but they still adhere to foundationalist habits of mind such as absolute rational certainty versus relativism as the only options. Clapp corrects this either/or habit of the evangelical mind, insisting, "It is only the lingering power of the foundationalist schema that makes us believe we must choose between the polar opposites of timeless and placeless objectivity and sheer, arbitrary and solipsistic relativism."[16]

Clapp maintains that evangelicals need to acknowledge that all their truth claims are contestable and that their confidence lies in the power of the Spirit and in faith rather than in some neutral and objective rationality divorced from the Christian perspective. In fact, he says, evangelicals need to become nonfoundationalists precisely because they are evangelicals—that

14. Ibid., 109.
15. Rodney Clapp, "How Firm a Foundation: Can Evangelicals Be Nonfoundationalists," in *The Nature of Confession: Evangelicals and Postliberals in Conversation*, ed. Timothy R. Phillips and Dennis L. Okholm (Downers Grove, IL: InterVarsity, 1996), 89.
16. Ibid.

is, because they embrace truth with trust rather than with logic or evidences, all of which are contestable and inevitably turn out to be operating within a particular perspective shaped by a narrative and tradition-community.[17] Furthermore, evangelical faith recognizes our own fallibility on biblical grounds: "Lest we forget, the Christian confession is that we all see through a glass darkly and it is only on the last day that every knee shall bow and every tongue confess."[18]

Murphy, Grenz, Franke, and Clapp share with most postconservative evangelicals a concern that traditional, conservative evangelical theology is by and large captivated by a modern quest for rational certainty that is living off the dregs of Enlightenment foundationalism if not explicitly working with it. The problem is that such indubitable foundations yielding rational certainty are nowhere to be found in the postmodern world; we now know that all knowledge arises within and hangs on beliefs shaped by perspectives shared by communities created by stories and traditions. Also, such rationalistic epistemology is basically unbiblical and sub-Christian. It ignores the roles of sin and the Holy Spirit and faith in knowing truth Christianly. Its main manifestation in conservative evangelical theology is insistent belief in the factual inerrancy of the Bible as necessary for authority such that without inerrancy authority would be absent. Belief in biblical inerrancy may still be present even within a nonfoundationalist theology, but foundationalism appears in the idea that inerrancy is a necessary postulate for biblical authority, on the grounds that without it theology would lack certainty because certainty requires solid and unshakable foundations.

What is the postconservative alternative to foundationalism in theology? There may not be any one "postconservative alternative" to foundationalism; postconservative evangelicals do not compose a monolithic block, party, or movement. They share a common dissatisfaction with scholasticism and foundationalism in evangelical theology, but they have not arrived at a unified alternative epistemology and may never do so. However, some common features appear as postconservatives develop postfoun-

17. Ibid., 92.
18. Ibid., 90.

dationalist theological methods. One is an embrace of what might be called "proper confidence" in place of foundationalism's search for certainty. Many postconservative evangelicals are influenced by Newbigin in this regard. Another common feature in spite of diversity of detailed methodology is recognition of the perspectival nature of all knowing. In this area many postconservative evangelicals are influenced by Newbigin and MacIntyre. Combining both these factors leads to *critical* realism in place of commonsense realism or naive realism, which postconservatives fear plagues much of evangelical theology.

Newbigin was a British missionary to India for many years. He also wrote books on theology, evangelism, and culture from the perspective of his experience embedded in the plurality of worldviews. He became convinced that modern Christianity in the West—both liberal and conservative—is more influenced by the Enlightenment and its philosophy than by the gospel story out of which Christianity originally grew. In *Proper Confidence* he explained, "I am writing this book as a missionary who is concerned to commend the truth of the gospel in a culture that has sought for absolute certainty."[19] He believed that this search for absolute Christian certainty through reason is a betrayal of faith and of revelation, and that it is a false hope because absolute certainty is not available to humans. For him, the search for certainty arose with Descartes and the Enlightenment and continues in projects of Christian apologetics that attempt to base belief on independent reason. But, says Newbigin, "Christian faith is not a matter of logically demonstrable certainties but of the total commitment of fallible human beings putting their trust in the faithful God who has called them."[20]

Newbigin argues against foundationalism in religion and particularly in Christianity because it posits a criterion of truth alien to the gospel itself; in foundationalism, evidence and logic become the bases for belief in the gospel. For Christianity, however, "the truth surely is not that we come to know God by reasoning from our unredeemed experience but that what God has done for us in Christ gives us the eyes through which we can

19. Newbigin, *Proper Confidence*, 93.
20. Ibid., 99.

begin to truly understand our experience of the world."[21] Not
only in religion but in every area of life there is no knowledge
unrelated to personal commitment. Every search for truth takes
place within an overarching story about reality that gives the
search shape and meaning. But this does not lead to relativism, contrary to some critics: "The (true) assertion that all truth
claims are culturally and historically embodied does not entail
the (false) assertion that none of them makes contact with a
reality beyond the human mind."[22] In other words, "true Truth"
(to borrow Francis Schaeffer's term) is "out there" even if we
are incapable of making truth claims that are not culturally and
historically embodied. This is critical realism, in which absolute
certainty must be replaced with the proper confidence of faith;
it is possible to believe even while recognizing that it is possible
to doubt one's beliefs.

Newbigin connects this humble approach to truth and knowledge with postmodernity while making a clear distinction between his Christian approach and postmodernity's chronic skepticism and antirealism:

> The church shares the postmodernists' replacement of eternal
> truths with a story. But there is a profound difference between
> the two. For the postmodernists [i.e., deconstructionists], there
> are many stories, but no overarching truth by which they can be
> assessed. They are simply stories. The church's affirmation is that
> the story it tells, embodies, and enacts is the true story and that
> others are to be evaluated by reference to it.[23]

Newbigin's postmodernism breaks with deconstructionist antirealism; for him and for postconservative evangelicals, acknowledgment that even the Christian operates out of a story that cannot
be proven true by no means entails relativism. The story is the
best account of reality even if it cannot be judged "true" by some
universal, objective criterion that is neutral with regard to stories.
No such thing exists. Contrary to the Enlightenment myth there
is no "view from nowhere."

21. Ibid., 97.
22. Ibid., 74.
23. Ibid., 76.

Another thinker who inspires many postconservative evangelicals is philosopher Alasdair MacIntyre, who argues that all searches for truth and all knowing take place within some story and the tradition it inspires. Probably MacIntyre has done more than anyone else to undermine foundationalism without falling into postmodern antirealism, deconstructionism, or relativism. For him and his followers, such as Rodney Clapp, "all inquiry is tradition-constituted and tradition-dependent."[24] This means that even Christians must admit that their "knowing" is a form of "believing" because it arises out of a perspective inspired by a story carried forth by a tradition-community. And it involves faith. But that is true of every "knowing." The result is a humility that acknowledges the possibility of being wrong and avoids the false triumphalism of foundationalist claims to unbiased, objectively certain knowledge.

Critics claim that even this soft postmodernism leads down the slippery slope to relativism; they often confuse antifoundationalism with antirealism. The two are not identical or even inextricably linked. Clapp anticipates the question: "What then? Are we all practically, if not rhetorically, rank relativists?" He answers, "It is only the lingering power of the foundationalist schema that makes us believe we must choose between the polar opposites of timeless and placeless objectivity and sheer, arbitrary and solipsistic relativism."[25] For MacIntyre and his postconservative disciples reality is there even if safely and absolutely secured knowledge is not. Even though "knowledge is particular and perspectival, and as such [it] is always contestable" absolute truth exists at least for the theist.[26] It is what God knows. Only our access to it is limited by our finitude and fallenness. But we do have access to it via the story God has given and our faith in its veracity. Also for MacIntyre, traditioned inquiry is not free to go anywhere; it is "constrained by many powerful checks and must always answer to the world around it, however that world is perceived."[27] In other words,

24. Clapp, "How Firm a Foundation," 89.
25. Ibid.
26. Ibid.
27. Ibid.

stories and traditions butt up against each other and have to take each other into account. Some stories wither and die away because they simply cannot explain lived experience as well as others.

For Clapp and others influenced by Newbigin and MacIntyre, this soft postmodernism—which is really perspectivalism— liberates Christian theology from the need to play the foundationalist game, which is largely discredited in the postmodern world. We now know that even foundationalism is itself part and parcel of a particular tradition and not an Archimedean pinnacle or "view from nowhere" standing above and apart from all stories and perspectives. Clapp concludes that by adopting a postfoundationalist epistemology, evangelical theology might become more evangelical: "So might evangelicals move from decontextualized propositions to traditioned, storied truths; from absolute certainty to humble confidence; from mathematical purity to the rich if less predictable world of relational trust."[28]

All this is to say that for many, if not most, postconservative evangelicals, Newbigin and MacIntyre (or at least their general approaches to knowledge) provide a better inspiration for evangelical thought in the postmodern world than does any form of foundationalism. Critical realism and narrative-dependency of knowing open the door to a revival of faith in theology. Proper confidence can replace the ephemeral absolute certainty so frustratingly sought by modernity. Christians can admit that, like every other set of truth claims, what they believe is open to correction and revision while they continue to believe and worship and practice their faith.

In the rest of this chapter we will examine some of the particular postconservative evangelical proposals for a postfoundationalist approach to theological knowledge. Some of them recommend what is sometimes called "holism" as the best replacement for foundationalism. Others turn to a "biblical foundationalism" quite different from classical foundationalism. As we will see, these are not really so different even if their practitioners do not seem to be aware of that.

28. Ibid., 92.

Evangelical Postfoundationalists

One of the first sustained evangelical encounters with postmodernity that reacted against foundationalism was the book *Truth Is Stranger than It Used to Be: Biblical Faith in a Postmodern World* by postconservative evangelical thinkers J. Richard Middleton and Brian J. Walsh. The book's title drew fire from conservative critics, some of whom did not seem to bother reading the entire book; several conservative evangelical critics who claimed to have read it told me the authors deny the truth of any metanarrative, including the biblical story—which is simply false. The authors begin with affirmation of MacIntyre's tradition- and narrative-dependency of all knowing: "Right and wrong can thus only be discerned from *within* a particular tradition."[29] Far from embracing the radical antirealism of deconstructionists such as Foucault and Derrida (to say nothing of Rorty), Middleton and Walsh recommend to evangelicals the softer and more modest perspectivalism of MacIntyre and other critical realists. They critically examine the deconstructionists' denials of grand metanarratives and accept the idea that such have totalizing tendencies. In other words, they tend to be used by would-be dictators, whether individuals or groups, to oppress minorities and marginalize people. They too often overwhelm and push aside local stories. However, according to Middleton and Walsh, "without a coherent metanarrative we are left morally adrift, at the mercy of random violence and brutality."[30] For Christians, the grand biblical epic of redemption provides meaning for all of life without falling prey to the temptation to totalize. In fact, they argue, it is the one metanarrative that resists totalizing because it includes the impulse toward liberation from totalitarianism and for freedom from violence.

Critics who accused Middleton and Walsh of denying the truth of the biblical metanarrative either did not read the book or read it with a hermeneutic of suspicion that missed the key clues to their faith in the Bible. Again, it seems some conservatives fail to distinguish between nonfoundationalism and antirealism; the

---

29. Middleton and Walsh, *Truth Is Stranger than It Used to Be*, 68.
30. Ibid., 77.

authors clearly are realists insofar as they believe the biblical "grand epic" tells the true story of "God's purposes for the world and for humanity . . . worked out through Israel, Jesus and the church."[31] For them, as for all postconservative evangelicals, this story is universally true. They adopt postmodernism in their rejection of rationalistic foundationalism and absolute certainty based on proof rather than faith. Middleton and Walsh argue for a covenantal, relational, dynamic, and progressive epistemology to replace foundationalism. It is an epistemology of indwelling and inhabiting the biblical story so that *it* rather than modernity becomes our Christian "normative plausibility structure."[32] This is what Hans Frei meant by the Bible "absorbing the world." The biblical story is not brought to the modern story (the world) of Enlightenment ideals and made to fit. Rather, for the Christian, the whole world is interpreted through the lens of the biblical story of God's redemption of the world in Christ, and that includes the Holy Spirit and faith.

Middleton and Walsh aver, "Because we are finite, our knowing is always limited, fallible and particular. We know from a particular perspective or world view that can function both to open the world up to us and to close it down."[33] Christians are *Christians* precisely because they find that the biblical story or worldview opens up the world and does not close it down. But they cannot prove this to someone else living out of a different story; all they can do is commend the biblical story to them and hope they will enter into it and be captivated by it. In the end, however, it is a matter of faith and not of proof.

Another postconservative evangelical theologian who critiques the modernity of conservative evangelical foundationalism and recommends a postfoundationalist theological method for evangelicalism is Henry Knight III. In *A Future for Truth: Evangelical Theology in a Postmodern World*, Knight argues that late twentieth-century evangelical apologetics and theology was captivated by lingering foundationalism, which evidenced its latent modernist underpinnings. He mentions John Warwick

31. Ibid., 69.
32. Ibid., 174.
33. Ibid., 170.

Montgomery and Carl F. H. Henry as case studies because they represent two evangelical epistemologies—evidentialism and rational presuppositionalism—both of which Knight regards as foundationalist and modern:

> What is modern about both is their distinctive understanding and use of reason to establish the truth of Christianity in a world shaped by the Enlightenment, making their apologetics more reflective of Descartes or Locke than classical theology. In a postmodern context, it puts rational apologetics in the peculiar position of arguing not only for Christianity but for Enlightenment rationality as well, as if the truth of the former depends on that of the latter.[34]

Knight believes theology at the end of modernity must be different; it must discover a new "future for truth" apart from the dying foundationalism of the Enlightenment. He examines five cultural transitions that require a postmodern perspective on knowledge and concludes that there are actually two postmodern approaches to postfoundationalism.[35] One is what we have here been calling "hard postmodernism." Knight calls it the "ultracritical approach" to postmodernity. It is also known as deconstructionism and may be found especially embodied in the works of Derrida, Rorty, and Foucault. In concert with all postconservative evangelicals Knight says of this ultracritical approach, which regards all truth claims as but masks for will to power, "Whether or not the ultra-critics are absolute relativists, it is evident that evangelical theology has a stake in making just the sort of overarching truth claims these thinkers fear. Insofar as they move to embrace relativism, I shall not be able to follow."[36]

The other approach to postmodern nonfoundationalism is "postcritical" rather than ultracritical. This is the approach charted by philosophers such as Ludwig Wittgenstein (and his followers) and Polanyi and MacIntyre. Knight does not mention

34. Henry H. Knight III, *A Future for Truth: Evangelical Theology in a Postmodern World* (Nashville: Abingdon, 1997), 51.
35. Ibid., 53–56.
36. Ibid., 60.

Newbigin, but he could. Knight shows quite conclusively that these thinkers and the theologians inspired by them are not relativists in spite of critics' claims about them. For them, "the Christian metanarrative does claim universality, but does not do so imperialistically."[37] Knight calls for a theology consistent with the postcritical approach to postmodern thought; it would be a postfoundationalism similar to John Wesley's "spiritual sense" epistemology.[38] Our knowledge of God is sensed in and through the mediated presence of Jesus Christ:

> Our experience of the identity of Jesus—if it is a living relationship and not simply recalling a past figure who is no longer present, like Socrates or Wesley—must therefore be indirect, or mediated. Presence and identity are one when we encounter the risen Jesus in the communal, liturgical, and devotional contexts which are at the very heart of the life of the church. That is, through the activity of the Spirit, the identity of the risen Jesus is experienced as we participate in word, sacrament, prayers, hymns, fellowship and other means of grace, and come to know him more deeply over time.[39]

Of course, all of this works only within the context of life absorbed in the narrative of God revealed in the history of Israel and Jesus and the church. Knowing the truth of Christianity takes place only within the context of faithful encounter with the biblical narrative: "By dwelling in the biblical narrative the Christian life receives its particular shape and the Christian believer is enabled to see the world as it truly is."[40]

Notice what is postfoundationalist and postmodern about this statement. For Knight the world can be "seen as" something only by dwelling in and viewing life through a particular narrative. Everyone does that. There is no "view from nowhere" or narrative that is not shaped by narrative. For the Christian, knowing

37. Ibid., 78. Surely, of course, Knight is referring to those postcritical thinkers who are Christians, which would not include Wittgenstein or Polanyi but would include their Christian disciples such as Newbigin.

38. Ibid., 83.

39. Ibid.

40. Ibid., 180.

God is not like knowing the existence of a distant planet or star; it is like knowing the love of another person. Even the scientist who knows the existence of a distant planet or star, however, is working out of a paradigm created by a story about the universe. And knowing God and proclaiming his truth to others follows personal involvement and commitment in community shaped by the story:

> Thus while the ultra-critics have raised the postmodern concern for "difference" and the "other," it is the post-critics' description of narratively-shaped communities—aided considerably by a vigorous doctrine of the Holy Spirit—which provides resources for a way to address that concern which is faithful to the gospel. For in a postmodern world, the persuasiveness of the truth claims of Christianity will depend on communities of persons whose characters reflect and who struggle to enact the love which was revealed in Christ.[41]

For Knight, then, as for most postconservative evangelicals, knowing truth Christianly is not a matter of independent, rational deduction but of having a spiritual sense created by life in community shaped by God's story. It is a matter of seeing reality "as" because of being grasped by the truth of a story in which one dwells and finds one's identity. This is similar to C. S. Lewis's famous nonfoundationalist apologetic statement that he believed in God as he believed in the sun—not because he can see it but because he can see everything else in its light. The "light" of the story of God in creation and in Christ enables the Christian to see reality "as" a world created and redeemed by God.

Another postconservative evangelical—although she does not like that label—who offers a postfoundationalist Christian epistemology for theology is Nancey Murphy. She and her late husband, James William McClendon, worked out of a postmodern perspective influenced by Knight's postcritical postmodern thinkers rather than the ultracritical philosophers so often associated with postmodernism. In *Beyond Liberalism and Fundamentalism: How Modern and Postmodern Philosophy Set the Theological Agenda*, Murphy argues

41. Ibid., 202.

that both conservative and liberal theologies of the modern world are tied inextricably to Enlightenment philosophy and especially foundationalism. Her thesis is that *epistemological holism* provides a better way forward for Christian theology. Holism rejects the idea of foundations for knowledge and replaces it with justification by means of coherence within a "web of beliefs." Murphy appeals to the philosophies of W. V. O. Quine, Imre Lakatos, and MacIntyre, all postcritical postmoderns and critical realists. In Quinean holism "each belief is supported by its ties to its neighboring beliefs and, ultimately, to the whole." Consequently, "justification consists in showing that problematic beliefs are closely tied to beliefs that we have no good reason to call into question."[42] Truth is a function of coherence within the web.[43] Knowledge exists when a belief is justified by its intrinsic connection with the entire web of justified beliefs or at least its close neighbors.

How is a web of belief supported? Not by foundations, because there are none—at least in the classical foundationalist sense of self-evidently true "objective" propositions. Rather, Murphy argues, following MacIntyre, webs of belief are paradigm dependent and arise within tradition communities. "We live in our traditions and can only think and perceive by means of the categories, images, stories they provide."[44] Does this mean they are immune to verification and falsification? Are they simply incorrigible? Murphy does not think so; she appeals to the philosophy of science of Lakatos, who rejected relativism as well as foundationalism. Webs of belief, like Lakatos's "research programs," can be either "progressive" or "degenerating."[45] They are amenable to testing with reference to lived experience; those that fail to account for lived experience ultimately fail to convince and die away. Those that fit experienced reality and illumine it successfully tend to progress over time and replace competitors. But there is no way to test individual beliefs within webs "from the outside in"; they can be tested only "from the inside out," which is the same way webs themselves are inevitably tested over time.

42. Murphy, *Beyond Liberalism and Fundamentalism*, 94.
43. Ibid., 95.
44. Ibid., 105.
45. Ibid., 102.

Murphy's thesis is that "historicist-holism [Quine's epistemology as modified by Lakatos and MacIntyre] will provide much more useful resources for understanding theological method—and perhaps for reforming the theological craft—than did the foundationalist model."[46] In a lengthy and somewhat abstruse paragraph Murphy explains how this might work out in theological methodology:

> The theologian can be imagined to be contributing to the reweaving of the doctrinal web as it has been handed on to her, whether this means minor repairs or a radical reformulation to meet an epistemological crisis in her tradition. In this reweaving she will be responsible to the formative texts, understood in light of the long development of communal practices of interpretation, but also responsible to that to which the texts are applied—the boundary conditions provided by current experience, in the broadest sense described above: the life of the church in the world.[47]

In other words, the theologian's "job" is to make the web of beliefs stronger by tightening up its coherence with an eye to the experienced world around the church (i.e., the culture). In this process the "formative texts" (Scripture) and tradition will play crucial roles. One may assume that logic would also come into play. This task cannot be oblivious to the external, experienced world (culture) to which theology's primary texts are to be applied.

Like many other postconservative evangelical thinkers,[48] Murphy looks to postliberal theology, the Yale School of Theology stemming from the work of Hans Frei, as an example of a postfoundationalist theology. For it, the primary criterion of truth is coherence between beliefs within the set that makes up the

46. Ibid., 89.
47. Ibid., 106.
48. Murphy takes exception to my label "postconservative evangelical" (ibid., 90n9). I must admit that I do not understand why. Her explanation is that "*postconservative* is not a suitable description since conservatism (favoring the past in a contest between traditional formulations and contemporary relevance) will continue to characterize one end of the spectrum." I hope that my explanation of "postconservative" here will convince her to adopt the label or at least consider it viable for the approach she takes to theological methodology.

tradition of the faith community shaped by the biblical narrative. Murphy says, "It remains to be seen what will develop when conservative theologians consciously adopt holist methodologies."[49] After she wrote this, two postconservative evangelical theologians took up the challenge: Stanley Grenz and Kevin Vanhoozer. Both have attempted to provide evangelical theology with nonfoundationalist methodologies, even though both acknowledged some value to the idea of foundations. For them, "foundations" are not indubitable, objective, and self-evident ideas from which all other ideas must be derived deductively. Nor are they historical or empirical facts or presuppositions rationally justified. Rather, such foundations as there are exist only within the story or drama of redemption from which Christianity derives its existence.

Although Grenz expressed his preference for a postmodern (i.e., postcritical) approach to theology in many articles and most of his later books, its most clear and detailed expression is in *Beyond Foundationalism: Shaping Theology in a Postmodern Context*, written with John R. Franke. Grenz picked up where Murphy left off—attempting to develop a Quinean holistic theological methodology for postconservative theology. The first step in the proposal of Grenz and Franke is to replace classical foundations and deductions from them with conversation. For them, theology is more a conversation among sources and norms than a logical system deduced from indubitable, authoritative foundational truths.[50] The task of theology is not to replace the Bible with a doctrinal system deduced from it but to "assist the Christian community in understanding the paradigmatic narrative and the Christian interpretive framework by means of which the Spirit creates in us a new identity through the appropriated text."[51] This takes place by means of a conversation between the Bible (or the Spirit speaking through the biblical text), the heritage of Christian thought (tradition), and contemporary culture.[52] In this conversation, or "trialogue," "the Bible serves as the norming

49. Ibid., 96.
50. Grenz and Franke, *Beyond Foundationalism*, 24.
51. Ibid., 83.
52. Ibid., 24.

norm."[53] The theological structure yielded by this conversation should not be conceived as a building on foundations but as a mosaic or "interpretive framework" of belief. This is analogous to Murphy's "web of beliefs." Theology is "the articulation of the cognitive mosaic of the Christian faith." "This mosaic consists of the interlocking doctrines that together comprise the specifically Christian way of viewing the world."[54]

Clearly, for Grenz and Franke the place of foundations in classical foundationalist theology is taken by what they call the "foundational narrative" that creates the identities of the self and community for Christians. This foundational narrative of God's redemptive acts and human responses is expressed in the Bible, which serves as theology's "classic text."[55] Compared to it, all our theological constructions are at best "partial, incomplete, subject to revision."[56] The foundational narrative is not a rational, indubitable, self-evident, or a priori concept or empirical experience as in classical foundationalism but a story that creates a tradition and its interpretive framework or mosaic of beliefs.

For Grenz and Franke the criterion of truth within the Christian interpretive framework or mosaic of beliefs is coherence; this is where Murphy's "holism" appears in their postconservative, postfoundationalist theological methodology. Grenz best describes this in his *Renewing the Center: Evangelical Theology in a Post-Theological Era*. There he endorses the holistic alternative to epistemological foundationalism: "Coherentist philosophers assert that knowledge is not a collection of isolated factual statements arising directly from first principles. Rather, beliefs form a system in which each is supported by its neighbors and, ultimately, by its presence within the whole."[57] This means that the enterprise of theology must be conceived differently than in foundationalism:

---

53. Ibid. Critics who think either Grenz or Franke has elevated culture to a status of authority equal with the Bible simply have not read them correctly.
54. Ibid., 51.
55. Ibid., 83.
56. Ibid., 86.
57. Stanley J. Grenz, *Renewing the Center: Evangelical Theology in a Post-Theological Era*, 2nd ed. (Grand Rapids: Baker Academic, 2006), 205.

Viewed from a perspective that takes the demise of foundationalism seriously, Christian doctrine comprises a "web of belief" or a
"mosaic," and theology is the articulation and exploration of the
interrelated, unified whole of Christian doctrine. Hence, a helpful
image for the nature of theological work is that of articulating the
belief-mosaic of the Christian community, a mosaic consisting of
interlocking pieces forming a single pattern (in which, of course,
some pieces are more central to the "picture" and others are more
peripheral). This mosaic consists of the set of interconnected
doctrines that together comprise what ought to be the specifically
Christian way of viewing the world.[58]

One result of this way of conceiving theology's task is that it
must be progressive. Theology must be the ever reformed and
reforming renewal and reconsideration of the belief mosaic of
Christianity in light of its primary sources and norms. The picture
is never perfect. "Theology is progressive in that it is an ongoing
discipline that repeatedly gives rise to new ways of looking at
old questions, brings into view previously undervalued aspects
of the Christian belief-mosaic, and occasionally even advances
the church's knowledge of theological truth."[59]

Clearly this is a postconservative vision of evangelical theology.
How so? Conservative evangelical theology is generally concerned with proper foundations for beliefs; true beliefs must be
connected back to more basic beliefs and ultimately to verbally
inspired, inerrant Scripture. The model of theology is a cathedral
rather than a mosaic. Each part of the cathedral is interconnected
with every other part and all are only as valid as the foundation
is strong. But the foundations have been shaken even as foundationalism itself shakes in the winds of postmodernity. As it turns
out, even the most basic foundation of all, inerrant Scripture,
is not available to us. And yet conservatives continue to appeal
to it as the only reliable support for assured Christian doctrine.
And even if Scripture is not considered inerrant or necessarily
inerrant the whole idea of a rationally supported foundation
upon which everything else is built (by deduction) is questionable because other foundations are conceivable. Perspective

58. Ibid.
59. Ibid., 343.

always intrudes in the form of faith. Conservatives have by and large substituted the internal testimony of the Holy Spirit with rationally supported foundations in the form of presuppositions or empirical and historical data. The point of it all, apparently, is to provide certainty and stability in the form of a total system of belief that needs no revision and is rationally justified.

Postconservatives are wary of this methodology because it tends to replace the biblical narrative and the Spirit speaking through Scripture with a rational system; something akin to a philosophy steps in where only the biblical story should be—as the center and core of Christianity. Also, as Murphy points out, the foundation is shaky if it is supposed to be universal and objective. Faith and belief lie at the heart of all knowing. Why should it be different with a religion that proclaims faith and belief? And it prematurely closes the system to revision and reconstruction, which means closure to reform. Such foundationalist systems of belief can hardly be kept open to reform in light of new visions of the mosaic or new insights from biblical study or from culture.

One evangelical theologian who has added his voice to the chorus of postconservatives complaining about foundationalism and seeking a new method for evangelical theology is Kevin Vanhoozer. Vanhoozer does not wish to reject foundations absolutely; in all his writings on theological method he embraces an idea of biblical foundations. His theological approach could be called "biblical foundationalism." However, it is quite different from classical foundationalism such as one finds implicitly at work in the tradition of evangelical theology indebted to Charles Hodge and Augustus Hopkins Strong. Vanhoozer recommends a postfoundationalist theology that consists of a "three-stranded epistemological cord": reliabilism, virtues, and fallibilism.[60]

"Reliabilism" simply means that persons are justified in believing reliable testimony without proof. "We are within our epistemic rights if we simply believe what we are told unless

---

60. Kevin J. Vanhoozer, "The Voice and the Actor: A Dramatic Proposal about the Ministry and Minstrelsy of Theology," in *Evangelical Futures: A Conversation on Theological Method*, ed. John G. Stackhouse, Jr. (Grand Rapids: Baker Academic, 2000), 87–88.

there is good reason to question the source."[61] "Virtues" simply means that epistemology—knowing rightly—can never be divorced from right living. A person's disposition plays a role in his or her knowing and can distort or enhance his or her perception of truth. "Fallibilism" is the recognition that one could be wrong and must therefore be open to correction. "Rationality is largely a matter of humility, or to be precise, of the willingness to put one's beliefs (and one's biblical interpretations) to the critical test."[62] On the basis of these three interrelated principles Vanhoozer describes theology's method:

> The procedure with which the theologian works is less a matter of building one's interpretation on some solid foundation (e.g., proof texts) as it is of reasoning to the best explanation. The rationality proper to systematic theology is neither a matter of making deductions from solid starting points nor of arriving at general principles from an inductive survey of biblical data. It is rather a hermeneutic rationality, involving what C. S. Peirce termed "abduction," or "inference to the best explanation." Those who lay their interpretations open to be criticized (e.g., by experience, by other disciplines, by other interpretative traditions) are rational; those who are unwilling to entertain criticism of their interpretations are not.[63]

For Vanhoozer the task of theology requires wisdom, imagination, apprenticeship to the texts, and "canonical competence." Its knowledge is "performance knowledge."[64] In other words, far from detached logical deduction, fine theological skill requires involvement, virtue, imagination, and wisdom. It also requires commitment. The theologian's task is not so much to look "at Scripture" as to look "along Scripture" in order to continue the action narrated therein.[65] Vanhoozer argues for substituting *theater* for *theory* as the basic metaphor for theological endeavor.[66]

61. Ibid., 87.

62. Ibid., 88.

63. Ibid., 88–89.

64. Kevin J. Vanhoozer, *First Theology: God, Scripture and Hermeneutics* (Downers Grove, IL: InterVarsity, 2002), 39.

65. Ibid., 37.

66. Kevin J. Vanhoozer, *The Drama of Doctrine: A Canonical-Linguistic Approach to Christian Theology* (Louisville: Westminster John Knox, 2005), 15.

> Christian theology seeks to *continue* the way of truth and life, not by admiring it from afar but by following and embodying it. . . . "Following" the way ultimately requires using the imagination as well, for the way of Jesus Christ is more an embodied story than it is an embodied argument, and as we shall see, it is largely thanks to the imagination that disciples are able to relate the story of Jesus to the story of their own lives.[67]

Thus the work of theology is really a form of play—which can involve work, as any actor knows! Through theology, as other practices, "the church continues to play out the final scenes of act 4" of the biblical theo-drama.[68] The theologian's task is closely related to practice; it is to "ensure that we fit into the action so that we are following rather than opposing Jesus Christ."[69] The biblical canon rules the dramatic action including theology not by functioning as a sure foundation for logical deduction but by serving as "the supreme norm and measure of dramatic consistency as we seek to assess the fidelity of our performances to the gospel."[70]

What does Vanhoozer have to say about foundations and foundationalism? For him Jesus Christ, the gospel, and the canon of Scripture are foundations for theology—but not of the type that characterizes classical foundationalism. "It need not follow from the church's having a foundation . . . that theology must be foundationalist."[71] He endorses Newbigin's vision of knowledge, including theology, as always taking place within a "fiduciary framework": "Knowing always takes place within the context of prior belief."[72] So theology is not a process of building on purely rational foundations but of faithfully following directions in a play and extending it with improvisation that is faithful to the script. Vanhoozer switches metaphors and describes the work of theology as following maps: "Knowing is neither a matter of building foundations nor of weaving webs of belief but of *following maps*."[73]

67. Ibid.
68. Ibid., 57.
69. Ibid.
70. Ibid., 146.
71. Ibid., 292.
72. Ibid., 295.
73. Ibid., 294.

Here one has to wonder if he has stated precisely what he means. Foundationalism is not building foundations but building *on* foundations; holism is not weaving webs of belief but justifying beliefs by their coherence with the whole web. He expresses his analogy more fully: "Scripture is neither a textbook of propositional truths that serves as the foundation for knowledge nor a narrative that relies on its position in the church's web of belief for its meaning and truth. Scripture is rather a canonical *atlas*: a collection of maps that variously render the way, the truth, and the life."[74]

Vanhoozer's alternative to foundationalism does not seem to be all that different from that of Grenz, although the imagery is different. In both cases Christian theology functions without "firm foundations" in the classical sense of foundationalism. In both cases theologians depend on a "fiduciary framework," to use Newbigin's language, to justify their conclusions and to revise and reconstruct theological formulations such as doctrines. Both regard "fittingness," to use Vanhoozer's term, as the criterion for such revision and reconstruction; a doctrine is right insofar as it fits with the web of belief and its narrated story or dramatic action of the play's script. Neither theologian appeals to inerrant Scripture as the foundation from which doctrines can and should be directly deduced or to tradition as the established source and norm beyond which theology should not move. Both encourage theological wisdom and practice of the faith as necessary for sound theological reflection and reject soulless deduction or closed-minded defense of past doctrinal formulas.

Postconservative theology is increasingly postfoundationalist in its approach to religious epistemology partly because of the postmodern ethos of the cultural context, but especially because foundationalism itself was a method of gaining and defending knowledge tied to a passing cultural ethos—that of modernity stemming from the Enlightenment. It was never the "biblical" epistemology or the epistemology of the church. It was drawn into theology because it was thought to be a bulwark against uncertainty in an uncertain age. But the cost was an arid scholasticism that chased the Holy Spirit, poetic imagination, virtue, wisdom, and faith out of theology.

74. Ibid.

5

Postconservative Revelation

Narrative before Propositions

We have seen that postfoundationalism is common in postconservative evangelical theology. In fact, it may not be a stretch to say that most postconservatives prefer a nonfoundationalist epistemology, but not out of any desire to accommodate to postmodernism. Postmodernism raises serious questions about foundationalism that occasion its reexamination among philosophers and theologians. Evangelicals are taking notice of the influence of foundationalist habits of the mind among their own and are moving toward holistic theories of knowledge because they find them more conducive to genuinely evangelical life and thought. This is a postconservative move even if not every postconservative makes it in the same way or to the same degree.

Problems with Propositionalism

So it is with postpropositionalism. Certain shifts in culture and philosophy are occasioning reexamination of traditional philosophical views about truth, knowledge, and communication. Philosophy of language is suggesting that straightforward assertions of simple facts may not be the only conveyers of truth; truth may be communicated even more effectively in some cases by means of images, symbols, and stories. And not all statements are meant primarily to communicate facts; some are "speech acts" that do more than that. They also, and even more importantly, alter reality; they make things happen.

Postconservative evangelicals are concerned that conventional evangelical theology has been captivated by an excessive concern for the propositional natures of divine revelation and of theology. They worry that this heavily propositional view stems more from the Enlightenment than from the gospel or even Christian tradition, and that it is evidence of an unintended capitulation to modernity, which prizes the communication of objective facts as the highest form of language. A proposition in this sense is a statement of fact interpreted as correspondence between word and objective reality. No postconservative evangelical wishes to deny a propositional element in revelation or empty theology of propositional content. Instead, postconservatives wish to explore other possible modes of revelation as valuable for theology and look into the possibility that theology itself may do more with words than simply communicate facts.

Alongside this concern to correct an overly propositional view of revelation and theology, many postconservatives are interested in the contributions of narrative hermeneutics and theology to evangelical thought. Put most simply, they wish to discover whether story might be an irreducible and irreplaceable mode of divine revelation. Perhaps propositions cannot express everything story can express. Perhaps a propositional system of thought—such as a systematic theology—cannot exhaust the tasks and goals of proper Christian theology. Where critics see faddish flirtation with subjectivism and relativism, postconservatives see sincere desire to rescue a crucial element of God's communication from obscurity in conservative theology. The fear that in much conservative theology a good systematic theology can replace the Bible is not entirely unrealistic. Postconservatives simply wish to raise up a forgotten dimension of revelation and see what happens when theology takes narrative seriously as a vehicle of truth.

What is propositional theology? Few conservative evangelical theologians explicitly call their theology "propositional," but it has become a common way of describing theologies that focus on the factual assertions of Scripture as the primary content of revelation and on rational knowledge expressed in statements of fact consistently arranged as the goal of every good theology. Furthermore, "propositional" usually indicates a belief that truth is a function of statements that assert facts that correspond with real states of affairs in the objective world. In addition, the term often indicates a concern for developing clear and distinct ideas that are univocally true; that is, an aversion to any dissimilarity between the concept and the reality it conceptualizes.

Like many postconservative evangelical thinkers, LeRon Shults complains that conventional, conservative evangelical theology is overly captivated by the notion of clear and distinct, univocal predication about God and other theological subjects. In other words, it is too concerned to strip away the symbolic and analogical dimensions of religious language to get at the clear and distinct ideas supposedly found in divine revelation. Often this is in reaction to liberal and neoorthodox theologies that have rejected propositional revelation in favor of personal revelation or revelation as action.[1] But it also predates that reaction and may have arisen as an unconscious accommodation to the Enlightenment, which was obsessed with such notions of knowledge and language. Shults traces evangelical reduction of revelation to propositions and elevation of the univocal aspect of theological language to primacy to a "Cartesian anxiety" among conservative theologians in the late eighteenth and early nineteenth centuries. Francis Turretin and Charles Hodge, stalwarts of conservative Calvinism in Europe and America, focused on propositional knowledge in theology and tended to underscore the univocity of attribution to God in their theologies in order to defend the

---

1. For a good overview of ideas of revelation as personal and historical—as opposed to propositional—see John Baillie, *The Idea of Revelation in Recent Thought* (New York: Columbia University Press, 1956).

rationality of Christian theology in the face of Enlightenment skepticism.[2] According to Shults,

> The temptation to rely upon univocal and quantitative predication in the doctrine of God has not always been sufficiently resisted among American theologians who find themselves in the current of this early modern theological stream. For example, Millard Erickson suggests that "whenever God has revealed himself, he has selected elements that are *univocal* in his universe and ours." Moreover, "God is powerful as humans are powerful, but *much more* so. . . . God has humans' knowledge *amplified* to an infinite *extent*. . . . Although what we know of him is *the same* as his knowledge of himself, the *degree* of our knowledge is *much less*."[3]

Like many other postconservatives, Shults is highly critical of this approach to religious language, which characterizes much conservative evangelical thought. He argues that such an approach "presupposes a basic dualism between God and the world, between two 'universes' that can be spanned by language, although one is 'much' larger."[4] In other words, according to Shults, the highly rationalistic, propositionalist, and univocal view of theological language carries metaphysical baggage that is very untheological in that it cannot do justice to the transcendence of God. It makes God part of the world, or a similar but "bigger" world. The reason behind this is the Enlightenment concern for clear and distinct ideas and words as determinative for rational discourse.

Evangelical theologian Alister McGrath complains that to a great extent conservative evangelical theology has denarrativized revelation and theology: "Throughout its history, evangelicalism has shown itself to be prone to lapse into a form of rationalism."[5] He lays this tendency directly at the feet of the Evangelical Enlightenment—an unconscious and often subtle

2. F. LeRon Shults, *Reforming the Doctrine of God* (Grand Rapids: Eerdmans, 2005), 25–26.

3. Ibid. Shults is quoting Millard Erickson, *Christian Theology*, 2nd ed. (Grand Rapids: Baker Academic, 1998), 205–6. Emphasis added by Shults.

4. Shults, *Reforming the Doctrine of God*, 206.

5. Alister McGrath, *A Passion for Truth: The Intellectual Coherence of Evangelical Theology* (Downers Grove, IL: InterVarsity, 1996), 106.

but clearly discernible accommodation of evangelical thought to the canons of modern thought:

> Despite all its criticisms of the theological and exegetical pro-grammes of the Enlightenment, evangelicalism seems to have chosen to follow it in this respect. The narrative character of Scrip-ture has been subtly marginalized, in order to facilitate its analysis purely as a repository of propositional statements, capable of with-standing the epistemological criteria of the Enlightenment.[6]

McGrath's critique is echoed by Kenneth Collins, who argues that much, if not most, conservative evangelical theology is cap-tivated by a "modernist reading" of Scripture's authority that evidences an "evangelical Enlightenment." He asks ironically:

> Does one have to be a modernist in order to be an evangelical? Does one have to genuflect before Enlightenment understandings in order to express the truth of the gospel? Is "objective," universal truth, the truth of facts, data, and "things," . . . the highest form of truth that is manifested in the life and ministry of Jesus Christ?[7]

Lest anyone worry that either McGrath or Collins or any other postconservative evangelical theologian wants to empty reve-lation or theology of objective truth, both warmly affirm the universal truth of God's Word. They are not interested in a purely personal, nonpropositional view of revelation à la Karl Barth or Emil Brunner—although it is questionable whether even they were able to pull that off entirely! Collins's qualifying explanation is typical of most postconservatives:

> Theology is a second-order activity as it reflects on the primary revelation that has already occurred in the decisive and liberat-ing acts of God in the history of Israel and in the life, death and resurrection of Jesus Christ. Revelation, then, embraces both historical event and revealed Word, elements that factor into any serious theological reflection.[8]

6. Ibid., 105–6.
7. Kenneth J. Collins, *The Evangelical Moment: The Promise of an American Religion* (Grand Rapids: Baker Academic, 2005), 77.
8. Ibid., 87.

In other words, revelation is multifaceted and contains both propositional and nonpropositional aspects. So theology takes propositional form without being reduced to propositions arranged in logically coherent order.

What exactly are the complaints of postconservative theologians on this topic? One way to pursue an answer to that question is by considering a fairly extreme example of propositionalism in conservative evangelical theology.

British evangelical philosopher and theologian Paul Helm argued for a purely propositional nature of revelation in *The Divine Revelation: The Basic Issues*.[9] Helm argues that the very concept of "revelation" implies propositional communication. Even though God's mighty acts are not directly propositional, the revelation of them must take propositional form. Thus, for Helm, "special revelation" is primarily propositional. Events without accompanying interpretation are not revelatory; intelligibility requires interpretation with words. Helm sums up his position:

> Granted that the Bible claims to be a special revelation giving knowledge about God not otherwise accessible, in what form does that knowledge come? The answer is: the basic form is an account, in propositions of divine actions and divinely-given interpretations of those actions. Any other revealed matters, such as commands, invitations and promises, logically presuppose the straight propositional account.[10]

This is about as good a description of what theologian George Lindbeck calls the "cognitive-propositionalist" theory of religion and doctrine as one can find.[11] Postconservatives fear that the view articulated by Helm tends to infect most conservative

9. Paul Helm, *The Divine Revelation: The Basic Issues* (Westchester, IL: Crossway, 1982).

10. Ibid., 35.

11. Actually, "cognitive-propositionalist" is a term used by Lindbeck's interpreters to create a parallel between what he variously calls the "cognitivist" or "propositionalist" account of doctrine and what he calls the "experiential-expressivist" theory of doctrine. See George A. Lindbeck, *The Nature of Doctrine: Religion and Theology in a Postliberal Age* (Philadelphia: Westminster, 1984), 16–19.

evangelical theology, even if other conservative evangelicals pay lip service to nonpropositional revelation. In other words, for all practical purposes his view tends functionally to swallow up any acknowledgment by conservatives of nonpropositional revelation or any nonpropositional nature to theology.

For Helm and those who follow him to one degree or another, "revelation" does not exist apart from straightforward propositions. Revelation may include other things such as "commands, invitations and promises," but without assertions of objective fact they are not revelatory.

The view of revelation held by Helm and other conservative evangelicals is plausible so long as one is focusing on communication of information. As we have already seen, however, postconservatives believe the main point of Christianity is transformation. Information is important and inescapable, but other uses of speech and other modes of revelation can be transformative. Helm's view seems to presuppose that the main thing about Christianity is communicating and gaining information about God. It also, however, tends to restrict the revelatory power of modes of speech other than propositions. Many people would argue, for example, that a good work of art or a musical score played well can be revelatory by evoking certain feelings and focusing the mind on something.

Symbols and images have the same power. Certainly stories, including parables, do the same. Jesus often communicated truths via parables, which contain propositions but are not propositions in the ordinary sense. They are not describing objective states of reality; they are extended metaphors that provoke thought. Their meaning is communicated indirectly and grasped by a disclosure event when the light goes on and the hearer says, "Aha! I get it."

Postconservatives worry that conservative theologians like Helm and Carl F. H. Henry tend to gloss over the disclosure power of stories and reduce their communicative efficacy to their propositional translations. This is why the didactic portions of Scripture and especially Paul's epistles take precedence over other kinds of literature in the Bible for theology. But the problem with this is that much of the Bible is nonpropositional in the usual sense. It contains parables, stories, images, symbols, and even myths or sagas. Are these only revelatory when linked with intelligible interpretations? What about those elements not so interpreted? Some of Jesus's parables contain no accompanying interpretation in the New Testament. Were they not revelatory anyway?

Surely no one could have presented the conservative, propositional view more powerfully and influentially than the "dean of evangelical theologians," Carl Henry, who referred to revelation as "intelligible disclosure" and "a mental activity."[12] In his magisterial exposition of conservative evangelical theology, *God, Revelation and Authority*, he defined revelation in contrast to much modern theology: "Evangelical theology, rather, affirms:
. . . That God's revelation is mediated always through the Logos and never unmediated; it is nonetheless direct rather than indirect, its content being objectively given and cognitively valid information about God and his purpose."[13] Surely this concise and programmatic statement begs some unpacking. According to Henry and most conservative theologians, the actual content of revelation, as opposed to its many material forms, is the cognitive or intellectual and factual information about God and his purposes that revelation communicates in intelligible language. This is propositionalism of revelation. Propositionalism of theology follows with the affirmation that theology's primary task is to put the cognitive, intellectual, factual content of revelation into systematic form in contemporary language. This is clearly conservative evangelical theologian Wayne Grudem's vision of his task and of the proper task of every evangelical theologian.[14]

Postconservatives complain about this propositionalist view of revelation and its accompanying propositionalist theology on several counts. For one thing, this view undermines or even denies any real distinction between revelation itself and even the best nonrevelational interpretation of revelation. This leaves the

12. Carl F. H. Henry, *Towards a Recovery of Christian Belief* (Wheaton: Crossway Books, 1990), 55.
13. Carl F. H. Henry, *God, Revelation and Authority*, vol. 2, *God Who Speaks and Shows* (Waco: Word Books, 1976), 310.
14. Wayne Grudem, *Systematic Theology: An Introduction to Biblical Doctrine* (Grand Rapids: Zondervan, 1994), 21–25.

door wide open to fundamentalistic assertions that "*MY* bible says. . . ." That is, it leads to confusion between the Bible itself (or revelation itself) and a particular interpretation of its message. Many postconservative evangelicals believe this tendency appears in the ways Grudem and other conservative evangelicals view their own theological affirmations; they present them as if they were not interpretations but simply restatements of the content of revelation itself. That leaves no room for disagreement without charges of heresy immediately resulting. Postconservatives think this is the true essence of fundamentalism: implicit if not explicit denial of the inevitable and universal gap between revelation and anyone's interpretation of it in nonrevelatory language. It infects too much conservative evangelical theology.

Alister McGrath, who operates along the boundary between conservative and postconservative evangelical theology and is highly esteemed by many conservatives, acknowledges the difference between interpretation and revelation. He avers that even the best interpretations must be examined and reconsidered in light of Scripture because "we may, through weakness or sheer cussedness, get our interpretations wrong from time to time and need correction."[15] He reminds conservatives, "The Bible is God's Word written, but our interpretations of it are not."[16] All interpretations are at best "approximations of God's truth" that do not call for "automatic conformity" but critical investigation to see if they are true.[17] McGrath raises serious questions about conventional, conservative evangelical treatments of revelation and Scripture, focusing especially on the Old Princeton School of theology, best represented by Charles Hodge, and also on Carl Henry. According to McGrath, Henry's theology, for all its strengths, allows the logic of sinful humans to rule and dictate theology and ignores or subsumes narrative to rational propositions.[18] Without taking on board narrative theology lock, stock,

15. Alister McGrath, "Evangelical Theological Method: The State of the Art," in *Evangelical Futures: A Conversation on Theological Method*, ed. John G. Stackhouse, Jr. (Grand Rapids: Baker Academic, 2000), 31.

16. Ibid., 47.

17. Ibid., 50.

18. Alister McGrath, *A Passion for Truth: The Intellectual Coherence of Evangelicalism* (Downers Grove, IL: InterVarsity, 1996), 170–72.

and barrel, McGrath says, "There is a tendency within evangelicalism to treat Scripture as simply a sourcebook of Christian doctrines, and to overlook, suppress or deny its narrative character."[19] To this postconservatives give a hearty "Amen!" and add that conservative evangelical theology also tends to pretend it is simply a restatement of biblical revelation, thereby denying its character as second-order, interpretive speech that is not in any way identical with or direct restatement of revelation itself.

To summarize, propositional theology is that form of theology that views revelation of God as primarily, not necessarily exclusively, a mental activity—communication of objective facts about God and God's purposes. It also views theology as the contemporary restatement of revelation in systematic form with expression of revealed doctrine as its main purpose. The content of revelation is primarily cognitive and propositional; the nature of theology is consistent arrangement and intelligible affirmation of revealed facts. This propositional theology tends to form the core of conservative evangelical thought, which focuses on the preservation and communication of biblical orthodoxy in coherent, factual statements that contain little or no distortion due to interpretation.

The complaint of many evangelical theologians, including some who would not accept the label postconservative, is that this is one-sided and possibly pernicious insofar as it ignores the nonfactual content of revelation, including narrative, and pretends that good contemporary theology is nothing more than restatement of revealed facts with no distorting mediation of human interpretation. The upshot is that the rationalistic, propositional approach tends to rule out the reform of theology. How can revelation itself be reformed? If good theology is simply restatement of revealed facts, no reform is needed. Reform is necessary only if interpretation colored by bias and perspective intrudes into theology. Conservatives like to think that such is true of liberal theology and bad evangelical theology but not of their own theologies. The fact that all their own theologies are particular and local and that there is no one, universal evangelical theology should indicate something wrong with this view.

19. Ibid., 173–74.

Actually, every conservative evangelical theology contains some striking particularities of the theologian's interpretation of revelation. How else to account for the differences among them?

Toward a Postconservative, Narrative View of Revelation and Theology

Postconservative theologians argue that the need for ongoing reform of theology to bring it more in line with the import of revelation itself presupposes that every theology is to some extent distorted by interpretation. And, they ask, if a system of doctrine could be constructed that perfectly reflects biblical revelation in all its factual assertions, would the Bible no longer be necessary? And yet the Bible does remain necessary.

Many more questions arise from postconservative evangelicals on this topic, but they all come back to the nature of revelation itself and to the nature of theology. Postconservatives tend to highlight the narrative character of revelation without denying its propositional aspect. They also tend to underscore theology's difference from revelation as Christianity's second-order speech. I would propose that theology be understood as the church's third-order speech, but in order to remain somewhat consistent with accepted language about all of this in contemporary evangelical discussion I will continue to refer to it as second-order speech. For me, the church's first order speech is the language of revelation itself—which is why every worship service contains the reading of Scripture. The church's second-order speech is the language of testimony, praise, and proclamation. Theology is the church's third-order speech, which reflects on Scripture in light of testimony, praise, and proclamation and comes back to testimony, praise, and proclamation with recommendations for correction and supplementation.

What is narrative theology? In some ways this is an essentially contested concept. There are many different interpretations of narrative theology and there is no magisterium to declare which one is best. Many different theologians have claimed the label and taken off in different directions. That's unfortunate because it leads to critics mistakenly treating all theological interest in narrative as the same and dismissing them by pointing out the worst features in the weakest approaches. That is the problem, for example, with Donald Bloesch's critique of narrative theology in his *Christian Foundations* series.[20] In its second volume the author takes on narrative theology. He admits it is "by no means a monolithic movement."[21] He then highlights that side of narrative theology that most wanders away from propositional theology into relativism and declares, "A strain of relativism runs through most narrative theology."[22]

While this may be true of some narrative theology—and especially that associated with so-called story theology—it is not true of much narrative theology and especially evangelical narrativists. Bloesch falls into the common conservative confusion between affirmation of truth as intrasystematic or intratextual and denial of truth as correspondence with extrasystematic or extratextual reality. In other words, like many critics, he fails to recognize the critical realism implicit in much, if not most, narrative theology. Truth can be "out there" even if our very best access to it is not direct, factual information that literally corresponds with it. Bloesch strays from correct or fair critique of narrative theology when he says, "In narrative theology the Bible is no longer a record of the mighty deeds of God but a collection of stories that throw light on the universal human predicament."[23] This is sad because it tars all narrative theology with the same brush—that of "story theology." Many narrative theologians— such as Gabriel Fackre—cannot fit that description.

Henry Knight is more nearly correct when he says that narrative theology is simply the idea that "narrativity is at the heart of human nature."[24] That is, this is just about all one can say of all narrative theologies except that they appropriate this insight into their views of revelation and the nature of theology. Narra-

20. Donald Bloesch, *Christian Foundations* series (Downers Grove, IL: Inter-Varsity, 1992–2004).

21. Ibid., 2:209.

22. Ibid., 2:210.

23. Ibid., 2:213.

24. Henry H. Knight III, *A Future for Truth: Evangelical Theology in a Postmodern World* (Nashville: Abingdon, 1997), 98.

tive theologians mean that human beings operate out of local and grand stories. Their lives are shaped by such stories, which cannot be reduced to or replaced by systems of propositions. Also, revelation is meant to meet humans at their point of need; narratives illumine life and give impetus to meaningful living. The heart of revelation, for narrative theologians, lies in its stories. The Bible is more like a great nonfictional novel than like a book of philosophy. It contains philosophy (or at least something like it), but only within the framework of a grand narrative. It is an epic more than a textbook of information or ideas. The diversity in narrative theology appears mainly in varying degrees of interest in the historicity of the biblical stories. But there is nothing inherent in narrative theology that militates against the Bible's historicity—contrary to Bloesch and other conservative and mediating critics.

Narrative theology ties in with postconservative theology's conviction that revelation is more about transformation than information, although it contains the latter. According to narrative theology in all its varieties, humans' lives and especially their spiritual lives are changed by stories more than by information. Humans live from stories. I know a young woman who read *Gone with the Wind* several times while a teenager; it forever impacted her life by shaping her outlook on what life is all about. The main character's repeated refrain, "There's always tomorrow," became not just a motto but her life attitude as a result of the power of the story. Narrative theologians say that to be human is to like stories because they give meaning to life in a way no other medium can or does. God knows this and communicated himself and his purposes to us via stories and the one grand epic told in the Bible that centers around creation, defection, covenant, correction, redemption, and consummation. To be Christian is to be caught up in that story and indwell it—which is much more than merely learning some facts about it. According to Knight,

> This is the reason scripture is the way it is—the divine Author has inspired it in such a way that it enables the Holy Spirit to use it to illumine our hearts and transform our lives. It is no accident that so much of scripture is narrative, metaphor, and the like—God is not simply sending us a memorandum but preparing a medium

through which we can have a true relationship with God, one in which we come to know God as God actually is.[25]

Of course, there is much more to narrative theology than this meager introduction can convey, but much of that "much more" involves diversity among theological narrativists. They all agree that revelation is history-like whether or not it is likely to be historical. Some revel in the story-quality of revelation and view theology as little more than the church's continuing actualization of the potential in the stories. Such narrativists care little or nothing about whether the stories or the grand epic itself are historically true. For them "true" is not related to historicity but refers to the story's ability to transform lives. Other narrative theologians such as Fackre, however, are concerned about the historical reality of the epic even if they are not particularly concerned about the historicity of every minor detail. Whether an ax head really floated on water is not particularly crucial to the gospel, but that Jesus really rose bodily from the dead is implied by the whole tenor and thrust of the grand story.

Postliberalism and Postconservative Evangelical Theology

This is the argument of Hans Frei, father of the postliberal school of theology, which is a form of narrative theology, in *The Identity of Jesus Christ: The Hermeneutical Bases of Dogmatic Theology*. According to Frei and his followers, revelation takes the form of "realistic narrative"; the question of the historicity of every detail is distracting and irrelevant, but the question of Jesus's resurrection is not. It is impossible to disclose all the reasons Frei gives here, but near the end of that book (to which many critical readers do not seem to have arrived) he says, "However impossible it may be to grasp the nature of the resurrection, it remains inconceivable that it should not have taken place."[26] For Frei, as for many narrative theologians, *some* connection

25. Ibid., 116.
26. Hans Frei, *The Identity of Jesus Christ: The Hermeneutical Bases of Dogmatic Theology* (Philadelphia: Fortress, 1975), 145.

between the realistic narrative of Scripture and historical time and space is necessary to the story itself; this is especially true of the passion-resurrection complex of events.

So it becomes evident that not all narrative theologians disconnect revelation's epic story from outer history even if all argue that revelation's primary mode is story and not historical account in the ordinary sense of textbook history. Knight is correct in his exposition of postliberal narrative theology, which he recommends as an alternative to liberal and conservative theologies. When he refers to Lindbeck he is also referring to Frei. Many conservatives claim that these narrativists, who are critical conversation partners for postconservative evangelicals, are sheer relativists or that they at least disconnect revelation from historical reality. Even McGrath worries about this.[27] Knight, however, rightly observes,

> The postliberal form of narrative theology is an attractive alternative to liberal and conservative theologies which are rooted in modernity. In contrast to the liberals postliberalism [one could say narrative theology in general] maintains the integrity of the text. The meaning of the text is found in what it says, rather than in either a highly speculative historical reconstruction or some ahistorical existential meaning. The identity of Jesus is not to be found by going behind the text but in the text, within the pattern of word and action in the biblical narrative.[28]

Knight acknowledges that this raises the question of truth as correspondence. If the main purpose of the text—the story—is to identify God for us and make Jesus present to us—what about the historicity of its accounts? Again, Knight correctly observes,

> What Lindbeck [with Frei and most narrative theologians] is saying is not that there is no correspondence of Christian claims to a reality external to the text or language, but that it is the biblical narrative and the practices of the Christian community which enable us to know what those claims are. And, to know those claims involves a way of life, a pattern of living, both as a mode

27. McGrath, *A Passion for Truth*, 119–61.
28. Knight, *A Future for Truth*, 103.

of learning the content of Christian claims about reality and as its expression.[29]

The point of narrative theology, including postliberalism and Knight's evangelical appropriation of these, is that the primary form of revelation for us—whatever its original forms in history may have been—is literature. The Bible is first and foremost great literature. And great literature transforms more than informs. But some great literature is historical. It will not be a straight-forward recounting of historical facts, as if there could be such a thing without the author's perspective intruding, but it may be rooted in history and may illuminate history. It can be and often is "truth-revealing" even if it contains some elements that are not necessarily historical. As an evangelical, Knight is convinced the Bible is basically historical in its general outlines if not in every detail. Literature like this cannot be reduced to propositional communication even if it contains propositions or gives rise to propositions. And there will always be a gap between the liter-ary work and the interpretations it provokes. Knight argues that revelatory literature—the canon—corresponds to external reality in that it truly reveals the character of God and our place in God's plan, but it does so in a manner that allows different interpre-tations and expressions, none of which are perfectly identical with the reality the canon discloses. Doctrine is the church's best attempt faithfully to interpret the implications of the literature for belief and life. And it sets some boundaries to how it may be interpreted. Not every interpretation is valid.

The point is that truth is not always correspondence with reality in the scientific sense. For narrative theology, truth is disclosure of a reality that transcends direct apprehension through the senses or reason and that transforms persons by absorbing them into a great epic story. It also absorbs the world for them. That means it becomes the explanatory framework or "lenses" through which they view the world in which they live. They interpret the world through the story rather than the story through the world. Too much conservative theology, like liberal theology, follows the latter strategy and regards the epic

29. Ibid., 107.

story of creation and redemption as true to the extent it fits the facts of the world. Narrative theology points out that "the facts of the world" are always already interpreted facts and that all interpretation and all facts are shaped by some story. Even the Enlightenment and modernity are a story from which much science and modern philosophy operate. That is not to pit the biblical narrative against them, but to say that for the Christian the biblical story is grander and more absorbing than anything else. That is what it means to be a Christian. It is not so much to give mental assent to some propositions as it is to live in and from the grand story of redemption.

Clark Pinnock on Narrative Revelation and Theology

Another evangelical theologian who embraces narrative theology and whose approach to theology is postpropositional is Clark Pinnock. In *Tracking the Maze: Finding Our Way through Modern Theology from an Evangelical Perspective* he explicates his vision of narrative theology in conversation with postliberalism.[30] For him, "the central message of Christianity and therefore its essence is the epic story of redemption, enshrined in its sacred texts and liturgies, that announces the salvation and God's liberation of the human race." "The essence of Christianity has to do with the greatest story ever told" and the teller is God.[31] He does not hesitate to declare that he believes the story is "true" as well as "wonderful."[32] "We must contend, in opposition to the existential theologians, that the heart of the Christian story is fact, not myth."[33] Of course, by "fact," Pinnock does not mean "objectively verifiable propositional fact." It is not "fact" as found in textbooks. Rather, he is pointing to the reality of the events narrated in the epic story of redemption that constitutes the heart of revelation. There is a method of verifying and falsifying

30. Clark H. Pinnock, *Tracking the Maze: Finding Our Way through Modern Theology from an Evangelical Perspective* (San Francisco: Harper & Row, 1990).
31. Ibid., 153.
32. Ibid.
33. Ibid., 160.

that reality, but it is not straightforward, rational, or evidential apologetics. Instead, for Pinnock the truth of the Christian story is grounded in experience. This story, as no other, illumines lived experience in the world.

Contrary to critics of narrative theology, Pinnock's approach does not wallow in subjectivism. For him, the epic story of redemption is "historically, publicly and ontologically true."[34] Its truth is not merely intratextual; it connects with reality outside the texts. He contrasts biblical narrative with myth, asserting, "Christianity is . . . more than fact without being less. . . . In Christianity, myth becomes fact without ceasing to be myth."[35] While this language is bound to provoke conservative critics, it is not far from C. S. Lewis's famous dictum that Christianity is true myth. Pinnock does not mean that Christianity is myth in the popular sense of myth as fable, or even the scholarly sense of myth as story that expresses universal human experience without being historical. For him, the story is historical even if not in every detail.

Pinnock's main point is that humans live from stories and God has given us a story that identifies who he is and what he wants with us. It is a powerful, true story that absorbs the world. It provides the interpretive framework that invests the greatest meaning in life. But stories cannot be replaced by concepts; even the most sophisticated doctrinal constructs cannot replace stories. According to Pinnock, for example, the Chalcedonian Definition of the person of Jesus Christ (two natures, one person) cannot replace the story of Jesus narrated in the gospels. "Stories are not just engaging ways of making a point that could really be better made by using abstract propositions."[36] This is where Pinnock's narrative approach to theology and his postpropositionalism merge. Together they make his theology postconservative. Propositions are inevitable; they are not to be avoided. But they are to be recognized for what they are: our feeble attempts to draw out the potential in the biblical story and express its meaning in interpretive statements. While the Bible is not a textbook of time-

34. Ibid.
35. Ibid., 164.
36. Ibid., 166.

less truths, it does contain propositions. Theology must draw on those as well as on the narratives to construct the best account possible of the interpretive framework. But theologians should never pretend that their systems are substitutes for the story.

This brings us to Pinnock's postpropositional theory of theology itself. For him theology is "a secondary language that reflects on the meaning of the primary story and not . . . a rational, doctrinal system that encourages people pretty well to dispense with the story."[37] This means that functionally the story is much more important than its propositional interpretations in doctrine. All doctrines are human creations; they are at best human attempts to express the epic story of redemption in concrete, propositional form. But they are open to revision and reconstruction in a way the story is not. And they should not be treated as litmus tests in the same way as the biblical drama itself:

> In so much evangelical theology, the test is not the Christian story but orthodox doctrines and traditional paradigms. Belief in plenary inspiration, vicarious atonement, the deity of Christ, etc., is the litmus test rather than the story on which they are doctrinal reflections. . . . It is high time we became less preoccupied with rational certainty and doctrinal precision and more concerned with telling the Christian story with its rich interplay of meanings that speak to all our human needs.[38]

Pinnock explains, "My point is not that doctrines are unimportant but that they are a second level of reflection upon what is truly primary—the biblically narrated promise."[39]

Some critics of Pinnock and other postconservatives have pointed to an imagined similarity with the theology of Friedrich Schleiermacher. Schleiermacher also spoke of doctrines as second-order or second-level reflection. He defined them as attempts to bring religious experiences to speech. For Pinnock doctrines are not attempts to bring "religious experiences" and especially not "universal God-consciousness" to speech; they are attempts to bring the meaning of the biblical narrative to

37. Ibid., 182.
38. Ibid., 184.
39. Ibid., 185.

speech.[40] This is a crucial difference. Universal religious experience lacks any objective content; the biblically narrated drama of redemption is objectively given. But if admitting that doctrines are less than revelation itself puts Pinnock in the same camp as Schleiermacher, I'm sure he would accept that company. In contrast to conservative theology Pinnock says,

> Christian doctrines are not absolute truths, free of contextual factors in formulation or infallible in and of themselves. Theology is the never-ending search for the intelligible meaning of the story so far as it can be known. Therefore, it will need to be more dynamic and flexible than can be a propositional theology.[41]

Critics fear that this narrative, postpropositional approach to theology makes it difficult if not impossible to mark heresy off from orthodoxy. Pinnock disagrees. For him, orthodoxy is "sound theology" and it can be recognized by its faithfulness to the biblically narrated story and by its respect for its original integrity. It is theology that lives from and works out of the original story and not some other story such as modernity or humanism or Greek philosophy. "Unsound theology [heresy] would be theology that strays away from the canonical narrative, operates out of another story, and inhabits a different universe of meaning [interpretive framework]."[42] This can and does happen on the "right" as well as on the "left."[43]

The thrust of Pinnock's postpropositional theology seems to be a "back to the Bible" project. What he and many other postconservatives are saying is: Perhaps we evangelicals can learn something from the postliberals (Yale theologians Frei and Lindbeck and their followers) about the primacy of the biblical narrative even as they can learn something from us about its historicity. What we can learn from postliberal, narrative theology is that story is fundamental and irreducible; some truths can be communicated by story in a way they cannot be communicated by rational propositions and systems. The biblical story in particular

40. Ibid., 186.
41. Ibid.
42. Ibid., 213.
43. Ibid.

is basic to Christianity. It refers to itself and the God whom it identifies, not to something more basic than itself such as secular history or science or universal human experience. To indwell the biblical narrative means to look at all of reality through its lenses or to bring every phenomenon to it for judgment about meaning. And to be Christian is to indwell the biblical story, to allow it to absorb the world. Pinnock believes this life of indwelling the biblical story in community will better guarantee orthodoxy (right belief) than formal assent to abstract sets of propositions, which may not touch the heart or transform the mind.

Stanley Grenz and Kevin Vanhoozer on Postpropositional Theology

Another postconservative evangelical theologian whose work was rooted in narrative theology and was postpropositional in character was Stanley Grenz. Toward the end of his life and career Grenz expressed his strong dissatisfaction with conservative, propositional evangelical theology, accusing its practitioners of returning to fundamentalism although lacking the separatistic mentality that characterizes that movement. Referring to Wayne Grudem's *Systematic Theology*, Grenz averred, "He appeared to have narrowed his forebears' [earlier evangelicals'] grand vision of a new evangelical engagement with the world to the fundamentalist quest for the delineation of the one, timeless, systematization of the doctrine that supposedly lies waiting to be discovered in the pages of the Bible."[44] His complaint was that the theological systems of Grudem, Erickson, and other conservative evangelicals seemed to aim at a collection and systematization of timeless truths of revelation as if such could then express the essence of the Bible and thus replace it. These conservative theologians, Grenz believed, misconstrued the nature of revelation and of the Bible as well as of theology.

For Grenz, "theology is not merely the systematic repetition of the content of the Bible" viewed as a set of hidden or disorganized

---

44. Stanley J. Grenz, *Renewing the Center: Evangelical Theology in a Post-Theological Era*, 2nd ed. (Grand Rapids: Baker Academic, 2006), 159.

timeless truths.[45] Rather it is a conversation between the biblical message, the Christian teaching tradition, and contemporary culture. The first source and norm is primary; its voice cannot be corrected or silenced in theology. Grenz's programmatic statement about theology's task is concise: "A truly helpful theology must articulate the biblical kerygma, in a way understandable by contemporary culture, while maintaining a fundamental unity with the one people of God throughout history."[46] He strongly rejected the "older evangelical propositionalism" that treated the Bible as a collection of timeless propositions and tended to ignore its narrative texture and that regarded theology as the repetition and systematization of biblical propositions. The Bible's purpose, he averred, is not to yield to a systematic theology but to be the Spirit's vehicle for instructing the Christian community as it faces the challenges of living in the contemporary world.[47] It does this by serving as the Christian community's "classic text" or "foundational narrative" that creates the individual Christian's and the Christian community's identity.[48] Compared to the Bible, Grenz declared, all our theological constructions are partial, incomplete, and subject to revision.[49]

For Grenz and his coauthor, John Franke, theology is not the authoritative collection of biblical propositions to create a closed system of truths to serve as a magisterium to rule the church. Rather, "theology seeks to assist the Christian community in understanding the paradigmatic narrative and the Christian interpretive framework by means of which the Spirit creates in us a new identity through the appropriated text."[50] Thus theology's role is ministerial and not magisterial; it is to be a servant to the Christian community and not to rule over it. Its products can

---

45. Stanley J. Grenz, *Revisioning Evangelical Theology: A Fresh Agenda for the 21st Century* (Downers Grove, IL: InterVarsity, 1993), 94.

46. Ibid., 104.

47. Stanley J. Grenz and John R. Franke, *Beyond Foundationalism: Shaping Theology in a Postmodern Context* (Louisville: Westminster John Knox, 2001), 67. In quoting from this book with such phrases as "Grenz said," I by no means wish to suggest that John Franke does not also say it. I merely wish to focus on Grenz's theology in this section.

48. Ibid., 82–83.

49. Ibid., 86.

50. Ibid., 83.

never replace the Bible or stand alongside it claiming to participate in its own authority, which is derived from the Spirit who
speaks through it. The Spirit does not normatively speak through
any systematic theology or creed or confessional statement.

Grenz's theology is postpropositional in the sense that he
wants to move beyond the limitations of the traditional evangelical propositional approach, which he finds rooted and grounded
in modernity. He maintains the ultimate authority for theology
is the Spirit speaking to the Christian community through the
biblical narrative. The biblical narrative contains propositions,
but they are not of the essence of the revelation itself, which
is narrative-shaped identification of God. Theology's propositions are at best local attempts to put that identification of
God through narrative into intelligible speech. It is second-
order discourse pursued "from within" the community shaped
around the narrative. It plays a servant role in relation to the
community.[51]

There is very little dissonance between Grenz's basic approach
to theology and Pinnock's. Together they serve as postconservative evangelicalism's twin theological giants. Both embody
the narrative approach that demotes rational propositions and
systems to second place in favor of the biblical narrative. Both
insist that God communicates himself to humans via stories that
transform more than inform, and that doctrine, though necessary and valuable, is open to revision as more light breaks forth
from the Spirit speaking through the Bible. While they both pay
lip service to the inerrancy of the Bible, neither one elevates that
concept to the status of a litmus test of evangelical fidelity. Both
regard Scripture as authoritative, theology's norming norm, while
admitting that it could function that way even if it contains minor
errors that do not affect the main story line.

John R. Franke has continued the general approach of Grenz
and Pinnock to postconservative theology by declaring, among
other things, that the theological and doctrinal language of the
church is "second order" compared to the language of revelation
without falling into Schleiermacher's pit of subjectivism. He
explains "second-order" by saying,

51. Grenz, *Revisioning Evangelical Theology*, 75, 78, 81.

The doctrinal, theological, and confessional formulations of theologians and particular communities are the products of human reflection on the primary stories, teachings, symbols, and practices of the Christian church. Therefore, these formulations must be distinguished from these "first-order" commitments of the Christian faith. For example, theological constructions and doctrines are always subservient to the content of Scripture and therefore must be held more lightly.[52]

Notice that for Franke and all postconservative evangelicals the first-order language of the church to which the second-order language is subservient includes above all Scripture. That is very unlike the God-consciousness that Schleiermacher placed in first-order and to which doctrine was subservient. Comparisons with Schleiermacher and liberal theology fail to do justice to the revelation-centered approach of postconservative evangelical theology.

Before delineating our final example of a postconservative theological use of narrative and postpropositional theology it will be useful to stop and consider what all this might mean in concrete terms. At the risk of offending some especially conservative readers and even some postconservatives, I choose to illustrate the narrative and postpropositional approach with open theism, which will be discussed in more detail in a later chapter. My point here is not to commend open theism but only to use it to illustrate how a narrative approach to postpropositional theology might and does work. Clark Pinnock uses it this way; Stanley Grenz does not. But Grenz uses it in similar ways in reconstructing certain doctrines and especially Christology. For Pinnock the narratives in which God is the primary actor in Scripture are not illustrative of the didactic portions of Scripture. If there is any conflict or dissonance between the portrait of God in narrative and statements about God in didactic teachings, Pinnock will lean toward the narratives. Traditional evangelical theology—influenced by Protestant orthodoxy and scholasticism, especially the Old Princeton School of Hodge and Warfield—will tend to go the other way; it

52. John R. Franke, *The Character of Theology: An Introduction to Its Nature, Task, and Purpose* (Grand Rapids: Baker Academic, 2005), 104.

will qualify the narrative portrait of God by means of the didactic statements about God's attributes and actions.

Pinnock came to believe that God does not know the future exhaustively and infallibly. This is known as open theism and is best expressed in his book *Most Moved Mover: A Theology of God's Openness.*[53] There he draws a "metaphysics of love" from the biblical narrative of God's covenant relationship with the world and interprets it as pointing ineluctably to God's self-limiting power and knowledge. He does not dismiss the biblical statements about God's unchanging nature and knowledge, but sets them under and interprets them in light of the powerful biblical drama of God's interactive relationship with the world. God changes his mind, repents or relents, is surprised, and even grieves in that unfolding, dynamic relationship. This is an example of how narrative can influence systematic theology. Critics of open theism such as Bruce Ware tend to appeal primarily to didactic statements of Scripture and to logic, tradition, and philosophical theism to interpret the troubling narratives in which God is portrayed as limited or self-limiting.[54]

Similarly Gregory Boyd turns to the sweep of biblical narrative to develop a spiritual warfare theology in which God and Satan, including demonic forces, are locked in deadly combat in history. Humans are given the responsibility to help God win.[55] Boyd does not dismiss didactic texts that appear to say that God cannot be limited or affected by what creatures do but interprets them in light of the overall drama of spiritual warfare in Scripture in which God allows himself and his plans to be defeated, at least temporarily, by the defection of creatures, including especially angels. Both Pinnock and Boyd are willing to overturn a tremendous weight of traditional theology heavily dependent on seemingly clear statements of Scripture about God's nature and power in order to do justice to the biblical dramatic story of interplay between God and creatures.

53. Clark Pinnock, *Most Moved Mover: A Theology of God's Openness* (Grand Rapids: Baker Academic, 2001).

54. Bruce Ware, *Their God Is Too Small: Open Theism and the Undermining of Confidence in God* (Wheaton: Crossway, 2003).

55. Gregory Boyd, *God at War: The Bible and Spiritual Conflict* (Downers Grove, IL: InterVarsity, 1997).

Of course, conservative evangelicals object that their account of God is not static and that they can account for the biblical drama in which God is grieved and appears to lose battles. They appeal to figurative language (anthropomorphisms) to qualify some of what the stories of the Bible say about God—for example, that God repents or changes his mind. This they do to retain the full force of didactic teachings of the Bible about God's transcendence in which he is not a man that he should change. But some postconservative evangelicals are not satisfied that conservatives have escaped the pull of the weight of philosophical theological tradition or taken with full seriousness the dramatic nature of revelation and the God-creature relationship. I do not mention this case to promote open theism or the spiritual warfare worldview but only to illustrate how narrative, postpropositional theology sometimes works itself out in concrete cases of hermeneutics and constructive theology.

Our final example of a postconservative evangelical theologian whose approach to theology is postpropositional is Kevin Vanhoozer. His theology is also similar to narrative hermeneutics, but he prefers what he calls a dramatic approach to revelation. Structurally they are the same. Vanhoozer's basic premise is that revelation is not primarily propositional, although it contains propositions, but "communicative action."[56] He calls this a "post-propositional approach" to revelation and evangelical theology.[57] He also refers to it as a "postconservative approach."[58] According to Vanhoozer, language does more than picture the world, and biblical revelation is more than simply a matter of conveying information.[59] "The Bible is not so much a handbook of revealed propositions as it is a set of divine communicative acts, of which statements and assertions—propositions that convey information about God—are an important subset."[60] Besides propositions, biblical revelation contains divine "speech acts" through which

56. Kevin J. Vanhoozer, "The Voice and the Actor: A Dramatic Proposal about the Ministry and Minstrelsy of Theology," in Stackhouse, ed., *Evangelical Futures*, 70–72.
57. Ibid., 75.
58. Ibid., 76.
59. Ibid., 75.
60. Ibid., 76.

God does things, thereby revealing himself.[61] Through his Word God "initiates, sustains, and nourishes covenantal relations."[62] Vanhoozer seeks to transcend both conservative propositionalism and postliberal narrativism. Revelation is a complex of genres, all of which can be subsumed under the category of speech acts. Therefore revelation should be conceived as drama and theology as theater. Vanhoozer is switching the metaphor from literature (as in narrative theology) to dramatic action (as in his own theater metaphor). He asserts,

> Scripture is neither simply the recital of the acts of God [as in narrative theology] nor merely a book of inert propositions [as in too much propositionalist theology]. Scripture is rather composed of divine-human speech acts that, through what they say, accomplish several authoritative cognitive, spiritual and social functions.[63]

God identifies himself and creates covenant by means of his speech acts. This goes far beyond the conservative view of revelation, which focuses primarily on communication of information. It also transcends the liberal and neoorthodox view, which focuses primarily on divine self-disclosure or "personal revelation" to the exclusion of propositions. For Vanhoozer revelation is both what God says and what God does. This is best captured in the metaphor of dramatic action. The difference is that revelation, in this understanding, *shows* and *does* more than it *tells*. "Theology must come to grips with the Bible as performative rather than simply informative discourse."[64] Vanhoozer accuses both liberal and conservative theologies of "de-dramatizing" revelation and thereby making it lifeless. Instead, the purpose of revelation is to be a means of transformation more than a carrier of information.[65] His critique of propositionalism is stringent:

61. Ibid., 70.
62. Ibid., 76.
63. Kevin J. Vanhoozer, *First Theology: God, Scripture and Hermeneutics* (Downers Grove, IL: InterVarsity, 2002), 131.
64. Kevin J. Vanhoozer, *The Drama of Doctrine: A Canonical-Linguistic Approach to Christian Theology* (Louisville: Westminster John Knox, 2005), 64.
65. Ibid., 70.

To equate God's Word with the content it conveys is to work with an abbreviated Scripture principle that reduces revelation to the propositional residue of its locutions. . . . It fails to see that what Scripture is doing is witnessing to and hence mediating Christ, and it fails to do justice to the role of the Holy Spirit in making sure that this witness is effective.[66]

Vanhoozer's model of revelation as drama and action is similar to narrative theology even as it attempts to do greater justice to the propositional and dynamic aspects of revelation. But his most radical proposal is that original revelation is not the be-all and end-all of the drama. Revelation in Scripture is only the first part of the drama that continues through the Spirit's work and human cooperation in the church and the world. Revelation's primary role is to draw us into the drama so that we participate in its continuation through faithful and creative canonical practices. The point of being Christian individually and collectively is not merely to believe and obey God's once-for-all given body of information and commands but to faithfully *perform* the theo-drama that lies at the heart of revelation. "Faithful performance responds to the author's direction with creativity and obedience, continuing the same (*ipse*) communicative action into new contexts."[67] Theology plays a crucial role in helping the church continue the unfinished drama with faithful and creative performance. "Christian theology is a matter of faithful improvisation on a theo-dramatic theme."[68] Vanhoozer insists, "Theology is . . . a matter not only of thinking God's thoughts after him but of improvising God's improvisations after him."[69] Theology discovers, examines, and reconstructs doctrines, which serve the church as director's prompts for dramatic action. Doctrines are not mere reiterations of biblical statements but even more "the realization of [previously hidden] canonical potential" that guides contextual performance.[70]

66. Ibid., 68.
67. Ibid., 185.
68. Ibid., 338.
69. Ibid., 341.
70. Ibid., 352.

All this is fairly radical because it shifts revelation and theology away from a primarily propositionalist interpretation to an action-oriented understanding in order to do justice to revelation's motive, which is to transform people more than to inform them. Of course, information comes along with the revelatory material, but it is not its essence. The essence of revelation, then, and continuing Christian performance based on it is dramatic action that, as in narrative theology, absorbs the world. For the Christian, the drama provides the interpretive framework for understanding the inner truth of all reality and participating in God's plan and purpose for covenantal relationships.

As we have seen, postconservative evangelical thinkers desire to move away from a focus on propositions in revelation and in theology to a more dynamic understanding of revelation that makes use of narrative or dramatic action (e.g., speech acts). They do not discard or neglect propositions, which they regard as part of the larger picture of revelation and theology. But they believe evangelical theology will be better off—that is, more biblical and contextually relevant—by shifting the center of understanding away from communication of information to action that draws persons into participation with God in transforming action. Revelation, then, aims at something more than knowledge and understanding. It goes beyond authoritative information to absorbing story and dramatic action. Theology goes beyond repetition and translation of past information to ongoing participation in the action of revelation. The anchor for all of this is God revealing himself in and through the canon of Scripture understood not as a set of propositions to be systematized but as a narrative or drama that sets in motion a performative process that continues through the church until the consummation.

6

Tradition and Orthodoxy in Postconservative Evangelical Theology

What person who has seen *Fiddler on the Roof* will ever forget the scene where the Russian Jewish peasant Tevye sings, "Tradition"? People over fifty tend to sympathize with the old man as he longs for the good old days when tradition was respected and the world did not constantly change. A younger generation is usually less enamored with the past and traditional ways; given time they too will come to value their roots and the traditions that remind them of who they are and where they came from. Philosopher Alasdair MacIntyre argues that identity and knowledge are both inextricably tied to community and tradition; all searches for knowledge and all truth claims arise within contexts bound to traditions of thought. All research projects are "tradition-constituted enquiry."[1] Without tradition-communities

1. Alisdair MacIntyre, *Whose Justice? Which Rationality?* (Notre Dame, IN: University of Notre Dame Press, 1988), 354.

we are lost in a swamp of solipsism. To think, to know, even to experience is to be enabled and conditioned by particular traditional forms of living and thinking. The modernist ideal of the purely objective, solitary individual who thinks outside of any context conditioned by tradition is exposed by postmodernity as a myth. Only in fiction does a Sherlock Holmes stand aloof and alone as he conducts his investigations and discovers the truth by pure, unadulterated reason working on the evidence without the hindrance of perspective or bias.

Tradition in Christian Theology

Christian theology has always known about the importance of tradition in thinking about God; the original sources of revelation with which theology works abound with references to community and tradition as mediators of God's truth to humanity. The apostles urged their followers to hold fast the traditions handed on to them, and the second-century church fathers appealed to apostolic tradition against innovators, including gnostics and Montanists.[2] Throughout the centuries of Christian thought, postbiblical tradition has been considered a source and norm of theological reflection; to be "orthodox" in one's beliefs and practices—that is, to believe and worship rightly—is virtually synonymous with consistency with the Great Tradition of Christian teaching throughout the centuries. Contemporary populist American Christianity often objects to reverence for tradition, which is too often treated as a poison that sucks the life out of authentic Christianity. Similarly, "orthodoxy" is often regarded as only half a word, the whole being "deadorthodoxy." The result, of course, is a rootless generation of Christians who have no memory of their Christian heritage and for that reason are vulnerable to every wind of heresy that blows through the churches and to every cult leader who stimulates spiritual sensations.

2. See the exposition of Irenaeus's and Tertullian's appeals to tradition in J. N. D. Kelly, *Early Christian Doctrines* (San Francisco: Harper & Row, 1978), 35–41.

In this milieu of antitraditionalism some evangelical Christians—including more than a few younger evangelicals—have gone on a search for roots and followed the Canterbury Trail to Anglicanism or the Road to Constantinople to Eastern Orthodoxy. A few have found that all roads lead to Rome. In response to those antitraditionalist Christians who decry tradition and dead orthodoxy, historical theologian Jaroslav Pelikan quipped, "Traditionalism is the dead faith of the living; tradition is the living faith of the dead." Other evangelicals, dismayed by antitraditionalism and historical amnesia rampant within the evangelical community, have turned to "the received evangelical tradition" to ward off doctrinal drift, unfettered theological experimentation, and acceptance of heresies within evangelical churches and organizations. It seems that among evangelical scholars, at least, tradition and orthodoxy have a new lease on life; some classical heritage of belief—ancient or modern—is being retrieved and with good intentions inadvertently hardened into a magisterium that rules out theological innovation and creativity.[3]

And yet Protestantism itself, of which evangelicalism is a part, contains a certain impulse toward suspicion of tradition. Some Protestant movements have taken that to extremes, resulting in what postconservative evangelical theologian John Franke terms "antitraditional traditionalism."[4] There is no escaping tradition; even antitraditionalism becomes a heritage passed down through the generations in certain Pentecostal churches, Churches of

3. Readers will know from previous chapters those to whom I am referring. Among other evangelicals who seem to me to want to harden traditional categories into a brittle orthodoxy impervious to revision even in light of God's Word are Thomas Oden, David Wells, and D. A. Carson, all of whose main works have been mentioned above. Some brief discussion of some of them will occur again here, but in this chapter I assume some familiarity with the discussions earlier in the book.

4. The very idea that postconservatives are against tradition is given the lie by John Franke's and others' strong affirmations of Christian tradition as a guide and norm for Christian theology. See John Franke, *The Character of Theology: A Postconservative Evangelical Approach* (Grand Rapids: Baker Academic, 2005), 143–60. Similarly strong statements about tradition's indispensable role in evangelical theology may be found in all the leading postconservative theologians' writings, including those of Clark Pinnock and Stanley J. Grenz.

Christ, and Baptist congregations. However, a certain ambiva-
lence about tradition is deeply embedded in the Protestant consciousness. Even liturgical, confessional Protestant communities
of the magisterial Reformation express some degree of caution
with regard to tradition insofar as it may conflict with Scripture.
A basic Protestant principle going back to Luther, Zwingli, and
Calvin is *sola scriptura*. Scripture alone is our ultimate authority. Another guiding Protestant principle is *reformata et semper
reformanda*—reformed and always reforming. Tradition, then,
must not usurp the place of Scripture itself. Evangelical traditionalists who wish to give impetus to a new evangelical appreciation of ancient orthodoxy love to quote Luther and Calvin on
the subject, but they usually neglect to mention Luther's harsh
words about some of the church fathers, including Augustine
(who he claimed did not understand salvation by faith) and Calvin's cautions about the errors of even the most ancient Christian
communities.

Eastern Orthodox and Roman Catholic churches refuse to
separate tradition from Scripture; they are two sides of the coin
of divine revelation—although at least since Vatican II in the early
1960s the Roman Catholic Church has officially subordinated tradition to Scripture. While traditions (with a small "t") may come
and go, Tradition provides stability and identity. Protestants, on
the contrary, see dangers in elevating even the Great Tradition of
Christian belief and practice, however that is defined, to such a
lofty status of revelation and infallible authority; even the most
hoary and revered elements of the Tradition can be partial and
distorted so as to stand in need of correction. Furthermore, humans all too easily confuse traditions with Tradition itself and end
up with their communities of faith in desperate need of renewal
and reform. That was the case in late medieval Europe; some
would say it is the case in some Protestant communities today.

A new mood is rising within evangelical Protestantism that
affects its valuation of tradition. Postconservative evangelicalism is an informal movement for reform and renewal that sees
evangelical Protestant theology as increasingly captivated by
tradition and rigid orthodoxy. As postconservative theologian
Stanley Grenz complained, conservative evangelicals seem de-

termined to boldly go only where they have always gone before. For much of conservative evangelicalism, "the received evangelical tradition" functions as an informal magisterium for setting "evangelical boundaries." At least this is true among evangelical scholars and theologians; it is hardly true at all in the pews (or folding chairs) of grassroots evangelicalism, which cares little about any tradition. The Evangelical Theological Society has approximately three thousand members and many of them, including many of the Society's leaders, are concerned with identifying and establishing "evangelical boundaries"—that is, with guarding what they perceive as evangelical orthodoxy.

The present traditionalist temperament of many conservative evangelical theologians leads them to seek rapid closure to any theological discussion of new proposals; they tend to reject any innovative interpretations of Scripture and constructive theological ideas as heterodox. The "received evangelical tradition"—including, for example, "classical Christian theism" with its emphasis on divine immutability, impassibility, and self-sufficiency—is protected against the encroachments of such new ideas as open theism, the belief that God does not know the future exhaustively and infallibly.[5] Since most evangelicals have always believed in the eternal suffering of the wicked, conservative evangelical theologians tend to react negatively to any suggestion of annihilationism. Inclusivism, which views God's mercy as wide enough to include many who never hear the gospel (the "unevangelized"), is rejected because it is not the traditional view of the majority of conservative evangelicals.[6]

5. For exposition of open theism see Clark Pinnock et al., *The Openness of God: A Biblical Challenge to the Traditional Understanding of God* (Downers Grove, IL: InterVarsity, 1994).

6. This traditionalist evangelical mentality is illustrated by conservative theologian Ronald Nash's appeal to a perceived evangelical consensus against inclusivism and for "restrictivism": "I know no one who denies that evangelicals commonly understand verses like these [viz., that seem to restrict salvation to the evangelized] to teach that since the death and resurrection of Jesus, explicit personal faith in Jesus is a necessary condition for salvation" (in John Sanders, ed., *What about Those Who Have Never Heard? Three Views of the Destiny of the Unevangelized* [Downers Grove, IL: InterVarsity, 1995], 108). Nash admits that occasionally the majority can be wrong, but he seems to believe that is not likely or possible on such an important subject as this. This is the usual traditionalist

Postconservative evangelicals are concerned that establishment, conservative evangelical theology is suffering from hardening of the categories due to a reverence for the authority of tradition that resembles that of Roman Catholicism. For some conservative evangelicals "tradition" may be perceived as an already accomplished and settled evangelical orthodoxy—"the received evangelical tradition"—impervious to challenge and change. They often appeal to the theological systems of the Old Princeton School thinkers Archibald Alexander, Charles Hodge, A. A. Hodge, and Benjamin B. Warfield, and to the agreements between more recent conservative evangelical theologians such as Carl F. H. Henry, E. J. Carnell, Bernard Ramm, Millard Erickson, and Wayne Grudem.[7] For other conservative evangelicals "tradition" is perceived as a broader and deeper consensus of ancient, classical Christianity, including the early church fathers, the ecumenical councils, and the great creeds of Christendom, especially the Nicene and Athanasian Creeds. These paleo-orthodox traditionalists include Thomas Oden, Daniel H. Williams, and Robert Webber. Postconservatives worry that both groups of doctrinally conservative evangelicals are limiting evangelical theological creativity and construction and that they may inadvertently be elevating tradition—however conceived—to the status of a theological norm that implicitly, if not explicitly, undermines the Protestant principle of *sola scriptura* and cuts the heart out of theological construction and creativity.

Conservative evangelicals worry that postconservatives are on a slippery slope toward liberal theological revisionism; they feel that only firm adherence to tradition keeps theological movements, institutions, and communities from drifting the "way

---

evangelical appeal to the received evangelical tradition: on important theological and doctrinal issues one should trust the historical consensus. One problem with this appeal is that cracks can usually be found in the consensus. Billy Graham expressed an inclusivist view in an interview with *McCalls* ("I Can't Play God Any More," *McCalls*, January 1978, 100, 154–58). The tradition is often not as monolithic as conservatives suggest.

7. An example of this attempt to bring closure to theological innovation by appeal to a perceived evangelical traditional consensus is Wayne Grudem's canon of thirty-four theologians who together constitute a "conservative evangelical tradition" (*Systematic Theology: An Introduction to Biblical Doctrine* [Grand Rapids: Zondervan, 1994], 17). The problem is that there is great diversity among these thirty-four theologians and their doctrinal and theology systems.

of all flesh" into culturally accommodated, compromised, and negotiated Christianity. Such postconservatives as Stanley J. Grenz, Clark H. Pinnock, James McClendon, and a host of lesser-known progressive evangelicals have begged to disagree with the accusation that postconservative evangelicalism fails to take tradition seriously enough.[8] Tradition is a good thing; without it we are rootless wanderers making up Christianity as we go along and repeating the mistakes of the past. Pinnock exhorts antitraditionalist evangelicals, "Let us drop our prejudice against tradition."[9] Without tradition Christianity is in danger of becoming compatible with anything and everything. Without it we are left to interpret Scripture anew without guidance from our faithful forebears, many of whom died for the truth they handed down to us. Grenz expressed tradition's powerful and indispensable role in evangelical theology well:

> Our theological heritage provides a reference point for us today. This heritage offers examples of previous attempts to fulfill the theological mandate, from which we can learn. Looking at the past alerts us to some of the pitfalls we should avoid, some of the landmines that could trip us up, and some of the cul-de-sacs or blind alleys that are not worth our exploration. In addition to warning us of possible dangers, past theological statements can point us in directions that hold promise as we engage in the theological calling.[10]

Postconservative Cautions about Tradition

In spite of its necessary role as theology's "hermeneutical trajectory,"[11] postconservatives warn that tradition can be dead-

8. See, for example, Stanley J. Grenz, *Renewing the Center: Evangelical Theology in a Post-Theological Era*, 2nd ed. (Grand Rapids: Baker Academic, 2006), 208–9; Clark H. Pinnock, *Flame of Love: A Theology of the Holy Spirit* (Downers Grove, IL: InterVarsity, 1996), 233; James W. McClendon Jr., *Doctrine: Systematic Theology*, vol. 2 (Nashville: Abingdon, 1994), 468–72.

9. Pinnock, *Flame of Love*, 233.

10. Grenz, *Renewing the Center*, 209.

11. Stanley J. Grenz and John R. Franke, *Beyond Foundationalism: Shaping Theology in a Postmodern Context* (Louisville: Westminster John Knox, 2001).

ening; it can easily become a cudgel to kill renewal and reform. McClendon especially warns against elevating any tradition to a level of infallibility or incorrigibility: "No one should deny that traditional biblical interpretation has proved inadequate to protect the Reformed Church in South Africa from the follies of Apartheid, inadequate to protect the medieval Catholic Church from the cruelty of the Inquisition—inadequate to protect American Christians from their twentieth-century military adventures."[12] As necessary as tradition is as a series of hermeneutical benchmarks, it can be used to protect the vested interests of the powerful guardians of the establishment. Postconservative evangelicalism is not opposed to tradition; it opposes traditionalism, which elevates either the received evangelical tradition or the ancient ecumenical consensus to a status alongside Scripture as a functionally authoritative source and norm for theological reflection. Grenz notes, "Understood properly . . . tradition plays an important albeit secondary role in theology. . . . The ultimate authority in the church is the Spirit speaking through the Scripture."[13] Of the great creeds and confessional statements he and John Franke write,

> They are helpful as they provide insight into the faith of the church in the past and as they make us aware of the presuppositions of our own context. In addition, they stand as monuments to the community's reception and proclamation of the voice of the Spirit. Despite their great stature, such resources do not take the place of canonical Scripture as the community's constitutive authority. Moreover, they must always and continually be tested by the norm of canonical Scripture.[14]

Postconservative evangelical theology relativizes tradition without discarding it; it distinguishes between the status quo and real tradition, the Great Tradition of Christian belief, as it also distinguishes between all tradition (including Tradition itself) and Scripture as God's inspired Word. It is a type of evangelical theology committed to the four hallmarks of evangelical

12. McClendon, *Doctrine*, 468–69.
13. Grenz, *Renewing the Center*, 208–9.
14. Grenz and Franke, *Beyond Foundationalism*, 124.

Protestantism: biblicism, conversionism, crucicentrism, and activism,[15] to which I have earlier added a fifth: respect for the orthodoxy of doctrine developed by the early Christian church and the Reformers of the sixteenth century. But postconservative theology is also committed to ongoing reform and renewal through critical theological examination of evangelical life and thought and constructive theological reflection that seeks to discover the "new light" (to use John Robinson's phrase) God always has yet to break forth from his Word. Tradition plays a vital role in the theological task, but it is not incontrovertible; tradition—ancient and modern—serves as a guide but not as a police officer. In the words of the founder of Reconstructionist Judaism, Rabbi Mordecai Kaplan, "Tradition has a vote but never a veto."

Many critics have overreacted to the label "postconservative evangelicalism." They have mistakenly equated it with radical revisionism and even "postevangelicalism." They assume, mistakenly, that "post-" automatically means "anti-." That is not always the case. "Post-" often indicates a sublation—a transcending of a category in which the best features are retained while the negative features are left behind. Contrary to some of its critics, postconservative evangelicalism is not antitradition or antiorthodox. It does not discard categories like doctrine and heresy. It does, however, approach them somewhat differently from conservative evangelicalism, which tends to defend the perceived status quo. Conservative evangelical theology tends to regard the constructive tasks of theology as finished; only the critical tasks remain.[16] Postconservative evangelical theology pursues

15. For detailed exposition of evangelicalism and the four hallmarks, see David Bebbington, *Evangelicalism in Modern Britain: A History from the 1730s to the 1980s* (London: Routledge, 1989); David Bebbington and Mark Noll, *Evangelicalism: Comparative Studies of Popular Protestantism in North America, the British Isles, and Beyond* (New York and Oxford: Oxford University Press, 1994).

16. My delineations of conservative and postconservative evangelical approaches to theology here are derived from composite impressions drawn from the writings of leading conservative evangelical theologians, many of whom are or have recently been officers of the Evangelical Theological Society. The reader is directed to the recent writings of David Wells, R. C. Sproul, Wayne Grudem, Roger Nicole, Millard Erickson, Al Mohler, Thomas Oden, D. A. Car-

the constructive tasks of theology as well as the critical tasks. It believes that no system of doctrine is final or complete.[17] Conservative evangelical theology regards evangelical Christianity as a bounded set category; one is either firmly within it or outside it. Postconservative evangelical theology views evangelicalism as a centered-set category; people and organizations are defined as more or less evangelical by their relation to its center: the gospel of Jesus Christ and conversion to him (an experience as well as a concept).

Conservative evangelical theology regards doctrine as the enduring essence of authentic evangelical Christianity; postconservative evangelical theology views the enduring essence as an experience, whereas doctrine is secondary, protective language developed to serve the experience of transformation by the Spirit of God into union with Christ. Conservative evangelical theology tends to treat "the received evangelical tradition," however precisely defined, as an absolute norm for determining evangelical identity.[18] Postconservative evangelical theology views tradition as a norm but not an absolute norm. For postconservative evangelical thought, when there is a conflict between Scripture and tradition, Scripture trumps tradition. And such conflicts are not assumed to be impossible. In fact, postconservative evangelicals assume that tradition will always stand in need of correction and reform, and that orthodoxy is dynamic. God always has more light to break forth from his Word.

---

son, Ronald Nash, et al., with the caution that no single one of them embodies everything attributed to conservative evangelical theology, which is a mood and not an organization.

17. My portrayal of postconservative evangelical theology is drawn from a composite impression of the writings of Stanley J. Grenz, Clark H. Pinnock, James W. McClendon Jr., Nancey Murphy, John Sanders, Henry (Hal) Knight, et al. The same caveat applies here as with regard to conservative evangelical theology and theologians in the preceding note.

18. This is not to say, of course, that they do not add other arguments to tradition to defend traditional interpretations. It is only to suggest that their appeal to tradition seems to settle the issue for many conservative evangelicals; exegetical and philosophical arguments appear to be aimed at nailing down the traditional consensus. Such arguments are often little more than repetitions of the same familiar hermeneutical moves that are being challenged.

Critical Orthodoxy

Postconservative evangelical theology aims at an orthodoxy that is *critical, generous, progressive*, and *dispositional*. A particular attitude toward tradition influences its approach to orthodoxy in each case. In concert with much of historical Protestantism and against the various traditionalisms of conservative evangelicalism, including especially the paleo-orthodoxy of Thomas Oden and the retrieval of patristic tradition espoused by D. H. Williams and Robert Webber, postconservative evangelical theology aims at a *critical orthodoxy* and not an orthodoxy borrowed from the past and defended by a contemporary, informal magisterium. Unlike fundamentalism, postconservative evangelicalism does not believe it is possible to jump over nineteen centuries of Christian thought and reflection to mine ancient meanings directly out of the biblical texts and re-create primitive Christianity "as it was." It is critical in its historical consciousness; postconservative evangelical theology regards history as a medium of ancient truth and community as the proper context for interpretation.[19] The past is never directly and immediately accessible to us; tradition informs and shapes our consciousness even if it does not control or determine it.

Orthodoxy, then, is critical in that it is always being shaped by tradition and never only by the Bible. It is also critical, however, in that any given vision of orthodoxy is always under scrutiny from Christianity's original source and norm, divine revelation, which we now have in the form of Scripture, and is always being examined in the light of reason and experience (secondary to Scripture). Our interpretation of Scripture may be influenced by tradition, but it is not determined exhaustively by tradition.

19. Especially Stanley Grenz emphasized community as the proper context for biblical interpretation and theological reflection. In *Revisioning Evangelical Theology: A Fresh Agenda for the 21st Century* (Downers Grove, IL: InterVarsity, 1993) and other books, he argued for an "epistemology of community" (p. 73) in which identity, including Christian identity, is mediated to persons by tradition-communities. Contrary to some critics, Grenz was not in favor of a slavish, continual negotiation of traditional theology with contemporary culture. However, he believed that revelation can and must correct tradition and community when they stand in need of reform.

It is possible to inhabit the Scriptural thought world to such an extent that portions of traditional interpretation—orthodoxy—can be recognized as defective by comparison. There is, then, a critical-dialectical process of interpreting Scripture in the light of tradition and examining tradition in the light of Scripture. It is possible that even the Great Tradition—the Christian consensus—has been wrong about some truths. Luther certainly thought so. He appealed to Paul against the church fathers and the entire consensual tradition of the church for justification by faith alone.[20]

Postconservatives value tradition, but they fear that paleo-orthodoxy's uncritical retrieval and reception of ancient ecumenical Christian tradition and conservative evangelicals' appeal to an authoritative received evangelical tradition make it impossible to reform the tradition itself; they elevate tradition to a status of functional infallibility, a status rightly accorded to Scripture alone. For postconservative evangelicals tradition is a guide but not a touchstone. It is to Scripture what the history of high court precedent decisions is to the US Constitution. Any Supreme Court decision can be overturned by a later Supreme Court and should be overturned if it is determined to be contrary to the letter or spirit of the Constitution itself. So any part of tradition can be overturned by the fresh theological reflection of the faithful community of God's people if it is determined to be inconsistent with the letter or spirit of Scripture. That is especially true if it also happens to be inconsistent with reason and/or experience.

20. Some paleo-orthodox evangelical thinkers such as Oden have attempted to argue that the Pauline doctrine of justification by grace through faith can be found in the early church fathers and that Luther was simply rediscovering it during the Reformation. Much depends, of course, on how one interprets justification, but I agree with Alister McGrath that the full-blown doctrine of justification by grace through faith alone including *simul justus et peccator* cannot be found except perhaps in fragments in Christian theology between the New Testament and Luther. This is the thrust of McGrath's treatment of justification in *Iustitia Dei: A History of the Christian Doctrine of Justification*, 2nd ed. (Cambridge: Cambridge University Press, 1996): "The most accurate description of the doctrines of justification associated with the Reformed and Lutheran churches from 1530 onwards is that they represent a radically new interpretation of the Pauline concept of 'imputed righteousness' set within an Augustinian soteriological framework" (p. 189).

However, just as law students should study Supreme Court decisions and precedents and not only the Constitution, so Christians who want to be thoughtful and informed in their faith should study tradition and not only the Bible.

Postconservative evangelical theology's antidote to liberal revisionism and doctrinal drift among evangelicals is not an appeal to infallible tradition but education inculcating respect for and appreciation of tradition within a greater appreciation for the sole supreme authority of Scripture. Postconservatives agree with Alister McGrath when he says, "Evangelicalism is principally about being biblical not about the uncritical repetition of past evangelical beliefs."[21] Of course, many conservative evangelical theologians agree with this, but their defensiveness of tradition and lack of interest in reexamining and revising traditionally orthodox beliefs betrays a different commitment or at least a divided one. Postconservatives regard orthodoxy as finally eschatological; all our orthodoxies on the way to the consummation are anticipatory and partial. Kevin Vanhoozer expresses this well: "'Final' or absolute biblical interpretations are properly eschatological. For the moment, we must cast our doctrines not in the language of heaven but in the time-bound, culture-bound languages of earth, governed, of course, by the dialogue we find in Scripture itself."[22] John Stackhouse sums up the postconservative approach to critical orthodoxy this way: "Evangelical biblicism at its best, then, is not only a conservative force but also a radical dynamic. It frees theology from automatic conformity to any such human approximations of God's truth—wonderful gifts to the church as many of these traditions may be."[23]

The critical principle of postconservative critical orthodoxy, then, is the Spirit speaking through the Scriptures that serve as theology's *norma normans* (norming norm) to which every tra-

21. Alister McGrath, "Evangelical Theological Method: The State of the Art," in *Evangelical Futures: A Conversation on Theological Method*, ed. John G. Stackhouse, Jr. (Grand Rapids: Baker Academic, 2000), 32.

22. Kevin J. Vanhoozer, "The Voice and the Actor: A Dramatic Proposal about the Ministry and Minstrelsy of Theology," in Stackhouse, ed., *Evangelical Futures*, 80.

23. John G. Stackhouse, Jr., "Evangelical Theology Should Be Evangelical," in Stackhouse, ed., *Evangelical Futures*, 50.

dition, including the Great Tradition, is secondary as theology's
norma normata (normed norm). Postconservatives put more dis-
tance between traditional interpretations or received orthodoxy
and Scripture itself than do most conservatives, who functionally
place them on the same level by treating some set of traditional
doctrinal affirmations as incorrigible. But conservatives believe
that what is really going on among postconservative evangelicals is a subtle tendency to elevate culture, whether modern or
postmodern, to the status of norm for critical examination and
reconstruction of orthodoxy. This seems to be the perception
and driving motive of D. A. Carson's *The Gagging of God: Christianity Confronts Pluralism*,[24] as well as of David Wells's *No Place
for Truth: or, Whatever Happened to Evangelical Theology?*[25] Both
argue for a renewal of traditional evangelical orthodoxy—which
seems to be the Calvinism of Charles Hodge—and decry what
they see as the accommodations of evangelicalism and evangelical theology to modern and postmodern culture.

Contrary to Carson, Wells, and other critics of progressive
or postconservative evangelical thought, however, the leading
postconservative evangelicals have made clear their superior
commitment to the voice of the Spirit speaking through Scripture. Kevin Vanhoozer speaks for all postconservative evangelicals when he argues that Scripture and tradition must not be
divided or set against one another, but one must be normative
over the other. It is not culture that norms theology or requires
revisions in tradition; it is Scripture. As Vanhoozer says, "What
is needed [in theology] is a critical principle to offset the naïveté
of tradition. This is precisely one of the purposes of the practice
of *sola scriptura*."[26]

One mistake by postconservative evangelicals has been to
refer to the Spirit speaking through culture; conservatives have
identified this as a fateful weakness in postconservative evangelical theology. Careful readers of Grenz and Franke, however,

24. D. A. Carson, *The Gagging of God: Christianity Confronts Pluralism* (Grand
Rapids: Zondervan, 1996).
25. David Wells, *No Place for Truth; or, Whatever Happened to Evangelical
Theology?* (Grand Rapids: Eerdmans, 1993).
26. Kevin J. Vanhoozer, *The Drama of Doctrine: A Canonical-Linguistic Approach
to Christian Theology* (Louisville: Westminster John Knox, 2005), 164.

will notice that even though they use this language[27] they also underscore the primacy of the Spirit speaking through the Word over the Spirit speaking through culture.[28] Every postconservative evangelical thinker, in concert with evangelicalism as a whole, always attributes ultimate, controlling theological authority to the Spirit speaking through Scripture. At best, "culture can be a means through which we gain theological insight."[29] Never do postconservative theologians elevate culture (including philosophy, science, or the arts) to the status of a norming source for the critical examination or reconstruction of orthodoxy.

Generous Orthodoxy

Postconservative evangelical theology regards true orthodoxy as *generous*. They worry that orthodoxy is too often used as a cudgel to attack and batter dissident and marginal voices even among the faithful. Orthodoxy should not be a weapon in the hands of heresy-hunters but a beacon to guide sojourners away from rocks and toward the shore of truth. It should be relatively simple and straightforward, attractive and welcoming, flexible and adjustible—not on demand but in response to new situations and contexts and especially in response to fresh and faithful biblical interpretation. That Jesus Christ is God incarnate is nonnegotiable for Christians, but that he has two wills rather than one, as decided by the Second Council of Constantinople in AD 553, is not. The truth that the Council of Chalcedon was trying to convey—that Jesus Christ is both truly human and truly divine without confusion and without change—is a precious truth of orthodoxy because it faithfully expresses what is revealed, but dyotheletism (the belief that Jesus Christ has two wills, one human and one divine) is not itself something to be imposed on everyone who would be a faithful follower of Christ.

27. See, for example, Franke, *The Character of Theology*, 141.
28. See, for example, Grenz, *Renewing the Center*, 211; Franke, *The Character of Theology*, 126.
29. Franke, *The Character of Theology*, 140.

Postconservative evangelicals are afraid that too much detail has been packed into orthodoxy by conservative evangelicals so that the evangelical faith as taught in many seminaries is suffering from hardening of the categories and being used to drive God-fearing, Jesus-loving, Bible-believing people away. Entire systematic theologies such as Charles Hodge's are esteemed by some conservatives as timeless standards of evangelical orthodoxy and are being used to define and defend boundaries that exclude people of faith. Alister McGrath recognizes this tendency and argues,

> An evangelical theologian should not be challenged concerning his evangelical credentials merely because he fails to agree completely with Jonathan Edwards, or B. B. Warfield, or John Stott. . . . We must acknowledge the provisionality of our interpretations of Scripture—which is, of course, what all good theology ultimately is—and be prepared to have them challenged and corrected by others as part of the corporate evangelical quest for biblical authenticity.[30]

Postconservatives would draw upon tradition—including Charles Hodge—but more especially upon Scripture to construct an orthodoxy that is basic and essential to the gospel of Jesus Christ, but not elaborate, detailed, and exclusive of everyone and everything that disagrees with some detail. "In essentials unity, in non-essentials liberty, in all things charity." In order to develop a generous orthodoxy we need to recognize the diversity within tradition. Authentic Christianity, including authentic evangelical Protestant faith, has always included, for example, monergists and synergists—believers in absolute divine sovereignty and believers in divine-human cooperation. Generous orthodoxy draws a circle around both and does not draw lines in the sand to exclude one viewpoint or the other. Both can be orthodox because, while they cannot both be true, they are both faithful and reasonable interpretations of Scripture and both exist throughout the Great Tradition.

30. Alister E. McGrath, "Engaging the Great Tradition: Evangelical Theology and the Role of Tradition," in Stackhouse, ed., *Evangelical Futures*, 150.

"Generous orthodoxy," a term coined by the father of postliberal theology Hans Frei, is as broad as it is deep and flexible as it is sturdy. It consists of doctrinal affirmations that are biblically based and not speculative or merely traditional. It is stated in such a way as to express openness to correction as required by fresh and faithful biblical investigation and it seeks to include as many biblically serious Christians as possible. One example of such a generously orthodox statement of faith is that of the National Association of Evangelicals (NAE). It consists of a few basic doctrinal affirmations drawn from the Bible and is expressed in such a way as to draw together evangelical Christians whose local theologies are more detailed and particular. It avoids shibboleths and the rhetoric of exclusion, including anathemas. The NAE Statement of Faith, to which about fifty denominations and hundreds of churches and organizations subscribe, is:

We believe the Bible to be the inspired, the only infallible, authoritative Word of God.

We believe that there is one God, eternally existent in three persons: Father, Son and Holy Spirit.

We believe in the deity of our Lord Jesus Christ, in His virgin birth, in His sinless life, in His miracles, in His vicarious and atoning death through His shed blood, in His bodily resurrection, in His ascension to the right hand of the Father, and in His personal return in power and glory.

We believe that for the salvation of lost and sinful people, regeneration by the Holy Spirit is absolutely essential.

We believe in the present ministry of the Holy Spirit by whose indwelling the Christian is enabled to live a godly life.

We believe in the resurrection of both the saved and the lost; they that are saved unto the resurrection of life and they that are lost unto the resurrection of damnation.

We believe in the spiritual unity of believers in our Lord Jesus Christ. (copyright NAE)

This is a model of generous orthodoxy in that it avoids identifying authentic Christianity or evangelical faith with any particular confessional tradition as it does not include secondary interpretations of Scripture (such as premillennialism, which some fundamentalists consider an evangelical if not Christian essential) as necessary for evangelical faith.

In contrast to the broad, generous NAE Statement of Faith, in 1999 a group of conservative evangelical leaders and thinkers drew up a statement of the gospel that was published in *Christianity Today* under the title "The Gospel of Jesus Christ: An Evangelical Celebration."[31] The consensual expression of the gospel itself was relatively brief, unifying, and restricted to biblical terms. However, the appended list of denials (anathemas, in traditional terminology) was garrulous, speculative, and divisive. It read like a document from an evangelical inquisition. Some evangelicals who would gladly have signed the gospel statement could not affirm the added list of rejections, which appended to the gospel an entire Reformed systematic theology reminiscent of Charles Hodge's. Generous orthodoxy seeks to draw together as many God-fearing, Jesus-loving, Bible-believing Christians as possible, leaving room for dissent on secondary matters and future revision from new biblical scholarship. Whereas the NAE Statement of Faith models generous orthodoxy, the 1999 gospel statement in *Christianity Today* models a narrow, brittle, divisive orthodoxy that seems destined, if not designed, more to exclude than to include.

Progressive Orthodoxy

Postconservative evangelical theology seeks to develop a *progressive orthodoxy* that is dynamic; the vision of truth changes as new light is discovered in God's Word by faithful, Spirit-led interpreters. Postconservatives remember that slavery was once vehemently defended as biblical and traditional by orthodox evangelicals; what might be an analogy today? What beliefs and

31. "The Gospel of Jesus Christ: An Evangelical Celebration," *Christianity Today*, June 14, 1999, 51–56.

practices that evangelicals hold dear today may stand in need of correction or revision? Most postconservatives would say that what many conservatives take to be orthodox Christianity is still largely held captive to patriarchal attitudes and habits, and that women need to be included fully and equally in every aspect of Christian ministry, including theological reflection. In terms of doctrine, many (not all) postconservatives would say that the orthodox doctrine of God needs to be liberated from its captivity to Greek philosophical theology so that God is viewed as more personal and relational instead of immutable, impassable, and entirely self-sufficient. Open theism is a new theological proposal supported by a postconservative approach to tradition and orthodoxy; not all postconservatives affirm it, but most consider it a valid evangelical opinion.

Such new points of view must not be excluded in knee-jerk fashion simply because they are new. Unfortunately, many conservative evangelicals do reject open theism on the grounds that its view of God's omniscience deviates from the classical account. Orthodoxy should be progressive because tradition is a living reality; it continues to grow and develop as the Word of God becomes fresh in each new generation. It is not a dead deposit; it is like a never-ending story with a stable plot but surprising twists and turns. Also, orthodoxy should be progressive because received tradition can be partial, distorted, and even false in certain aspects. It is not an infallible or complete guide, but like a map: not the territory itself, but a more or less reliable guide to the territory. Maps can always be improved. Progressive orthodoxy is not an attempt to abolish maps but to improve them in light of a closer examination of the territory using reason and experience as guides.

British New Testament scholar and Bishop of Durham N. T. Wright offers an analogy that many postconservative evangelicals find helpful to illustrate progressive orthodoxy. It informs the dramatic account of doctrine presented by postconservative evangelical theologian Vanhoozer and is also mentioned favorably by Grenz and Franke. The analogy asks readers to imagine the discovery of a lost Shakespeare play that has only two or three acts.[32] It is an

32. N. T. Wright, "How Can the Bible Be Authoritative?" *Vox Evangelica* 21 (1991): 7–32.

unfinished play. As contemporary Shakespearian actors, our task is to perform the whole play, which means imagining what the rest of the play should look like. As a troupe of actors we improvise the missing act or acts based on what we know of Shakespeare and based on the finished portion of the play. We must be both faithful and creative as we finish the play. Similarly, progressive orthodoxy means that the church's task is not merely to parrot ancient prescriptions but to perform Christianity in a way that is both contemporary and faithful to the original, given revelation and tradition. That takes immersion in the ancient texts plus imagination and creativity within our own modern or postmodern contexts. The final acts of the play would be marked by continuity and innovation; so it should be with contemporary orthodoxy.

Dispositional Orthodoxy

Finally, postconservative orthodoxy is dispositional. That means it is as much a matter of the affections as of the intellect. *Orthopathy* must not be separated from *orthodoxy*; the two should be inseparably linked together. The intellect follows the affections or dispositions as much as they are shaped by the intellect. A person is orthodox in his or her Christianity insofar as he or she is seeking faithfully to follow the light of Scripture led by the Holy Spirit using the Great Tradition of Christian belief as a guide or map. Orthodoxy is not a matter of "either-or," "in or out." It is a matter of the direction of a person's steps as led by the affections and intellect together. Love for truth combined with commitment to Scripture is the first step; the rest of the journey is a trajectory toward God's own truth along a path of faithful reflection.

Some will inevitably object that this definition could allow, for example, a Jehovah's Witness to be considered orthodox. The response is that a Jehovah's Witness may be more orthodox than a conservative evangelical who knows Hodge's theology forward and backward but cares more about Hodge's thoughts than about God. It is as much a matter of direction and intention as of propositional affirmation. Of course, postconservative evangelicals do believe that a person is only orthodox insofar as he or she is thinking about God with the Great Tradition and not against it; wholesale rejection of and complete departure from Christian tradition is not compatible with orthodoxy, but slavish adherence to a set of propositions does not make one orthodox either. Rather, consistent and steady movement toward truth, guided by Scripture and tradition critically received, does make one orthodox.[33] What makes one dispositionally orthodox includes love for the Great Tradition as well as for Scripture. Love of the Great Tradition does not rule out criticism, but it does rule out disrespect and dismissal. An orthodox Christian is one who regards the Great Tradition of Christian teaching—the consensus of faithful Christian belief throughout the centuries—as a "canon outside the canon" and not as apostasy or irrelevant chatter. Love for it should come close to love for Scripture itself without rivaling love for Scripture as God's inspired, written Word.

This postconservative account of orthodoxy inevitably raises the question of heresy. Does postconservative evangelical theology recognize the category of heresy, or must it be discarded once orthodoxy is interpreted as critical, generous, progressive, and dispositional? To be sure, postconservative evangelicals are not as quick to cry "Heresy!" as are many conservative evangelicals. Conservative theology is concerned with boundaries and whatever lies outside the boundaries is heresy; therefore identifying and exposing heresy is crucial for conservative theology's project. Postconservative theology does not eschew the category heresy even though its practitioners are not particularly anxious to hunt for heretics. For postconservatives, heresy is belief that contradicts the basic impulses of the Christian story—the redemptive drama of God with us recorded in Scripture and lived out in the community of God's people. In Pinnock's inimitable description heresy is "unsound teaching that ruins the story in radical

33. An example is the pilgrimage of the Worldwide Church of God founded by Herbert W. Armstrong. After the founder's death his successor led the church toward and into Trinitarian orthodoxy. What was once considered a cult by most evangelicals is now a member denomination of the National Association of Evangelicals. At what point did the WCG become "orthodox"? From a postconservative perspective, it was orthodox before it arrived at orthodoxy. See Joseph Tkach, *Transformed by Truth* (Sisters, OR: Multnomah Books, 1997).

ways."[34] Not everything that goes against tradition is automatically heretical; whatever overthrows the Great Tradition is likely to be heretical. Postconservatives regard denial of the Trinity, for example, as heresy because it contradicts the redemptive story, which includes God with us in Jesus Christ, in us as the Holy Spirit, and over us as Father. To deny the Trinity is to deny the truth of the Christian story; it is also to reject a core aspect and linchpin of the Great Tradition of Christian reflection and teaching. Furthermore, all the denials of the Trinity are incoherent and contrary to Christian experience.

A powerful case can be made that the Trinity is part and parcel of Christian orthodoxy—faithfulness to the gospel and to the redemptive drama of our salvation. Postconservative evangelicals, however, do not think there is any single model of the Trinity that is the only orthodox option; both the so-called psychological model and the social model or analogy are well within the field of orthodoxy. Both are faithful interpretations of the basic impulses of the divine redemptive drama and the Great Tradition of Christian reflection and teaching about the triune God. Furthermore, a person or church organization that is moving steadily toward embrace of the Trinity *may* be considered dispositionally orthodox. To admit lack of understanding within a steady pilgrimage toward truth is not the same as denial of truth; a modalist who is simply confused and open to correction and enlightenment about the Trinity is more orthodox than a Trinitarian who is bored with and uninterested in Trinitarian life.

Some case studies may shed light on what is meant here by "critical, generous, progressive, and dispositional orthodoxy" within a postconservative evangelical framework. The February 2003 issue of *Christianity Today* reported on a peculiar situation at what many people consider evangelicalism's flagship college—Wheaton College of Wheaton, Illinois.[35] The college, which includes a graduate school of theology, revised its statement of faith in 1990. The new confessional statement, signed

---

34. Clark Pinnock, *Tracking the Maze: Finding Our Way through Modern Theology from an Evangelical Perspective* (San Francisco: Harper & Row, 1990), 213.
35. "Heresy at Wheaton?" *Christianity Today*, February 2003, 18.

by all faculty members and administrators, says, "Jesus Christ was begotten of the Holy Spirit." The Niceno-Constantinopolitan Creed, however, says that Jesus Christ was "begotten of his Father," not "begotten of the Holy Spirit." Jesus Christ was conceived by the Holy Spirit, not begotten of him. The article title in *Christianity Today* raises the question whether Wheaton College had fallen into heresy and the article itself calls it "theological error." It is difficult to tell but entirely possible that the article is somewhat tongue-in-cheek. A conservative approach inevitably raises the question of Wheaton College's orthodoxy during the decade and more that its official confessional statement was in theological error. A postconservative approach applauds the attention to detail that brought about the change in the statement of faith to "conceived by the Holy Spirit" rather than "begotten of the Holy Spirit," but questions the scrupulosity that would seriously suggest the college fell into heresy for more than a decade. A postconservative evangelical trusts the college's intentions; its disposition is love for the Scriptures and for the Great Tradition.

The same issue of *Christianity Today* contained an article about a small religious movement that claims to be evangelical and would like to be accepted as such by evangelicals, but which some evangelical critics have labeled a cult.[36] The group points to its statement of faith as evidence of its orthodoxy. A conservative approach would be to examine its confessional statement's wording to make sure it contains no theological errors. Or, alternatively, some conservative critics would examine its publications in an effort to show that they contain theological errors. Orthodoxy in this view depends on scrupulous adherence to traditional evangelical beliefs.

A postconservative approach would be to examine the movement's disposition with regard to Scripture, the gospel of Jesus Christ, and the Great Tradition. Since it is a movement rooted in China we might expect it to express biblical and traditional beliefs differently than they would be expressed in European-based cultures. One must look beneath the surface of language

36. "Local Church Fights for Evangelical ID Card," *Christianity Today*, February 2003, 24–25.

to the deeper grammar of faith that expresses the group's disposition. Furthermore, a postconservative evangelical would argue, it may be that the group is not yet fully orthodox but is moving in the right direction. What should the evangelical attitude toward such a group be? Should evangelicals shun the group because of theological error, assuming error is present, or nurture its blossoming faith and draw it lovingly into the circle of the evangelical community?

A conservative attitude tends to be rooted in suspicion; a relatively unknown movement or group must prove its complete orthodoxy—meaning absence of theological errors by traditionalist standards—before it is accepted at all. A postconservative attitude assumes everyone harbors some theological errors and gives a person, movement, or group the benefit of the doubt insofar as it claims to be evangelical and displays signs of being in love with Scripture, the gospel of Jesus Christ, and the Great Tradition of Christian belief. A postconservative approach to such a situation would be to enter into dialogue with such a new religious movement and get to know it beyond just reading its statement of faith and its literature. It is possible that a religious group whose teachings are completely consistent with classical Christian orthodoxy and the received evangelical tradition is not truly orthodox because it is dispositionally uninterested in the "living faith of the dead." Dead orthodoxy is not true orthodoxy from an evangelical perspective, but a form of heresy. It is also possible that a religious group whose beliefs are not yet completely consistent with the received tradition—and thus possibly harbors some theological errors—is orthodox because it is dispositionally alive toward the gospel of Jesus Christ, including the essential biblical teachings of historic Christianity about God, Jesus Christ, and salvation. Wheaton College was not sub-Christian for a decade because its statement of faith contained theological error; its disposition was right. A new religious movement may or may not be authentically Christian, and examination of its printed statements alone does not settle the issue.

A postconservative evangelical suspects that we all harbor heresies in our thoughts; we are all at best mixtures of orthodoxy and heresy. No church or denomination has a perfect, complete vision of truth; every church and denomination needs reform of life and theology. Heresy that breaks fellowship appears when a Christian or group of Christians reject the core of the Christian story—the gospel of Jesus Christ—and live instead by another story—such as salvation by human effort (Pelagianism), or salvation through a savior other than Jesus Christ (pluralism), or denial of the deity of Jesus Christ (Arianism). There is plenty of room within the Christian story—and thus within the evangelical community—for different interpretations of such matters as the roles of human decision and divine sovereignty in salvation, the possibility of salvation for the unevangelized, and Jesus's consciousness of his own deity during his sojourn on earth. Furthermore, a postconservative evangelical knows that there is more than one way to say the same thing and different cultural and ecclesiastical traditions express truth in different ways. Often careful, patient, sympathetic dialogue leads to acknowledgment of agreement about substance even where disagreement about terminology abounds. Should a person who affirms that the Bible is the inspired, authoritative, infallible, supreme source and norm for Christian life and faith have to affirm "inerrancy" as well to be considered authentically evangelical? Some conservatives say, "Yes." A postconservative is likely to say, "No," because the substance of belief about the Bible is the same in each case, especially when "inerrancy" is qualified the way most conservative evangelicals qualify it. A postconservative evangelical is unimpressed by the conservative claim that "inerrancy" is part of the received evangelical tradition insofar as that claim is supposed to settle the issue once and for all; perhaps that tradition simply needs to be expanded, revised, and reformed.

Postconservative evangelical theology, then, is not antitraditional or postorthodox. It receives tradition critically with great love and respect and seeks to improve on the current understanding of orthodox belief. Scripture is its first source and norm; tradition its second. The first is absolute and the second is relative. It avoids two extremes with regard to tradition: dismissal as irrelevant and elevation as absolutely authoritative. Tradition guides but does not control; orthodoxy is a growing, dynamic identity rather than a static deposit. Heresy is not any and every nontraditional theological opinion but blatant denial of the central impulses of the redemption story of God in Christ for us. Orthodoxy is not tied slavishly to tradition but finds guides rather than masters in the Great Tradition of Christian belief and in the received evangelical tradition. The only master is the voice of Jesus Christ speaking through the Holy Spirit in Scripture.

7

New Horizons in Evangelical Thinking about God

The doctrine of God has in recent years become a battleground among evangelicals. Some conservative evangelicals have a heightened concern to defend and protect what they regard as classical Christian theism. One evangelical guardian of conventional theism in evangelical theology greeted open theism—belief that God does not know the future exhaustively and infallibly—with scorn, declaring it heresy. According to him, the "fantasy" that God does not know the future flies in the face of early Christian orthodoxy and therefore cannot be taught as legitimate Christian doctrine. Even as a theologoumenon—mere theological opinion—he and many other conservative evangelical thinkers reject it as little more than process theology—the liberal belief that God evolves along with the universe—and therefore contrary to authentic Christian teaching.

Classical Theism and Its Discontents

The classical tradition in the Christian doctrine of God has many defenders among evangelicals. Norman Geisler coauthored a book titled *The Battle for God* that condemns open theism and other revisions in the doctrine of God as "neotheism."[1] Geisler commends and defends what postconservative evangelical theologian Clark Pinnock calls the classical "package of divine attributes" that makes up traditional Christian theism—omnipotence, omniscience, simplicity, immutability, impassibility, and eternity as timelessness.

Geisler's book title is revealing of the heat surrounding evangelical thinking about God. *The Battle for God* is reminiscent of Harold Lindsell's *The Battle for the Bible*.[2] Many evangelicals have joined the fray and heaped anathemas on open theism and other revisions of classical Christian theism as if the latter were part of the gospel itself. This has not deterred many evangelical theologians from continuing their quest for the new light that God always has yet to break forth from his Word; they are confident that conventional ideas about God can be improved through fresh and faithful research and reflection on divine revelation. Postconservative evangelical theologians are not anxious to break from traditional theological thinking; doctrinal correction and revision is not an end in itself. In fact, it can be agonizing and deeply troubling. Postconservative evangelicals respect the Great Tradition of Christian doctrine while having the courage to examine any part of it critically in the light of Scripture. Tradition is worthy of respect, but if it is found incompatible with God's own revelation through Jesus Christ and Scripture it must be revised.

Postconservative evangelicals are driven by the conviction that the reforms begun by Luther and Calvin and the radical Reformers of the sixteenth century were not finished then and are still not finished. Fresh thinking is shedding light on past mistakes that need correction. N. T. Wright is leading the way in rethinking

1. Norman Geisler, *The Battle for God* (Grand Rapids: Kregel, 2001).
2. Harold Lindsell, *The Battle for the Bible* (Grand Rapids: Zondervan, 1976).

the doctrine of justification; Joel Green and Mark Baker are forging new paths in Protestant belief about the atonement; Stanley Grenz offered an alternative evangelical Christology.[3] These and many more postconservative evangelical scholars insist on exercising the freedom so hard won by the Reformers to rethink old doctrines in light of God's Word. To them the conservative guardians of tradition seem like the bishops and theologians of the Roman Catholic Church in the sixteenth century who resisted change regardless of how biblically founded it was.

Of course, one danger in my portrayal of the current situation in evangelical theology is dualism. Some Canadian evangelical commentators have complained that US evangelicals tend to divide everything into two parties along the lines of the two-party political system. In fact, however, it is quite clear to me and others that contemporary evangelical thought is divided roughly into two broad camps—those who see their proper theological task primarily as defending tradition and those who see one major task of evangelical theology as reconstructing conventional ideas in light of God's Word using tools such as tradition, reason, experience, and culture. Of course, each of these camps is diverse within itself. But at a most basic and simple level US evangelical theologians are divided into two groups and that is nowhere clearer than in their approaches to the doctrine of God.

Of course there are more than two positions on almost every theological issue, but on one issue there seems to be only two options: whether reformulation of traditional beliefs is legitimate or not. Even though most conservative evangelical theologians pay lip service to some limited reconstruction of old doctrines such as God's immutability, at the end of the day they are more defensive than constructive. An example is John Feinberg's massive volume on the doctrine of God, titled *No One Like Him: The Doctrine of God*.[4] There the Trinity Evangelical Divinity School philosophical theologian allows some minor revision of classical theism, but in general his work represents a repudiation of

3. Stanley Grenz, *Theology for the Community of God* (Grand Rapids: Eerdmans, 2000).

4. John Feinberg, *No One Like Him: The Doctrine of God* (Wheaton: Crossway, 2001).

change and a defense of tradition; it is a classical evangelical philosophical and theological recommendation of traditional Christian theism. Early in his career Southern Baptist theologian Bruce Ware, a major conservative evangelical opponent of open theism, presented some intriguing and fairly far-reaching suggestions for altering the classical theistic doctrine of God's immutability using German mediating theologian I. A. Dorner's nineteenth-century reformulations of theism (drawn heavily from Hegel's philosophy). Without repudiating that earlier postconservative move, Ware later became an outspoken defender of classical theism against open theism.[5]

Especially in the doctrine of God one can see a division within evangelical theological ranks. There are those who stand solidly together against revision and reform of classical Christian theism in spite of some slight diversity, and there are those who stand together in spite of much diversity for the freedom and the necessity to make some significant changes in traditional Christian thinking about God. The latter evangelicals agree that process theology is a dead end; it departs too radically from Scripture and is hopelessly mired in modernity—in spite of some process theologians, like David Ray Griffin, who think it is postmodern. The biblical story of God hardly plays a governing or regulative role in process theology; that role is played by Whitehead's or Hartshorne's philosophy. But postconservative evangelical revisioners of the doctrine of God share a conviction that classical theism is based too heavily on ancient Greek modes of thought about reality; it is out of touch with both the Hebrew worldview of the Bible and with contemporary culture, both of which are relational and personalistic. Conservative thinkers, including Thomas Oden, Norman Geisler, and Bruce Ware, believe something important and precious is at stake; for them classical theism is not unduly influenced by Greek philosophy, but represents biblical thinking. They are convinced that only on the foundation of classical Christian theism that depicts God as simple, immutable substance, timelessly eternal being, and the all-determining reality can the gospel itself be

5. See Bruce Ware, *God's Lesser Glory: The Diminished God of Open Theism* (Wheaton: Crossway, 2000).

safely ensconced against the ravages of modern humanism and postmodern relativism.

At a 2001 convocation on the doctrine of God sponsored by the conservative Alliance of Confessing Evangelicals, a keynote speaker argued that even classical Arminian theology, to say nothing of open theism, is probably not a form of classical Christian theism because the latter requires belief in God as the all-determining reality. He attempted to demonstrate that salvation by grace alone through faith alone requires monergism (the belief that God is the sole determining cause of salvation), and monergism depends on classical theism. His argument was greeted with agreement and appreciation by the members of the alliance. It seems to me that conservative belief in classical Christian theism generally includes the idea that God is the all-determining reality, even though some conservative evangelicals such as Geisler have attempted to find ways to include some element of free will within it. His own approach to the matter is heavily influenced by Thomas Aquinas, who considered free will a secondary cause within God's primary all-determining causation. In the end, most conservative evangelical thinkers adopt a compatibilist account of free will; free will is judged to be compatible with divine determinism. Compatibilists maintain that free will means doing what you want to do, but you are controlled by your strongest motives and cannot do otherwise than you do. So long as you are not being coerced by forces outside your own motive-driven and controlled volition, you are "free" even if you could not do otherwise. Conservative evangelical thinkers often include this belief within the penumbra, if not the core, of classical Christian theism.

Postconservative evangelical thinkers believe that classical theism had its virtues when it was being developed in the early centuries of the Christian church and in the medieval philosophies of Anselm and Aquinas. But they point out that there was always some diversity within it as there still is today. Even such a conservative evangelical thinker as Ronald Nash expressed serious qualms about the doctrine of divine simplicity.[6] Different accounts of immutability have been offered by classical Christian thinkers.

6. Ronald Nash, *The Concept of God: An Exploration of Contemporary Difficulties with the Attributes of God* (Grand Rapids: Zondervan, 1983).

And Luther did not express strong appreciation for the scholastic doctrine of God, although he retained much of Augustine's theism. The point is that classical Christian theism may itself be something of an abstraction, a concept that admits of serious differences of interpretation. And what about those attributes so passionately defended by conservative evangelical thinkers? They argue that God's omniscience must be absolute, without qualifications or limitations. But what about God's omnipotence? Only Luther seemed to think God could do the logically absurd. Most conservative theologians working out of the Protestant orthodox scholastic tradition admit that God cannot, for example, change the past. But why not? Does that not represent a limitation of God's power? If God is omnipotent and timelessly eternal such that all times are simultaneously before his eyes, where is the logical difficulty in affirming that God can change the past? And yet even the most passionate defenders of classical theism rarely if ever hold prayer meetings to persuade God to undo the holocaust or the events of September 11, 2001.

My point is simply that classical Christian theism is not a monolithic belief system that admits of no development or variation. It has always been under construction. Perhaps conservative evangelicals are defending it as incorrigible now out of fear that open theism and other reconstructions of the doctrine of God may lead to "finite godism," or process theology, or worse. Some, like Geisler and Ware, have certainly expressed that anxiety. Postconservatives simply do not evaluate the situation in the same way; they have great respect for the various historical accounts of classical Christian theism, but they believe there is room within the growing tradition for alteration and the process that led to classical theism is still open. Development through fresh, faithful research and reflection is never finished; the kingdom has not yet come.

Divine Temporality and Relationality in Postconservative Thought

It is not difficult to put a finger on the single main issue driving postconservative evangelical thinking about God. In 2003 a group of evangelical theologians established a program unit of the American Academy of Religion (AAR) called "Relational Theologies." It received the endorsement of the AAR and is now a regular feature of its national meeting. Postconservatives are concerned that classical theism was and is inadequate as an expression of the biblical portrayal of God—often through narratives—as personally involved with people in history. To put it bluntly: God has a history. Or in the words of German Catholic theologian Hans Küng, God has a career. God's career is his path toward the kingdom that winds in and through and around the paths of his people. God is a responsive and personal God of love who in creation embarked on a journey and a project that is not yet finished. Relational thinking is largely replacing substantialist thinking or essentialism in postmodern culture. That by itself does not require any alteration in conventional Christian theological thinking. Nor does it represent a capitulation to culture. We are not led around by culture like a cow with a nose ring. Nevertheless, as Clark Pinnock has pointed out, culture often does push our theological noses down into Scripture to look at it in new and fresh ways.

Many postconservative thinkers come up from that exercise convinced that conventional Christian thinking about God is too closely tied to a substantialist and essentialist cosmology and metaphysics that cannot do justice to the biblical portrait of God as passionately involved and affected by what goes on in history. Also, the doctrine of the Trinity reveals God as eminently, immanently relational. Western theology especially has tended to emphasize God's single subjectivity or single essence over the threeness of persons; our encounters with Eastern Orthodoxy and the Greek church fathers, especially the Cappadocians, is showing us that this has been a mistake. It has led to what Roman Catholic thinker Karl Rahner called a mere monotheism in the practical lives of most Christians: "We must be willing to admit that, should the doctrine of the Trinity have to be dropped as false, the major part of religious literature could well remain virtually unchanged."[7] Under the influences of such Roman Catholic

7. Karl Rahner, *The Trinity*, trans. Joseph Donceel (New York: Seabury Press, 1974), 10–11.

and Protestant thinkers as Rahner, Walter Kasper, Catherine LaCugna, Jürgen Moltmann, Nicholas Wolterstorff, Adrio König, Hendrikus Berkhof, Vincent Brümmer, and led by a concern to be truly biblical, postconservative evangelical theologians are moving toward new horizons in theological thinking about God as relational and personal. Along the way they respectfully leave behind some of the baggage of classical theism in order to discover a more biblical picture of God.

At this point some conservative evangelicals, and perhaps other Christians, will become worried that postconservative revisions of classical theism might be driven by process theology. My own study of the matter leads me to believe this is not the case. To be sure, parallels between postconservative relational thinking about God and process theology exist, but for the most part they are coincidental. With few exceptions postconservative evangelicals are not enamored with process theology. One leading conservative evangelical theologian complained that open theist Gregory A. Boyd more than flirted with process theology in his book *Trinity and Process: A Critical Evaluation and Reconstruction of Hartshorne's Di-Polar Theism Towards a Trinitarian Metaphysic*.[8] However, a close reading of the book reveals that Boyd is more critical of process theology than appreciative of it. He admits to a very general and broad agreement between his vision of God and that of process theology in that both are relational and dynamic. But beyond that, Boyd pits dynamic Trinitarianism, a social model of God, against process theology's di-polar theism, which he finds seriously deficient for developing a truly relational ontology.

Norman Geisler, a leading conservative evangelical critic of open theism charged that postconservative evangelical philosopher William Hasker admitted that open theism is influenced by process theology.[9] He even cited the page in Hasker's *God, Time and Knowledge*.[10] However, Hasker does not make any such

8. Gregory A. Boyd, *Trinity and Process: A Critical Evaluation and Reconstruction of Hartshorne's Di-Polar Theism Towards a Trinitarian Metaphysic* (New York: Peter Lang, 1992).

9. Norman Geisler, *Creating God in the Image of Man?* (Minneapolis: Bethany House, 1997), 107.

10. William Hasker, *God, Time and Knowledge* (Ithaca, NY, and London: Cornell University Press, 1989).

admission either on the page cited or anywhere in the book. On the contrary, he specifically denies influence from process theology while admitting some general, accidental similarities and parallels between open theism and process theology. One should note that such general, accidental similarities also exist between classical theism and certain non-Christian views of God such as Vedanta (philosophical) Hinduism. That does not imply influence of the latter on the former. The volume *Searching for an Adequate God*, edited by process theologian John Cobb and postconservative evangelical Clark Pinnock, clearly reveals the gulf between evangelical open theists and process theologians.[11] The book is more debate than dialogue. Specifically, the evangelical authors insist on *creatio ex nihilo*, while the process authors deny it. Nowhere do postconservative evangelicals give in to panentheism (the idea that God and the world are interdependent realities); all accept wholeheartedly the biblical concept of God as creator and ruler over all, even as they appeal to God's voluntary self-limitation in relation to creation.

It is probably safe to say that much postconservative evangelical reconstruction of the doctrine of God was stimulated by a single essay by an evangelical philosopher who has never been accused of being influenced by process theology: Nicholas Wolterstorff. His essay "God Everlasting" developed Oscar Cullman's thesis about the Hebrew concept of God's relationship with time. There Wolterstorff argued cogently and convincingly that a timeless being who lives in a purely nontemporal realm cannot interact with or be affected by temporal beings and events. He also displayed the biblical evidence that the God of the Bible is temporal and not timeless and connected God's temporality with God's personal being. A timeless being may be the first cause of the universe and everything in it, but such a being cannot be personally involved in history in the way described in the Bible. According to Wolterstorff,

> If we are to accept this [biblical] picture of God as acting for the renewal of human life, we must conceive of him as everlasting

11. John Cobb and Clark Pinnock, eds., *Searching for an Adequate God* (Grand Rapids: Eerdmans, 2000).

rather than eternal [i.e., timeless]. God the Redeemer cannot be a God eternal. This is so because God the Redeemer is a God who *changes*. And any being which changes is a being among whose states there is temporal succession. Of course, there is an important sense in which God as presented in the Scriptures is changeless: he is steadfast in his redeeming intent and ever faithful to his children. Yet, *ontologically*, God cannot be a redeeming God without there being changeful variation among his states.[12]

Wolterstorff's essay slowly gained the attention of evangelical scholars eager to emphasize God's personal and relational nature. This essay, more than process theology, stimulated the discovery of new horizons in the doctrine of God by postconservative evangelical theologians.

One manifestation of that discovery is open theism; others include Stanley J. Grenz's social God project, F. LeRon Shults's reformation of the doctrine of God's relationality, and Miroslav Volf's concept of God as reconciling love. All of these are working along the same lines even though they draw somewhat different conclusions in the details. They are all projects to reconceive God as relational rather than immutable substance. One thing important to notice in all these postconservative projects is that they move away from abstraction and depersonalization toward a rediscovery of the full personhood of God. Postconservatives have shown no interest in immanentist idealism or panentheistic reduction of God to a field of force. Their interest is solidly personalistic even if their proposals take different approaches. Their God is more like Buber's Thou than Hegel's Absolute Spirit or Tillich's Ground of Being. Yet they show little interest in Whitehead's reduction of God to the Fellow Sufferer Who Understands. They seek to combine biblical personalism with biblical transcendence in a way that avoids the problems of classical theism, which tends to make God remote, invulnerable, and even tyrannical. They regard the God of classical Christian theism as specializing in power and control rather than love and compassion—at least the latter take a back seat to the former.

12. Nicholas Wolterstorff, "God Everlasting," in *God and the Good*, ed. Clifton J. Orlebeke and Lewis B. Smedes (Grand Rapids: Eerdmans, 1975), 181–82.

Postconservative evangelical theologians want to change that and put divine love, compassion, and even suffering-with above domination and control.

Henry Knight's Nonprocessive View of God's Relationality

One postconservative evangelical theologian who has written in a general way about reconstructing the doctrine of God is Henry Knight III. In his *A Future for Truth: Evangelical Theology in a Postmodern World*, the evangelical Methodist thinker argues for a new emphasis on the love of God in evangelical thought; for him such an emphasis will inevitably bring about revisions in classical Christian theism and draw it away from its Greek philosophical roots and more toward biblical personalism. For Knight, as for most postconservative theologians, what is at stake in the reconstruction of the doctrine of God is God's character, which is revealed primarily in a pattern of activity communicated through the biblical narrative.[13] The God of the biblical narratives is a personal God whose main "reigning attribute" is love:

> This is the central scriptural claim about God, and while biblical accounts of God's loving intention and action abound, the culmination and the depth of God's love is revealed in Jesus Christ. It is to the revelation of God in Christ I now turn, first with a consideration of the incarnation followed by a discussion of atonement. It is here more than anywhere else that we not only find that God is love, but come to know the particular nature of that love as it was manifested in Jesus Christ.[14]

Knight is convinced that too much conservative thinking about God is not based on the biblically narrated pattern of intention and action culminating in the incarnation and God's manifested love in Jesus Christ but on philosophical theism heavily influenced by Greek thought. There, as in modern philosophical theism, a dualism reigns that divides time from eternity so that

13. Henry H. Knight III, *A Future for Truth: Evangelical Theology in a Postmodern World* (Nashville: Abingdon, 1997), 139–40.
14. Ibid., 143–44.

God is not able to be fully revealed in temporal manifestations such as the incarnation. According to Knight, "It is essential for a faithful biblical orthodoxy to maintain the distinction between eternity and time while upholding their God initiated relationship."[15] Knight echoes most postconservative evangelical theologians with his critique of classical theism's infection by Greek metaphysics of perfection:

> While it was entirely natural and appropriate for the intellectual defenders of Christianity to borrow from Greek philosophy to make their case, they nonetheless permitted those concepts of divinity to take root within Christian theology and seriously modify its doctrine of God. . . . In spite of their commitment to biblical revelation, classical theologians to a greater or lesser extent began to interpret that revelation through the lens of Neo-platonic and (later) Aristotelian philosophy.[16]

For Knight, as for most postconservative evangelicals, God is identified in Jesus Christ. Or it may be better to say that God is identified *by* Jesus Christ. It is from him and not from philosophy or tradition that we should take our clues as to the nature and character of God.

> To know who Jesus is—to know his character through his intentions and actions as portrayed in the biblical narrative—is to know the character of God. Jesus reveals God as the One whose will is life, not death, and who is characterized by a love which willingly accepts humility and suffering. This pattern of divine love is shown in Jesus' teaching ministry, and death.[17]

This means, then, that some of the attributes of God in classical theism must be discarded or radically revised. One example Knight cites is *divine impassibility* (the idea that God cannot suffer). "In spite of their [i.e., the church fathers'] intentions, the doctrine of impassibility has historically invited a less than

15. Ibid., 147.
16. Ibid., 166.
17. Ibid., 150.

biblical picture of God."[18] Knight admits an element of truth in impassibility while affirming a greater truth about God's ability to suffer:

> The truth of impassibility—that God cannot be affected and changed by anything outside of God except by God's own will—must continue to be affirmed, for the cross of Jesus Christ is the strongest possible evidence of God's unchangeable love. But at the same time it must not prevent our saying that God can and did choose to enter into our history and share in our suffering. God is not impassive, but full of compassion; God is pained by evil and suffering but rejoices at righteousness. God is affected by the world, not out of deficiency or weakness but because God chooses to be so affected out of love.[19]

Knight's insistence on God's love, compassion, and capacity for suffering is crucial to the postconservative reconstruction of the doctrine of God. Traditional, conservative theology has always affirmed God's love and compassion, but those attributes have been undermined by the greater emphasis on God's power and immutability. For Knight, as for most postconservatives, taking with full seriousness Jesus Christ as our best clue to God forces us to jettison the most extreme theistic notions of God's power and immutability and allow them to be tempered by God's self-limiting vulnerability, which stems from his love.

For Knight and most postconservative evangelicals, necessary biblical revision of the doctrine of God will inevitably lead to a lessening of ideas about God's all-determining or all-controlling power. "It makes little sense to speak of sin as a violation of God's will if in fact on some higher level everything that happens is God's will."[20] Rather, Knight asserts, "God does not control all that happens [because this would be inconsistent with love], at least not in the usual sense, but God is actively and powerfully engaged in creation to bring about genuine redemption."[21] Knight sharply contrasts this view, shared by most postconservatives,

18. Ibid., 152.
19. Ibid.
20. Ibid., 166.
21. Ibid., 172.

with process theology, which empties God of power and super-natural action. Contrary to process theology, Knight says, the God of biblical revelation is powerfully and supernaturally involved in the course of events, but he does not determine everything. All limitations of God's power are self-limitations that arise naturally from divine faithfulness.[22] God is not essentially limited by any-thing outside himself. And yet, God is limited and does change. His limitations are self-imposed and his changes are voluntary; both flow from his love.

Although Knight does not explicitly say so, his account of the doctrine of God seems to imply that God is temporal. Many, if not most, postconservative evangelical thinkers are ready and willing to move in that direction. God is not limited by time as if time were a container in which God lives, but God enters into time to experience real relationships that include being vulner-able and affected by persons outside himself. Scottish theologian Thomas F. Torrance was perhaps the first to speak of the "open-ness of God" in this regard. He is not usually thought of as an evangelical (whether conservative or postconservative), but his influence on evangelical theology has been important in the last decades of the twentieth century and continues into the twenty-first century. In *Space, Time and Incarnation*, writing about the world's openness to God, he asked,

> But what of the same relationship the other way around, in the *openness of God* for the world that He has made? Does the inter-section of His reality with our this-worldly reality in Jesus Christ mean anything for God? We have noted already that it means that space and time are affirmed as real for God in the actuality of His relations with us, which binds us to space and time, so that neither we nor God can contract out of them. Does this not mean that God has so opened Himself to our world that our this-worldly experiences must have import for Him in such a way, for example, that we must think of Him as taking our hurt and pain into Him-self? . . . If God is merely impassible He has not made room for Himself in our agonied existence, and if He is merely immutable He has neither place nor time for frail, evanescent creatures in His unchanging existence. But the God who has revealed Himself

22. Ibid., 176.

in Jesus Christ as sharing our lot is the God who is really free to make Himself poor, that we through His poverty might be made rich, the God invariant in love but not impassible, constant in faithfulness but not immutable.[23]

Torrance cannot be accused of being influenced by process theology. He is more a disciple of Karl Barth, who is hardly a process theologian. Torrance's assertions closely resemble those of postconservatives like Knight. The emphasis is on God's love and relational compassion as well as his ability to be affected by what creatures do. This is what classical, conservative theism and the theologies of most conservative evangelical thinkers cannot account for. Their God is impervious to change and invulnerable to pain. Such a God, postconservatives fear, is not the God of Abraham, Isaac, and Jacob, or the God supremely revealed in Jesus Christ and his cross.

Open Theism

Most people who pay attention to the current evangelical theological scene are aware of open theism; it certainly is the most controversial new horizon in postconservative evangelical thinking about God. It builds on the relational turn in evangelical thinking about God and goes further than Wolterstorff, Torrance, or Knight. And yet open theists would argue it is implied in the accounts of God's relationship with the world. In brief, open theism is the belief that God knows the future as partly settled and partly open, as a realm of actualities and possibilities.[24] God does not know exhaustively and infallibly which possibilities will become actualities, but he knows all the factors that exist right now going into that process. The fact that his knowledge of the future includes possibilities is no limitation on his power or even

23. Thomas F. Torrance, *Space, Time and Incarnation* (Oxford, London, and New York: Oxford University Press, 1969), 74–75.

24. The main books of open theism are by Clark Pinnock, William Hasker, John Sanders, Gregory Boyd, and Richard Rice, but others who share the basic vision of open theism include philosophers and theologians Dallas Willard, Richard Swineburne, and John Polkinghorne.

his knowledge since that which he does not yet know absolutely is not possible to know. Even the most conservative classical theist would admit that God does not know the DNA of unicorns. Like the DNA of unicorns, open theists say, the undetermined parts of the future are not knowable because they do not exist in any sense for anyone to know. God's knowledge is coextensive with everything real as real and coextensive with everything possible as possible. How is that a limitation? It would be a limitation only if there was something to be known that God did not know. It is no more a limitation of God's knowledge than the fact that God cannot change the past is a limitation of his power!

But what is the point? Why do open theists say these troubling things about God? Is it a spirit of rebellion against tradition? Are they merely dabbling in theological experimentation? Are they under the spell of process theology? I don't think so. Open theism's primary concern is for God's personal and relational nature as love. Dutch philosopher Vincent Brümmer has argued convincingly that the very natures of "person" and "love" require time and change; without some degree of vulnerability and capacity for suffering, both of which require temporality and openness to a future, a being cannot interact with other persons in love.[25] Although this argument runs directly counter to classical theism, postconservatives find it convincing on biblical as well as philosophical grounds. The basic impulse of open theists is not to adjust to the culture of change and relativity; they are certainly not interested in taking away any of God's glory or majesty or holiness. Rather, they regard God's glory, majesty, and righteousness as manifested in his voluntary self-limitation to vulnerability in creation out of love.

Like a good parent God lays aside his prerogatives of power and self-sufficiency and enters into covenants with people that lay him open to grief and suffering. But to go on this journey with creation God has to enter fully into time, and that is exactly how the Bible describes God. God journeys with his people and suffers their idolatry and disobedience. The biblical portrayal of God is thoroughly relational even as it is also majestic. In the words

---

25. Vincent Brümmer, *Speaking of a Personal God: An Essay in Philosophical Theology* (Cambridge: Cambridge University Press, 1992).

of Dutch theologian Hendrikus Berkhof, God is the "defenseless superior power" in the "monopluristic covenant" between God and humanity.[26] Postconservatives are not afraid to talk of God's vulnerability and humility without diminishing God's glory and power. The concept of divine self-limitation resolves the paradox. Insofar as God faces an open future with us it is because he chooses to and not because of any intrinsic limit the world places on God; he chooses to for the sake of a reciprocal loving relationship. All open theists affirm that God has the ability to control the world and does occasionally exercise control for the sake of the coming kingdom; God is in charge of history without having to exercise a dominating control that robs history and humanity of contingency and freedom. God is, open theists say, "omniresourceful." He can and does meet every unexpected situation with the full resources of his wisdom, love, and power.

Some conservative evangelicals have reacted to open theism, if not to the relational revolution in theism generally, with harsh criticism. Among other things the God of open theism has been described by conservative evangelical critics as a pathetic, hand-wringing God who gives bad advice. To be sure, on the one hand, some open theists have not been as careful in describing God's openness to the future as one might wish. On the other hand, many conservative critics have inflated rhetorical flaws in open theism out of all proportion and ignored open theists' positive statements about God's self-sufficiency, creation out of nothing, omnipotence, and self-restriction as the foundation for any limits God experiences. It seems to me that the conservative evangelical reaction to open theism has been nothing short of hysterical. Some conservatives tried to expel open theists from the Evangelical Theological Society. Others have worked hard to get open theists fired from their teaching positions in evangelical colleges, universities, and seminaries. Open theists have generally made clear that what they are proposing is a research project in theology; their vision of God's futurity is a theologoumenon—a proposal for discussion—and not a dogma to be adopted by

26. Hendrikus Berkhof, *Christian Faith: An Introduction to the Study of the Faith*, trans. Sierd Woudstra, rev. ed. (Grand Rapids: Eerdmans, 1986), 140–47.

everyone and certainly not without lengthy discussion and even debate.

Not all postconservative evangelicals are sympathetic with open theism, but most believe it is an opportunity for constructive reconsideration of some aspects of traditional evangelical belief about God and that it is not as harmful as conservatives make it out to be. After all, how does open theism affect Christian practice? Will it harm evangelism? Certainly no more predictably than Calvinism! Does it damage trust in God's ability to fulfill his promises? It should not. Open theists affirm God's complete omnipotence and ability to turn history any way he wishes to. Does it make God less worshipful or majestic? I do not see how that could be, as long as any limitation of God's knowledge of the future is voluntary and not due to an essential limitation of God's nature. All in all, it seems that the open view of God needs much more careful study and dialogue among evangelicals, whereas many conservatives seem to wish to halt study and dialogue and focus energies on drawing boundaries that exclude open theists from evangelical communities. That is not to say conservatives have not presented strong arguments against it; some have. But too often mixed in with the biblical and theological arguments is the rhetoric of exclusion that subtly engages in ad hominem arguments about open theists' lack of piety or biblical fidelity.

Miroslav Volf's Embracing God

Open theism is not the only relational option for postconservative theism. Miroslav Volf is a postconservative evangelical thinker who draws heavily on the theology of Jürgen Moltmann. For Volf, as for Moltmann, the root metaphor for God is father or parent; God is primarily love and reconciling will and power. But God is not dominating power even if he does know the future exhaustively and infallibly. After all, Moltmann's God is the power of the future, who in some sense already dwells where we are going. But Moltmann's and Volf's God is not a prisoner of the future; he enters lovingly and powerfully into history to suffer and die on the cross and enter into the church as the transforming Spirit of the kingdom. This God lures and persuades and suffers for the cause of canceling out the reluctance of finitude and sin; God pushes and pulls the world toward the kingdom, all the while voluntarily depending on human partners to achieve the consummation.

Volf appropriates Moltmann's vision in a general way but introduces his own distinctive contribution: God as the power of reconciliation through embrace between enemies. This is more implicitly than explicitly expressed in *Exclusion and Embrace*, where the focus is on the ethics of reconciling love.[27] But lurking not far in the background of Volf's call for Christians to adjust their personalities into a stance of willingness to embrace the foreigner, the alien, and the enemy stands the very personal, vulnerable, and relational God of Jesus's parable of the prodigal son, a God who grieves and suffers in order to meet the rebellious child with outstretched arms. Volf is not particularly interested in metaphysics in any traditional sense, but one can clearly discern in his theology a turn away from the *actus purus* of classical theism who cannot be affected by the world because he has no potential. The God of Volf's vision is thoroughly relational; he lives for the embrace of his people and seeks every path of reconciliation with them. But he does not coerce or dominate them; he works only through the power of suffering love to pull them into his arms. According to Volf, especially the cross reveals that "God will not be God without humanity. . . . The cross is the giving up of God's self in order not to give up on humanity."[28]

Open theism's and Volf's visions of God may not seem on the surface to have much in common. The former revels in metaphysical speculation rooted in the biblical narratives of God's interactions with people in history. The latter borrows on Hegel's legacy as mediated through Moltmann; God is seen as one who comes to himself through a dialectical process of love that involves going out of himself toward the other and embracing the other and returning to himself more full and complete in his being. Of course, nowhere does Volf fully reveal this dialectical vision of God or his indebtedness to Hegel. Nor is it pure Hege-

27. Miroslav Volf, *Exclusion and Embrace* (Nashville: Abingdon, 1996).
28. Ibid., 126.

lianism, for Volf's God is not the Absolute Spirit who needs the world for self-actualization and self-knowledge. Rather, God is Trinitarian and complete in himself but self-limiting for the sake of loving relationship with persons. But that means God does voluntarily embark on a journey in creating men and women; that God has a history is his own choice, but he does have a history. Because of human defection God is not God in the same way and he will be God yet differently when the reconciling embrace is achieved. In the process God takes risks and is hurt and experiences new things—just like parents raising adolescents. This is a thoroughly relational vision of God that takes up the best of classical theism and leaves the rest. Yes, God is omnipotent. Yes, God is omniscient. Yes, God is immutable from the perspective of faithfulness to his promises. But God is not the all-determining reality; God chooses to let people have a role even in how God feels. Impassibility if not immutability must go.

F. LeRon Shults's Reformation of the Doctrine of God

Another postconservative revisionist of the doctrine of God is F. LeRon Shults who, after years teaching at evangelical institutions in the United States, has moved to Norway to teach theology. His influence among North American evangelicals remains strong. The title of Shults's main book on the doctrine of God reveals his postconservative bent: *Reforming the Doctrine of God*. There Shults explains the need for reforming theology, including the doctrine of God: "Much of our theological language is imprisoned by particular philosophical and scientific categories that constrain our proclamation of the good news about the biblical God. It is love for the gospel that leads us to take up the task of reforming theology, to protest whenever and wherever it is being fettered."[29] Further, he expounds on postconservative evangelical methodology beautifully; almost all postconservative evangelical theologians would applaud this explanation of theology's proper style and method:

29. F. LeRon Shults, *Reforming the Doctrine of God* (Grand Rapids: Eerdmans, 2005), 2.

The reconstructive theological presentation that follows [in Shults's book] is guided by four interwoven desiderata: a faithful interpretation of the biblical witness, a critical appropriation of the theological tradition, a conceptual resolution of relevant philosophical issues, and a plausible elucidation of contemporary human experience. Reforming theology is both dangerous and difficult, but it is also delightful—insofar as it serves the gospel of God.[30]

As in most postconservative approaches to revisioning God, Shults centers around the concept of relationality, which he sees as crucial both to the biblical witness and to contemporary philosophy. He believes that too much conservative (and liberal Christian) thinking about God is unnecessarily influenced by early modern philosophy stemming from the Enlightenment. Early modern philosophical theism was captivated by rationalistic notions of God as single, immaterial substance, single subject, and first cause. These ideas of God bled into conservative evangelical theology from the eighteenth-century Reformed theologian Francis Turretin and nineteenth-century Princeton theologian Charles Hodge to contemporary theologians like Millard Erickson. Shults recommends a rediscovery of the fully relational God of the Bible under the guidance of postmodern philosophical thinking about relationality:

> We need a concept of the Absolute that is essentially relational, an eternal being-in-relation that constitutes the finite by distinguishing it from the infinite, incursively upholding the structures of the finite and evocatively opening up the finite to an intensification of its differentiated union with the infinite. This brings us to the doctrine of the Trinity.[31]

Shults then expounds a relational doctrine of God centered around a "robust Trinity." This doctrine rests on an understanding of reality as personal being-in-relation and not as immaterial substance. The implications of this for an evangelical doctrine of God are far-reaching. God is no longer to be understood pri-

30. Ibid., 4.
31. Ibid., 132.

marily as controlling power but as empowering relationship that creates room for creatures to develop as creatures within the overarching creative sovereignty of God. The infinite, Trinitarian God does not control the world so much as he embraces it and constitutes its becoming. The presence of God must be rethought in relation to the world as "the gracious liberation of creation in and to the possibility of sharing the eternal life of the Trinitarian persons."[32] The result is a vision of God and the world that keeps them distinct while bringing them into intimate relationship—a relationship that is not merely external to either one.

For Shults this vision of a relational God has far-reaching consequences for understanding God's power. Conservative evangelical theology has inflated God's power at the expense of creaturely self-determination and God's love. Shults goes so far as to suggest that for much traditional Christian theology God's power is like that of a pagan god.[33] Instead God's power must be conceived as "the power of Trinitarian love that holds the other in being and calls the other (in)to being—truly omnipotent love."[34] God's power, then, should be conceived as formational rather than dominating and controlling. In love God forms human acting, ordering it toward the good without extrinsically controlling it.

Shults seems to be arguing for a sort of evangelical panentheism—if there can be such a thing. Panentheism is generally understood to be a view of God and the world that sets them in an interdependent relationship. Shults rejects that understanding, but he accepts and argues for God as the "truly infinite" who does not operate on the world from outside but includes the world in his own Trinitarian life and works on it from within. He is opposed to the implicit dualism of traditional theism that pits God and the world against each other so that if one is active the other is passive. The biblical and contemporary vision of God and the world is fully relational so that there is no question of domination or controlling but rather of personal agencies interacting with each other where one (God) is the superior influence. For Shults, God's complete sovereignty is eschatological; only in the

32. Ibid., 200.
33. Ibid., 242.
34. Ibid., 243.

eschaton will God be all in all or everything to everyone. On the way to that future God acts on the world from within by liberating creatures from independence and autonomy and drawing them into the loving life of the Trinity.

Stanley J. Grenz and the Social God

Stanley Grenz was working on a relational vision of God when he died. He had already published the first volume of a projected six- or seven-volume set of monographs on loci of theology. It was titled *The Social God and the Relational Self: A Trinitarian Theology of the Imago Dei*.[35] His second volume, *The Named God and the Question of Being: A Trinitarian Theo-Ontology*, was completed just before his untimely death in March, 2005.[36] Grenz's project was to draw on the resources of the doctrine of the Trinity to create a social or relational ontology including God as essentially other-oriented—which is another way of saying essentially love. In *The Social God and the Relational Self* he drew heavily on the social Trinitarian lineage of theology stemming from the Cappadocian Fathers through Richard of St. Victor to Moltmann, Wolfhart Pannenberg, Catherine LaCugna, and John Zizioulas. From them—and in dialogue with Scripture, of course—Grenz developed a concept of God as "ecclesial self," by which he meant communion.

This communal nature of God is not, however, God's necessary relationship with creation as in Hegel and the panentheism that stems from his speculative metaphysic. Rather, God's communal or ecclesial nature is his eternal intratrinitarian bond of love that is also dynamic in its interplay between the three persons. Grenz summarizes as follows:

> The eternal generation of the Son constitutes the first trinitarian person as the Father of the Son and the second person as the Son of the Father, yet the two are bound together by the love they

35. Stanley J. Grenz, *The Social God and the Relational Self: A Trinitarian Theology of the Imago Dei* (Louisville: Westminster John Knox, 2001).

36. Stanley J. Grenz, *The Named God and the Question of Being: A Trinitarian Theo-Ontology* (Louisville: Westminster John Knox, 2006).

share, a bond that characterizes the divine nature as a whole but also emerges as a separate hypostasis in the third person, the Holy Spirit. In this way, the love that characterizes the relationship of the Father and the Son in the differentiation of each from the other means that they likewise share the sameness of the divine nature—that is, love. This shared love is the Holy Spirit, who nevertheless is neither the Son nor the Father and therefore differs from both. In this manner, the doctrine of the Trinity teaches that the trinitarian persons share in the one divine essence, for there is but one God; yet they differ from one another, for each is a distinct person who cannot be equated with, or subsumed within, the others.[37]

The gist of Grenz's reflections lies in the idea of being as relationship; even God must not be conceived of as a monad, which is a perennial danger in Western theology inspired by Augustine. To be is to be related; that is true for God as well as for creatures. It is true for creatures because it is true for God. Furthermore, relatedness is always purposive. That is, it has a teleological character; it aims toward a goal. The lively divine life of Father, Son, and Holy Spirit is no static self-enclosed circle in heaven (to use Moltmann's words) but a communal life driven by the greater unity of the future consummation of creation. God created out of the overflowing love between Father, Son, and Spirit. The triune persons enter into history in varying patterns of the kingdom; this economic Trinity within history is also the immanent Trinity, although it does not exhaust God's eternal being. God does not lose himself in history. The community of love that constitutes the divine life creates little ecclesial selves and welcomes them into the community of the church, which is the prototype of the kingdom in which God will be united with creation.

Grenz embraced the idea of a history of God; not only is God essentially relational so that even the Father depends on the Son and the Spirit for his being, but the community that is God has a history with the world. Grenz appealed to his mentor Wolfhart Pannenberg in this regard and especially in what I have called "Pannenberg's Principle," which is that God's deity is at stake in the coming of his kingdom. In other words, once the world exists,

37. Grenz, *The Social God and the Relational Self*, 321.

because God is ecclesial love within himself, he cannot let go of the world. God's deity—which is relational—drives him to bring about his goal of an ecclesial world, but not without participation of created persons. Love does not dominate or control but works with the beloved to achieve the highest good for both the lover and the beloved. Thus there is a sense for Grenz in which God is both relational and dynamic, both communal and historical. The immanent Trinity of eternal bliss in heaven does not go on above the historical process of the kingdom as if that were not happening; rather, it becomes the economic Trinity within history through the incarnation and the sending of the Spirit in order to return to itself, enfolding the world in its loving embrace. The world makes a difference to God. Yes, God could have remained fulfilled as Father, Son, and Holy Spirit without the world; God does not need the world to be God. But the creation of objects of love outside the divine life is the most natural thing imaginable. Once that happens, the world is part of God's life.

Not Panentheism but Relational Theism

Conservatives ask whether this new postconservative evangelical vision of God as relational does not constitute panentheism. Traditionally, panentheism, a term coined in the early nineteenth century by Karl Friedrich Christian Kraus, means God-world interdependence. In true panentheism, without the world God is not God. Whether the term should be applied to any form of relational ontology that portrays God as lovingly and voluntarily interdependent with the world is questionable. In open theism, Volf's vision of God, Shults's reconstructed theism, and Grenz's ecclesial, Trinitarian ontology, God is not dependent on the world necessarily but voluntarily, out of love. All three make clear that God does not need the world to be God or even to come to self-realization. However, once the world exists, they imply, God is not God in exactly the same way but is affected by what happens in it and especially in grief at its defection and joy at its return through the missions of the Son and the Spirit. The world is drawn by God into his own life just as a parent draws the child into his or her own life. God wills not to be a worldless God and wills the world not to be godless. Their union is important to God and affects his own experience and identity because he wills it to be so. In my judgment, this does not constitute panentheism. Some, however, have labeled it "Christian panentheism" and "Trinitarian panentheism."[38]

Postconservative evangelicals have not settled into a stable doctrine of God; that is not in the nature of the postconservative mood. Even the doctrine of God is a pilgrimage and a conversation. Neither, however, is postconservative thinking about God unfettered theological experimentation. It is rooted in serious biblical research and reflection and driven by a concern to have a doctrine of God that does justice to the revelation of God as love in Jesus Christ. To a great extent classical Christian theism has not been so driven but has thought about God's being apart from Jesus Christ. Postconservatives are determined to interpret God through the best clue we have: the incarnation.

---

38. See Philip Clayton and Arthur Peacocke, eds., *In Whom We Live and Move and Have Our Being: Panentheistic Reflections on God's Presence in a Scientific World* (Grand Rapids: Eerdmans, 2004), especially Niels Henrik Gregersen, "Three Varieties of Panentheism," in ibid., 19–35.

Conclusion

This book has attempted to point the way to a new approach to evangelical theology that is less conservative than conventional evangelical theology without being more liberal. That seems impossible to many people who are locked into the old paradigm of mapping theologies on a rightward-leftward spectrum based on responses to the Enlightenment and modernity. The chapters included here fall short of presenting a comprehensive account of postconservative evangelical theology, but I hope they have at least intimated the possibility of this new approach and cleared up some of the confusion surrounding it.

Astute readers trained in contemporary theology will recognize some similarities between what I here call postconservative theology and what has been known as postliberal theology for the last couple of decades. They are certainly not the same; evangelicals of all types will at least struggle with the New Yale Theology's (postliberalism's) cavalier attitude toward the historicity of the biblical narratives. That is not to say all postliberal theologians are equally guilty of treating the historicity of biblical narratives in such a manner, but only that evangelicals of all types are wary of any purely intratextual approach to theology. Postconservative evangelicals share this concern but believe the postliberal theologians (e.g., Hans Frei and George Lindbeck) have something valuable to say to evangelicals too caught up in rationalistic apologetics and hermeneutics.

A way forward is for evangelicals and postliberals to engage in constructive dialogue. Some of that has already happened. More would be beneficial to both sides that share so much in common and yet cannot quite meet on common ground. They share a common concern to treat the Bible as realistic narrative rather than a collection of not-yet-systematized, rationalistic propositions waiting to be organized into a coherent system. They have difficulty coming to agreement on the importance of the objective referential nature of biblical narratives as historical. They agree that some biblical narratives are history-like without necessarily being historical (in the modern sense of objective descriptions of what "really happened"), but they fail to agree on how important it is that at least key events communicated in the biblical narratives refer to events in space and time.

I also believe postconservative and conservative evangelicals need to engage in dialogue with each other. They, too, have much in common including a supernatural life and worldview, fidelity to the authority of the Bible above all other human sources and norms, respect for the Great Tradition of Christian teaching, belief in the deity of Jesus Christ and the Trinity, experience of the transforming power of God in conversion, and a personal relationship with Jesus Christ. It pains postconservatives to hear and read some conservative evangelicals treating them as if they did not believe in or experience these things. This common ground should form the basis for constructive dialogue drawing all evangelicals together rather than driving them apart. The dialogue is difficult, though, because of tensions between conservatives and postconservatives. The former tend to elevate some tradition alongside Scripture as authoritative and incorrigible whereas the latter tend to question tradition in the light of fresh and faithful biblical research and hermeneutical discoveries. The former invest great interest and faith in propositions organized into coherent systems of theology whereas the latter view theology more as an endless pilgrimage never arriving at a final system of doctrinal beliefs.

Evangelicals need to practice a hermeneutic of charity toward each other's (and everyone else's) writings; too often we begin with a hermeneutic of suspicion when reading and then expounding (too often exposing!) other evangelicals' views. I labor under no illusion that conservative evangelicals will appreciate the postconservative approach I have outlined in this book, but I do hope that they and others who encounter it will give it a fair hearing and not distort it in their own minds or as they communicate and critique it to others. I hope and pray that I have been as generous and fair to the conservative approach to evangelical theology as I want conservatives to be to my own and others' postconservative approach. If I have failed in that at any point I apologize and ask for correction and guidance to a better understanding of that approach to evangelical theology in which I was tutored and out of which I worked for many years.

Index